T5-BPZ-663

A Sociology of Johannine Christianity

Anthony J. Blasi

Texts and Studies in Religion
Volume 69

The Edwin Mellen Press
Lewiston/Queenston/Lampeter

BS
2615.2
.B535
1996

Library of Congress Cataloging-in-Publication Data

Blasi, Anthony J.
A sociology of Johannine Christianity / Anthony J. Blasi.
p. cm. -- (Texts and studies in religion ; v. 69)
Includes bibliographical references and indexes.
ISBN 0-7734-8753-0 (hard)
1. Bible. N.T. John--Criticism, interpretation, etc.
2. Sociology, Biblical. I. Title. II. Series.
BS2615.2.B535 1997
226.5'067--dc20 96-41014
CIP

This is volume 69 in the continuing series
Texts and Studies in Religion
Volume 69 ISBN 0-7734-8753-0
TSR Series ISBN 0-88946-976-8

A CIP catalog record for this book is available from the British Library.

Copyright © 1996 Anthony J. Blasi

All rights reserved. For information contact

The Edwin Mellen Press
Box 450
Lewiston, New York
USA 14092-0450

The Edwin Mellen Press
Box 67
Queenston, Ontario
CANADA L0S 1L0

The Edwin Mellen Press, Ltd.
Lampeter, Dyfed, Wales
UNITED KINGDOM SA48 7DY

Printed in the United States of America

A SOCIOLOGY OF JOHANNINE CHRISTIANITY

For

Stella Marshall

Table of Contents

Preface

This is a work in more than one discipline. It involves New Testament studies as well as sociology. I admit to having less background in the former than in the latter, and consequently I have consulted widely among New Testament scholars. Naturally, I have faced the disconcerting fact that the New Testament specialists whom I consulted disagree among themselves on some matters and are quite tentative about that on which they do agree. There is also the troubling fact that some of what publishers have chosen to disseminate as sociological or social scientific inquiries into early Christianity would be rejected out of hand by most bona fide sociologists of religion and social scientists in general. These two circumstances not only create difficulties for a sociologist working on early Christian materials but also for readers in the field.

Some observations about New Testament studies can provide the reader with a helpful context for what follows. "There was a great deal of interest in source criticism in the middle of the century," one of my consultants writes me, "which seems to have petered out since 1970 or so." In the case of the Gospel of John, this diminution of interest came from the fact that New Testament studies shifted "towards literary and social-scientific studies that focused on the final form of the text," and from the fact that a consensus about the fourth gospel had been settled upon, about its having been based on a "signs source" and its having undergone a "series of editions and amplifications that reflect...the history of the community" for which it was written "and the development of its eschatology and christology." Another consultant notes that most New Testament specialists place materials together as reflecting the same stage in the editing of the gospel when they form a literary unit, such as the pattern in which "a) Jesus gives a short and somewhat enigmatic saying, b) his interlocutor expresses a misunderstanding, and c) Jesus then provides a lengthy disquisition on the subject."

The work that follows is no doubt out of step with these trends in New Testament studies, and that it is so should not be taken as evidence of any lack of respect for contemporary studies of the fourth gospel. Rather, it is a matter of a continued interest in source criticism on my part. First, the final form of an extended work such as the Gospel of John, which had undergone several revisions, reflects the literary devices and intent of the final editor, or at best previous literary devices and intents of that the final editor chose to retain. If the early Christian movement could be properly depicted by the social world, the time and place, of the last editor alone, focusing on the gospel's final form would suffice for scientific and historical purposes. However, social movements tend to undergo changes, and any account needs depict those changes. Consequently it is necessary to examine closely and separately the materials from editorial stages that were earlier than the final one. This led me to break with one of the post 1970 trends, and to embrace another trend - the focus on the series of editions and amplifications that reflected the history of the Johannine community.

Second, to my way of thinking the formation of literary units such as the enigmatic statement-misunderstanding-disquisition pattern mentioned above was itself an event that occurred in a time and place. If evidence of a literary seam appears in such a unit, evidence that two or more pre-existing texts had been "sewn" together, then the texts themselves reflect earlier times and places of composition than does the unit taken as a whole. I found it necessary to "break up" a number of units, the kind of which literary critics love to identify, in order to focus on the separate elements that an editor had brought together. This will be jarring to some contemporary scholars; it tends to locate more literary stratagems at later stages of the composition history of the gospel than has been traditional in Johannine studies. For example, the "signs source" becomes no longer a source but a redactional pattern that was applied to earlier material. Am I right or wrong headed in doing this? I cannot say, but I offer the (jarring) results as hypotheses.

Third, the present attempt is not one of finding something either new and of interest because of its novelty, or something that coheres with scholarly consensus. Here is where the sociologist in me comes through. I am interested in the way patterned human actions fit together, why certain attitudes and situations, for example, go together. If what I find is altogether new, I am probably wrong; for surely someone before me would have observed it before. However, if by different means of analysis I arrive at a depiction that in some way coheres with what others have seen, I may be onto something. The very fact that I use different means will prevent my creating a simple duplication of what others have done; exact replications are very difficult to create anyway. Rather, it is a matter of methodological triangulation; we social scientists tend to be curious about how social patterns come to appear when approached in different times and places and in different ways. More than one of my New Testament consultants has observed that my findings cohere with those already present in the literature, though I arrived at those findings on the basis of different source critical conclusions. (In one instance, when upon invitation I presented a chapter as a paper in an interdisciplinary setting, an unduly hostile critic alleged that my work was "derivative" from that of someone whose work I found helpful but not always persuasive, and whom I cite reasonably often in the pages that follow.)

Fourth, and again I proceeded as a sociologist, the conceptual framework that appears in the work, beginning in Chapter 3, is related to theories that are to be found in the history of sociology but is not a mere restatement of those theories. Grand theories serve to sensitize us to general questions and issues, but they rarely fit evidence - literary or otherwise - in any simple way. Rather, "theories of the middle range" emerge in the course of contending with evidence. Such modest theories constitute the specialties within sociology, such as the sociology of law, the sociology of education, the sociology of the family, urban sociology, and the sociology of religion. Primarily in

Chapter 3 I have done some "middle range" conceptual work in the sociology of religion.

* * *

I am immensely grateful to the New Testament specialists who lent their expertise to this project. Contrary to the impression that might be given by the preceding observations, I usually followed their advice and always acted upon their encouragement. I should mention first Robert Fortna, who encouraged me to "play" with source critical alternatives in the fourth gospel rather than take any one prior study, including his own studies, as the final word. Jack T. Sanders and Adele Reinhartz were kind enough to read through the whole of an early draft of my manuscript and to lay out a series of issues that I needed to address. Amy Jill Levine and Shawn Kelley helped greatly at critical junctures in clarifying a number of questions.

Whenever one works in a new subject area such as the sociology of early Christianity, the formation of a specialized subculture is of critical importance in separating the personally idiosyncratic from what would be generally common to a wider universe of discourse among informed observers. In order for me to know what needs be argued and demonstrated, versus what can be assumed, I have needed to discuss with others who do similar work the issues that arise in a study such as this one. Fortunately, the annual Sociology of Early Christianity Workshop has enabled such discussions to take place. Several of the chapters included in this study were first presented at the workshops. I wish to thank publicly the Workshop participants, including Richard Fenn, Peter Staples, Nicholas Taylor, Willi Braun, Donald Nielsen, David Horrell, Harry Eberts, and many others.

Others as well have been of material assistance in my pursuit of this study, providing time, space, equipment, and other resources. I would like to mention Jeffrey Crane, now Dean of Arts and Sciences at Northern State University in South Dakota, and David Broad, chairperson of the sociology department at Tennessee State University.

There are no doubt many imperfections in this complex study; they are, of course, my responsibility.

A.J.B.

Nashville

July 1996

Ch. 1. Introduction and Separation of the Text into Sources

This is a sociological study of the Johannine Christian community. By "sociological," I refer to the quest to find forms of interaction with which to understand substantive historical materials better; this problematic is characteristic not only of sociology in a narrow sense, the academic discipline, but also of sociology in a broader sense that designates as well anthropology and social history.[1] By "Johannine Christian community," I mean that grouping in the early Christian movement of the first century C.E. for which the biblical Gospel of John, or fourth gospel, was written, and in which that gospel was read and heard. To speak of them as "Christians" is not to assume that there was already existent a world religion call "Christianity" but that there was a religious movement that had accepted Jesus of Nazareth as a messiah in some sense; the term "Christian" had already been used to refer to the followers of Jesus by the time the Gospel of John was published (see Acts 11.26). The Johannine Christians, of course, can only be spoken of as a community in a loose sense of that term, since it remains to be demonstrated that they constituted a single social network. I do not intend to carry the inquiry into the other biblical materials that are often termed "Johannine," except when the inquiry into the fourth gospel brings me to them. This is not to deny that one or more of these other works was from the same social context but simply to keep the project down to reasonable dimensions.

If it was the case that many or even most early Christians were in fact Jews who wished to assimilate into the hellenistic/Roman world while retaining a serious religiosity,[2] the experiences of the Johannine Christians may have been typical of a large portion of the early Christian population. As will be shown in later chapters, much of the fourth gospel reflects the dynamics of developing a new religious identity from within the sphere of a Jewish one. Others besides the Johannine Christians may have gone through similar or at least parallel experiences.

The Gospel of John is one of four accounts of the life of Jesus of Nazareth that date from the earliest decades of Christianity and appear in Christian Bibles. It resembles the other three accounts[3] insofar as it narrates Jesus' ministry of teaching and wonder working, then recounts a passion consisting of Jesus' arrest, trial, and crucifixion, and concludes with resurrection accounts. However, it differs from the other three insofar as it describes largely different wonders, or miracles, includes some quite unique discourses, and in numerous other respects. Nineteenth century scholars considered John to be a second century inspirational work having less grounding in history than the other gospels, but more recent scholars see it as a late first century work that includes both early traditions and later inspirational discourses. This change in scholarly opinion had been occasioned by papyrus finds that suggest an earlier date of composition, by archeological evidence from Jerusalem that accords with references in the gospel itself, and by an attentiveness to the variety of materials that had been incorporated into the gospel. I will focus on the date of composition - or more precisely, dates of incorporating materials into the text - in the next chapter.

In commentaries on biblical books, it is customary to distinguish between "internal" and "external" evidence about a work's authorship and time, place, and circumstances of composition. The internal evidence is what one can ascertain from the text of the work itself - in this case, from the text of the Gospel of John - while the external evidence is what other ancient writings tell us. Most of what follows in subsequent chapters below is a sociological study of internal evidence. Here, I want to review some of the external evidence. Many of the references in antiquity to the origin of the Gospel of John are derivative from the writings of Papias of Hieropolis, who wrote in Asia Minor about 140 C.E. His book, *Interpretations of the Sayings of the Lord*, which is no longer extant, was not highly regarded, but the fact that Papias made inquiries of the second generation (his elders) of Christians about the first followers of Jesus was of historical interest to church writers. Irenaeus of Lyons (c. 130 - c. 202), who had an apologetical interest in connecting the canonical books of the Christian New Testament to the immediate followers of Jesus, is the earliest writer who refers to Papias' work. After quoting a passage he says:

> This is also attested in writing by Papias, who was a hearer of John and a comrade of Polycarp, an ancient man, in his fourth book, for there are five books that were composed by him.[4]

What was important to Irenaeus was the claim that Papias in Asia (modern day Turkey) was a hearer of John. Irenaeus may have confounded John son of Zebedee, a disciple of Jesus, and John the Presbyter, resident of Ephesus and evidently author of the Second and Third Letters of John and the Revelation of John.

Nevertheless the Johannine writings, including these works, the First Letter of John, and the Gospel of John, were taken to be Asian (and more precisely, Ephesian) in origin, and the effort was to link John son of Zebedee with Asia. Irenaeus notes that John "gave out" his gospel in Ephesus.

Eusebius of Caesarea (c. 260 - c. 340) also provides quotations from Papias. In one of them, Papias related how he collected his information:

> But I will not hesitate to put down along with my interpretations whatever I carefully learned at any time from the elders.... And if anyone should come my way who had been a follower of the elders, I would ask for the accounts given by the elders - what Andrew or what Peter said, or what Philip or what Thomas or James, or what John or Matthew said, or any other of the disciples of the Lord, and what Aristion and the elder John, the disciples of the Lord, say.[5]

Note that Papias lists two persons named John, one of them a disciple of Jesus about whom elders gave him reports and another, the "elder" or "presbyter" John, who (judging from the tense of the verb) was a contemporary of Papias. Elsewhere, Papias as quoted by Eusebius places John the Presbyter in Ephesus. It is also noteworthy that reports about John son of Zebedee, the disciple of Jesus, reached

Papias in Asia. Moreover, Eusebius goes on to say in the same passage that there were two tombs in Ephesus, both tombs of John; the implication is that not only John the Presbyter but also John the son of Zebedee had resided and died there. Eusebius may have relied on the letter of the Ephesian bishop Polycrates (c. 190) to Pope Victor, for this information. The connection between the Gospel of John and Ephesian Christianity seems to have been taken as fact by these early writers; the issue for them was whether John son of Zebedee, an immediate disciple of Jesus, could be claimed as its author.[6]

Methodology in the sociology of early Christianity[7]

It is commonplace in sociology to distinguish between research methodology and techniques of inquiry. Both pertain to the movement from observable data to interpretive conclusion, but techniques differ from methodology in that they are separate little stories, tactics of observation, while methodology is the strategy of appealing to useful conceptualizations. Without techniques, one would be deaf and blind, but without a conceptual methodology one might attempt to hear images or see sounds. One who would conduct adequate research obviously needs both the right empirical grasp and the right conceptual one, but it is largely about the latter that I wish to speak here and now.

Most sociologists are well trained in one or more techniques of inquiry. Typically, they learn how to construct questionnaires, conduct interviews, and make unobtrusive observations in live social settings. Many become expert in quantifying data and partialing out the independent associations between several thusly constructed categories of quantity. A few may have established some familiarity with the techniques of the systematic content analysis of texts or the art of historical reconstruction. These techniques can be useful in the study of early Christianity in some instances; I myself in other works have used content analysis and historical reconstruction in this pursuit. But in general New Testament and ancient historical scholarship does not need to learn much in the way of this kind of technique from sociologists; the arts of text criticism, source criticism, redaction criticism, and form criticism provide a perfectly adequate foundation for research. We can bring a few additional sensitivities to the field, suggested by analogies with our more accustomed questionnaire work,[8] but that which is essentially sociological is to be found more in methodology than in a given collection of research techniques.

A first insight into the sociological methodology can come in the realization that all interpretations of the early Christian movement are sociological. In Dieter Georgi's **Theocracy in Paul's Praxis and Theology**,[9] which is an engaging synthesis of a large body of research, it is made plain that Paul's rejection of law as a means of salvation is predicated on a more general antinomianism. The Christians' now famous missionary systematically subverted political authority even while encouraging his readers to comply with those of its demands that are just, and, according to Georgi, the Romans knew what they were doing when they executed him. The fact that this has not been obvious to Christians since the fourth century can be accounted for by the sociological presuppositions with which the apostle's letters have customarily been read. It is people loyal to governments who have supplied the social hermeneutic for reading the Pauline letters, not people who were rebels, malcontents, misfits, anarchists, or leftists. The view of the larger world that a reader has is nothing less than a sociology, albeit a folk sociology; and as such that view shapes the interpretation of the evidence about early Christianity that is at hand. Now for the professional sociologist the question is, How useful a sociology is it that is being used? Is the folk sociology in question an unreflective projection? Granted that every sociology will be "folkish" insofar as it is comprehensible to some competent member of some society, how much is the folk aspect of an inquirer's sociology a problem rather than a help? I would propose that we acknowledge our own social locations and use those interpretive models that we admittedly can understand, but that we refrain from defining interpreted objects into existence. That is, we use our familiar models for interpreting data, not creating it. For example, the re-election by acclamation of a totalitarian tyrant can be interpreted against a template of true democracy or be interpreted as being an instance of true democracy. The former, yielding a contrast, depends on our folk category, "democracy"; the latter, yielding a lie, imposes our folk category on the data. Let us call this first insight into sociological methodology **the anti-procrustean principle**. We have beds, as Procrustes is said to have had, but we need not size people to them.

A second insight comes from reading studies that make much of their sociological nature but need not have done so. It is not that such works should not have been produced; their authors were on to something but had not yet found a well chosen battle for their strategy. Sociology as a professional pursuit should come into play where interpretation is not easy, where the chasm between two social worlds widens and deepens enough to require a bridge. As in the case of the anti-procrustean principle, this insight suggests that self-knowledge is as important as the knowledge of antiquities. We might call this insight **the reflexivity principle**, since it calls for a reflection upon our social selves.

At this juncture, we could proceed to examine the inherently hermeneutic nature of any sociology. There is the living social process in the society under study, with a dialectic of its own; there is the living social process in our own society, with its peculiar dialectic; and then there is the dialectic of the process of mediating between those two processes.[10] I have elaborated this view of sociology for non-specialists elsewhere, raising no little unanticipated controversy in the process.[11] A necessary conclusion one reaches when taking such an approach is that one cannot simply seize upon concepts that have proven to be useful in the study of one social world and apply them without change to another. We might call this **the dedogmatization principle**.

There is an evident family resemblance among these principles. They all suggest a strategy that is more thoroughly inductive than the "scientific method" often presented in introductory science texts. That textbook method, which I prefer to call the "scientistic method," begins with a general theory, the origin of which is left unexamined. From the general theory, one derives operational propositions that can be "tested" with an experiment, or if an experiment is not feasible, some selective record of evidence that is linguistically framed in an experiment-like presentation. If the results of the experiment accord with the propositions, credibility is said to be gained for the general theory. For example, the law of gravity is a general theory. If one could determine the masses of two material bodies and the distance between them, one should be able to predict the gravitational attraction between them. If in fact they repel each other, less credibility is supposed to be accorded the law of gravity. Now such an approach to science is fraught with problems, especially if it were to be applied to the social world; but the one problem upon which I would have us focus here is the prior statement of a general theory. From where is such a theory to come? If it is formulated before the sociological investigation, it must be dependent upon a folk sociology. In plain language, the scientistic method imposes prejudices upon the evidence because rather than using a concept as a model or template for comparative purposes it uses it to describe an object, a thing, for which one would look. There is a force of gravity or not a force of gravity; one is simply not asking about magnetic charges or alternative tropic processes. Using this methodology, a totalitarian tyrant can readily produce the appearance of a democracy.

Rather than begin with a general theory, many sociologists speak of beginning with deliberately fuzzy concepts, called "sensitizing concepts."[12] These are necessarily based on empirical observations, but their initial lack of precision leaves it relatively unimportant whose observations engender them. They could fit about anywhere - rank, attitude, self, other, interaction, situation, sign, etc. What is important is that they can be nuanced in the life world that one is studying. We speak of them being "grounded" in that world in the course of our giving them greater content and precision. As this process occurs, it may become necessary to create neologisms, in order to speak of these concepts in their thusly nuanced senses. We know that we have done this adequately once repeated inspection of the social world in question add little or nothing to the concepts that seem important in the evidence. Thus the inductive character of the inquiry is present in the very formulation of any interpretive statement about that social world, not delayed for some test of such a statement.

How to use sensitizing concepts has not been established definitively, in part because their applications are themselves situational, contingent on the nature of the evidence and on the life worlds of those for whom information is to be made evident. It should be noted, however, that there are two general kinds of error that statistical logic brings to our attention and that could be applied in the present kind of work. In one kind of error, one accepts a statement as true that is actually false, and in the other kind one rejects a statement as false that is actually true. New Testament scholars, fearful that real or alleged faith commitments will appear to interfere with their critical judgment, sometimes become fixated with avoiding the first kind of error, forgetting about the second kind. They would be overly reluctant to make any historical inference from a religious text, employing something of a methodological hostility toward texts. I frankly do not see this approach to be a sound one; as I learned in statistics, the second kind of error is as mistaken as the first.[13] Those who mistake a hyper-skepticism for induction will be dissatisfied with my procedure. While the study that follows requires no faith commitment and harbors no apologetical intent, neither does it identify induction and empirical procedure with positivism.[14]

In what follows, I propose and expand upon some sociological sensitizing concepts that I believe could be very useful in the interpretive study of early Christianity. These concepts are discussed only rarely in sociology because they are usually taken for granted in the field. One finds them only in the most foundational, quasi-philosophical treatises in the discipline because it is usually not necessary to make resort to them in research, given the fact that most sociological research does not focus on evidence from as far back as the first and second centuries, C.E.

Religious texts, such as the writings of the New Testament, are particularly interesting social phenomena. First, they are intended to be symbolic of an order of reality that is other than that of the everyday world; that intent is what makes them religious texts, in contradistinction to other literary products. Second, though their intended referents may be remote, their origins are not; the authors who create them, the editors who contextualize them, the images that inhabit their metaphors, the presuppositions that render them comprehensible, and the values that make them attractive are this-worldly. Indeed, the more articulate a religious text is, the greater its tension and irony, its tendency to speak of the unspeakable and therefore to communicate by indirection and implication. Third, the dynamics of indirection by which religious texts must work are social dynamics; their very indirectness constrains the subject who creates them to be other than a sole author, to assume an authorial humility whereby the voice that speaks in the text is the voice of tradition, revelation, recollection, and repetition, the voice of mere testimony to a not so mere insight. Consequently, the sociology of such texts needs begin with the phenomenon of anonymity.

Anonymity as understood in the present context is a social achievement. It is not the mere absence of an identity but the presence of a social world that encompasses without constraining and thus supports a cultural ambience without giving notice. Such an achievement cannot be intended since it transcends the compass of a deliberating subject; it is rather the byproduct of collective life. Where there is a "we," a sense of fusion wherein what befalls or is beheld by one member of a grouping holds import for all, such an achievement is possible. The more intense is the fusion in such a "we," the less that those actions that are taken on behalf of another member and attitudes assumed because of another are experienced as constraining.[15] Such "we" feelings, are more characteristic of small collectivities than large, and hence engender new religious contents in an unforced, unauthoritarian or unauthorized manner. This kind of anonymity is not the authoritativeness of traditionalism that speaks voicelessly for the ages through ambience and rite but the authorship of the effervescent, spontaneous, surprise of the present. It is more analogous to the non-individual pursuit of a gathering of friends at a hardly-planned party than the comfortable but routine processes of a mature religion.

As a methodological point, it is obvious that using New Testament texts as evidence for the social existence of the early Christians must begin with what those texts would have been understood to say from their vantage rather than from ours. And sociological models, even relatively content-free forms that are useful as sensitizing concepts, are no substitute for the literary methods of arriving at such non-anachronistic understandings. But who would it have been who held such understandings? What kind of social life was it that could support the creation of such understandings? How could the necessary indirection and spontaneity come about? Given the nature of our evidence, i.e. given the fact that we have religious texts with which to begin, it is here that I would propose a sociology of early Christianity begin. That is why I propose further that a methodology needs be articulated for such inquiry that is strategic rather than tactical in nature; that is, the methodology cannot be a matter of techniques of inquiry - though these too merit attention - pursued in a framework of sociological research business-as-usual. Rather, the sociology of early Christianity is an unusual business that needs begin with a meta-methodology that is up to the research challenges that social spontaneity, anonymity, and indirection pose.

I have been considering New Testament texts as social symbols. As such they are examples of but one face of the social dynamics of which they were a part. It was a basic principle of the "meta-methodology" of the profound Russian French thinker, Georges Gurvitch, that social dynamics have many faces, some of which are more accessible to unsubtle observation than others. The most readily observable are such features as population size, the density of residential settlements, and the like. More subtle features are such things as the values of a people and mental states and acts that grip a population. Social symbols such as religious texts fall somewhere between the most and least accessible; comprehending them requires greater sophistication and study than does a mere census count, but one is likely to confront them as physical texts before having a good grasp of mental states and acts.[16] Now the peculiarly sociological question is not on the order of a census count or an exegesis of a text or an apprehension of values; these are different modalities of data collection, or more precisely, different objects of observation. They are necessary but not sufficient for sociological analysis proper. According to Gurvitch, the peculiarly sociological question pertains to the relationships **among** the different faces of such social dynamics. To what extent can we better understand one of them by placing it into the context of one or more other ones?

A methodological strategy that is up to the task at hand would therefore relate authorial and audience understandings of New Testament texts to a variety of faces of first century social dynamics. This cannot be a matter of some fixed formula because the number of relevant faces is a variable rather than fixed quantity. In order to sensitize sociologists to what I have been calling "faces," Gurvitch wrote about no less than ten "levels in depth" proper to the social world. I have used his model - I think to some profit

- in approaching the issue of charisma in my study of the posthumous early Christian career of Saint Paul. Paul, his letters, and stories about him became social symbols for the author of the Acts of the Apostles, the authors of the deutero pauline letters, the author of the Acts of Paul and Thecla, the Marcionites, and many others. I tried to make the upward trajectory of Paul's charisma comprehensible in terms of likely events pertaining to the other faces of the early Christian movement - for example, the spontaneous conduct of those first generations of Christians who were raised in the faith and who therefore needed to look to a founding personage rather than to a personal conversion. The charisma of Paul could, I proposed, be understood in terms of Paul as a symbol coming to stand for something at a less visible level of social reality. This was a sociological - as opposed to a literary or theological - appreciation of the symbolic reality of Paul to some generations of early Christians.[17]

It is not the case that one can only proceed from the more visible to the less, in this kind of problematic; one can also proceed from the more subtle to the more readily observable. In my study of the social world of the authentic pauline letters, for example, I suggested the theological archetypes that Paul used were especially suited to the household situation common in early Christianity, wherein persons of vastly different ethnicity and status dwelt together amidst the immediate tensions of family and business, insofar as they transcended the natural divides that could threaten the church.[18] The more evident pluralism of early Christianity comes to mind well after a reading of Paul's theology of the new Adam and of newly-established heirs of God the Father, yet Paul's theological strategy itself becomes manifest only after one has considered the problems that arise from such a pluralism.

So as a matter of strategy one must plot out the operative "levels in depth" of the social dynamics in question, and see what and how many faces there were in a given situation. Was the morphological or ecological surface relevant? What was the organized apparatus? What social models and collective signs were in force, and what kinds of rule constituted them and brought them into play? Were there patterned kinds of collective activity? What social roles were there, and how were they played out? What collective attitudes were there? In everyday life these are more readily apprehended than are religious texts, but if we have largely textual evidence to begin with we must work towards these from that textual evidence, and then establish reasonable connections among all of these faces, but more particularly between each of these and the religious text. We might also infer what is usually less tangible - spontaneous, creative conduct, collective ideas and values, and collective mental states and acts - and then connect these with the religious texts and also with the other levels. All this amounts to a tall order and would be too complex a project to pursue if done, as it were, by formula. However, the informal procedures of human intelligence handle this kind of complexity quite well, once one is attuned to the sociological problematic. Sociologists who have survived the first study after the guided dissertation come to expect a stage of creative perplexity that follows the collection and summation of data. When things work in the end, when we manage to make connections that both surprise us yet seem obvious in a peculiar way, and when they reveal the ironic dialectic across the different faces or levels of the social world, we speak of "the sociological imagination."[19] This imagination is, of course, meta-methodological, and not much is said about it in research methodology texts.

The fact that the sociological truth about one given social phenomenon is to be found not in itself but in another one to which it is related and which is more tangible or less tangible than itself, leads to a most disconcerting result: a well-formulated definition of one's object of inquiry will not necessarily bring to the fore the considerations that will ultimately lead to insights about the phenomenon, because the insight may well pertain to some other but related social face, or level. In this sense, sociological method contrasts that of propositional philosophy. For example, early Christianity was a movement, not a church, sect, cult, or denomination. Before proceeding with our inquiries, we need to explain to ourselves what we mean by "social movement," so that we can separate what we are studying from what we are not.[20] But having done that, we cannot assume that we have at hand a conceptualization of the most important dynamics impinging upon early Christianity. Unlike philosophy, we cannot proceed in such an essentialistic fashion. Rather, our conceptualization will ultimately be subject to the vagaries of the multiple layers or faces of first century life. Similarly, definitions of religion, of text, of tradition, of ritual, and so forth may be of great assistance at various junctures in our research, and I myself have taken great pains to define these terms and nuance them at one time or another; however, no inquiry should be imprisoned within the boundaries of a concept or two. In short, I heartily recommend an avoidance of linguistic philosophy and its conceptual and propositional apparatus like the plague it is, for it is of the very nature of science to be open to insights that are not defined, conceptualized, operationalized, and set up for test in advance. Prior conceptualizations should be lights, not blinders - sensitizers rather than procrustean beds. We have no reason to believe that the subtle dialectics of the social world ever did or ever will follow the stilted procedures of professional philosophy of science, and a sociological strategy must follow the former where it leads, irrespective of the "methodological," or at least methodical, inhibitions of the latter.

I hope in a peculiar sort of way that these brief remarks disappoint as much as satisfy. What they should disappoint is any hope for a formulaic sociology of religion to be lifted out of a textbook. There are many good texts, and I recommend them for an introduction to the field. But sociological research is best advanced in the messy business of seeing the real social world as it is - a fluid, multi-leveled complex of related movements, fronts, systems, and ironies. Such a seeing develops as one becomes familiar with more and more studies, not as one commits formulae to memory. So I put forward the recommendation that one read not only an introductory text and a few classic theories, but also a good number of diverse sociological studies of diverse religious phenomena, in order to develop thereby a sixth sense of when to link phenomena from different-but-related social faces. In the way that baseball and many other sports are experience-intensive rather than feats of speed and strength, sociological research is experience-intensive; it is learned by doing and by following what others are doing. Its successes are generally successes of inference rather than deduction; they require a perverse sort of wisdom that asks how the obvious can be so - in evidence but not noted. Such successes usually find social complexes tied together by tangents, connections among phenomena that are as obvious but as protean as the course of a conversation.

Technique: separation of the textual layers

The sociology of the early Christian movement has literary materials as its "data." Much of this material takes the form of tradition documents, wherein previous formulations are handed down in a somewhat updated form.[21] Research using such material entails source criticism, wherein texts are examined in order to separate different sources and strata from one another.[22] Such work is easier when versions of the source material appear in separate works, so that one would basically look at what the different works have in common, as, for example, the "Q" texts found in the Gospel of Matthew and the Gospel of Luke. It is easier yet when a source that is extant, as, for example, the Gospel of Mark, is used in other gospels. It is very difficult in the case of the Gospel of John, since none of its sources is extant and no other gospel **readily** appears to have used any of the fourth gospel's sources.[23]

After I have separated the textual materials of the fourth gospel's sources, I will set out in Chapter Two to ascertain their respective times of composition. This will enable me to set up something of a trajectory of the Johannine community's history. Then I will be able to proceed with the more sociological aspect of the project, and describe the Johannine part of the early Christian movement in terms of its structural dynamics and place in the social world. That part of the project would not differ essentially from studies of modern new religious movements.[24]

A sociological inquiry of any kind needs to focus on evidence that presents one or more social entities. Each piece of evidence should pertain, however, to only one such entity. Thus, if we were to study modern life style movements, we would be careful not to confound information from any two different movements - say, for example, the background information about the leaders of the pro-life movement and the feminist movement. We might want to compare the two sets of information, but not mix them together. This is a methodological question of representativeness; it is necessary to know who, or what social entity, each piece of information represents. In survey technology, this takes the form of defining a target population and sampling from it.

In the present study we cannot define our population ahead of time in a simple fashion. In one sense, we can say we are interested in the authors and originally intended audiences of the Gospel of John, or "fourth gospel," but that definition does not tell us anything about who these people were and what their religious movement was like. That kind of information is one of the things we might hope to obtain as an outcome of our research. So we have our evidence at hand, a religious literary text traditionally attributed to "John," before rather than after we have a defined population. If the gospel were the product of an author who wrote in one period of time for the benefit of one audience, we could straightway set out looking for clues; but this gospel seems to have been written for more than one audience and to have been written during an extended period of composition. The text of the work is fraught with "aporias," jumps and abrupt changes that, except for a general unity of style, would suggest a multiple authorship; even if there were one author, these "aporias" suggest a second hand had been at work editing together texts that were not originally written as a single work. Alternatively, a revered source person's utterances may have been written down by followers or students, and gathered together in a way that left "seams" between different utterances.

In order to deal with this complex text in a satisfactory manner, we need to understand it to be a **tradition text**.[25] The editor of the published, more or less final version of the gospel evidently thought that certain prior written materials were important, even sacred, presentations of tradition; one could have juxtaposed these materials, producing a sequence of unrelated sayings, as did some other ancients who published gospels, thereby preserving the traditions precisely as received.[26] However, the person responsible for the publication of John thought for some reason that the received materials should be woven together; they may have been the work of the same writer at different junctures of a literary career.[27]

Or they may have been one set of materials useful for appreciating another set. In any case, they were edited together. One may have added an explanation or clarification of one's own here and there, and one may have wanted to make a point or develop a theme by organizing the material in a certain way, but essentially the first editor was working with received traditions that were deemed valuable and worthy of re-presentation.[28]

If this editor of the published gospel, whom I shall call the "redactor," wanted to be true to these traditions, the redactor would leave them sufficiently intact within their earlier arrangement so that they could retain their respective characteristics. This explains the jumps and changes to be found in the text. In order for us to keep from confounding evidence from different writings of these materials, with their differing audiences and different times of composition, we need to un-edit them. That is, we need to sort them out according to their several originary situations. I will speak of these as "sources" for purposes of convenience, even though it could hypothetically have been a matter of the same writer addressing different audiences.

On what basis might these materials be sorted out? First, wherever there is an abrupt change, a jump, the texts on either side of the jump can be assumed to belong to different sources. For example, if Jesus is replying to someone else in a dialogue and suddenly shifts to the second person plural, only to return to the singular a little later, we might assume that the plural material had been inserted into the dialogue. Such jumps can come about either in linguistic features, such as the singular versus plural "you" in the Greek, or in the content of the material, such as a statement expecting the end of all things to come some time in the future, followed by one suggesting that the end had come already in the life of Jesus (future versus "realized" eschatology).[29] In general, it is safest to stick to the more obvious and awkward aporia than to strain theological gnats to look for inconsistencies.

Second, the texts reflect quite different social worlds. In some passages the reader is expected to know something about Palestinian Judaism. Factions and personages are named, such as Pharisees and the high priest, and typical events are mentioned, such as named feasts. (Sometimes after naming one of these, an explanation is given for a reader who might not know anything about Palestinian Judaism, and these explanations are so unnaturally forced into the text that they are obvious insertions of the redactor.) These passages also betray a detailed knowledge of features at architectural sites in Jerusalem that modern archaeology has in general verified.[30] In any instance, these texts tell their story about Jesus, a Jewish teacher in Palestine, from an insider's or local's perspective. Quite in contrast, other passages seem to be socially distant from Palestinian Judaism; they betray a "we/they" stance with respect to "the Jews."[31] Parties and personages are not distinguished or identified, but merely lumped together under that ethnic label. The writer, or at least the writer's intended audience, does not seem to know the details about Palestinian Judaism, much less present anything that the redactor needs to explain to the unknowledgeable reader.

The very fact that there are jumps and skips, inconsistencies, and even repetitions in slightly changed phraseology in the Gospel of John suggests that the redactor who was responsible for the present text left most of the earlier traditional material as found, rather than rewrite the material to eliminate such problems. This is quite in contrast to the stylistic improvements Matthew and Luke made on the text of the Gospel of Mark, which they incorporated into their gospels. If the suggestion that the redactor of John did little if any rewriting is correct - and I think it is - then the text of the gospel can be aproached as comprised of blocks or segments; this would lead us to avoid attributing one word or phrase of a sentence to one source and other parts of the same sentence or phrase to another.

Such a lack of rewriting on the part of the redactor also changes the probabilities involved in hypothesizing about sources ("source criticism") compared to the probabilities involved in hypothesizing about the purposes of the redactor ("redaction criticism"). Not too long ago, it was faddish to focus on source criticism, but then dealing with New Testament texts as "finished products" displaced such source criticism. Such trends, of course, are entirely arbitrary and should not be accorded much attention. Moreover, there is no reason why both kinds of inquiry could not be pursued without affecting their mutual validity. The two approaches need be considered together, however, to make a point about the levels of probability involved in putting forth hypotheses. In the case of the synoptic gospels, the "Q" source common to Matthew and Luke is a hypothesis, and proposals about the audience and users of the Q material are even more hypothetical; however, by juxtaposing the treatment of similar material by the respective authors/redactors of Matthew and Luke one can speak of their redactive purposes with a high level of confidence. That is to say, the probability of accurately recreating Q and its world is lowered by the practice of Matthew and Luke of rewriting their source material, but the probability of correctly ascertaining Matthew's and Luke's purposes is raised by their having rewritten their source material. In the case of the Gospel of John we have the reverse situation; the reluctance of the author to rewrite leaves us with passages that allow us to recreate the worlds of earlier versions of the gospel with greater confidence than in the case of Q, but our efforts to understand any purposes of the final redactor need to be received with greater skepticism than is the case with our readings of Matthew and Luke.

Using the few, simple criteria discussed above, I have sorted out the passages of the fourth gospel. I am certainly not the first person to try to do this; in modern times it has been done by a number of biblical scholars.[32] Working from the vantage point of the 1990's, I have the benefit of these scholars' work, with the earlier endeavors frequently being commented upon by the later ones.[33] In the course of my work, I found that I had sorted the texts into three general categories, which I labeled "A," "B," and "C." "A" material evinced an insider's knowledge of Palestinian Judaism and sites in Jerusalem. It had much to say about companions of Jesus, whom it named, and it professed to be the work of a disciple whom Jesus loved.[34] Some "A" material, the present Chapter 21 of the gospel, seems to have been an early addition to the rest of that layer of tradition;[35] I label this "A_1" in the Appendix. "C" material contained narratives and disputations between Jesus and his critics; it often used the expression, "the Jews," and spoke of the Palestinian Jews within a "we/they" perspective. "B" material consisted of sayings and discourses that the redactor attributed to Jesus; often the "B" passages had textual parallels in the First Letter of John, a work that was probably written some time after most of the materials in the Gospel of John had been composed.[36] These sayings and discourses often turned on a key word that the "A" or "C" material cued in, as it were. When I came upon these sayings, I found myself visualizing something like the layout of Talmudic texts, with the passages to be explained written on one part of a page and explanations written on another part. In the case of the Gospel of John, I thought of the "B" material as written out on the margins, giving insights or presenting meditations on topics that came up in the "A" and "C" material. Sometimes I found parallel passages, with two of the three categories of material presenting different versions of the same saying or narrative.[37] As a matter of convenience, I arranged the text of the gospel in parallel columns, with "A" on the left, "B" usually in the center, and "C" usually on the right. On a few occasions it seemed that there were more than one "B"-like source and more than one "C"-like source, so that I had to use subscript identifiers, such as "B_1" and "B_2" to distinguish them.

The full gospel, as separated into strata columns, can be found in the Appendix. At this juncture, we cannot assume that any given stratum is older than any other; we do not know their times of origin yet. I will take up the question of the temporal ordering of the strata later. In the notes to the text in the Appendix, where I comment on why I placed a text in a given column, I refer to the "A" material as the "primitive narrative" because it seems to provide the narrated order for the whole, with "B" and "C" material inserted into it. Speaking of "A" as "primitive" in that sense does not mean that an insertion might not itself be older, though when I was doing the initial sorting out I was thinking in terms of "A" **probably** being earlier than most of them.

My analysis was done from the Greek text of the gospel,[38] but the presentation in the Appendix and the quotations in the chapters below are my own translations. As with any translation, there are tradeoffs between precision and style; I have leaned toward precision, and where possible without losing the sense of a passage I employ different English synonyms when the Greek text uses different Greek synonyms. This proves to be awkward here and there, but since I am focusing on differences among sources I want the linguistic differences in the original to show through as much as possible. The purpose of the translation is to convey relationships among the three kinds of text to the reader, especially to sociologists who may have no background in Greek. There is no suggestion that my translation would be a better one, or even a good one, for other purposes.

At this point, I recommend that the reader turn to the Appendix and establish a familiarity with the text as presented there. It is not necessary to read through its entirety to follow the discussion in the later chapters below, but becoming familiar with the three kinds of material that turn up in the "A," "B," and "C" columns will be helpful. Those readers whose main interest is in source criticism will want to go through the entire text, however. Those who would separate the texts differently may reach some different conclusions from what are presented in later chapters below, and those who see no grounds for separating texts at all would likely not agree to anything that follows in my discussion. In general, I try to avoid relying on controverted points in source criticism in my sociological depictions, but no doubt some readers will separate differently texts that I do use.

NOTES

1. While the conceptual apparatus of anthropology and sociology are largely the same, anthropologists tend to study tribal peoples by means of participant observation and by interviewing informants while sociologists tend to study larger societies and to use surveys and quantitative analyses. It is not unusual for either kind of scholar to use historical materials. Historical sociologists tend to develop interpretive concepts and engage in comparative analyses more readily than do social historians. Efforts to draw sharp lines between these fields reveal a great deal of concern with what some academics are willing and not willing to read or accept, and little about that into which they purport to make inquiry. This writer has formal training in all three fields, but usually writes as a sociologist.

2. See Rodney Stark, The Rise of Christianity. A Sociologist Reconsiders History (Princeton, New Jersey: Princeton University Press, 1996); pp. 49-71. I am at present unable to evaluate Stark's hypothesis of the prevalence of ethnic Jews among the early Christians.

3. The Gospel of Mark, or second gospel; the Gospel of Matthew, or first gospel; and the

Gospel of Luke, or third gospel - listed here in their probable sequence of composition.

4. By "book" Irenaeus means "chapter" or "section," not a separate work. See Irenaeus of Lyons, Against Heresies 5.33.3-4; quoted here from The Apostolic Fathers. An American Translation, by Edgar J. Goodspeed (London: Independent Press, 1950), p. 263.

5. Eusebius of Caesarea, Church History 3.39, quoting Papias; translation quoted from The Apostolic Fathers, p. 264.

6. For a thorough critique of the view that John son of Zebedee could be the source behind the fourth gospel, See James H. Charlesworth, The Beloved Disciple. Whose Witness Validates the Gospel of John? (Valley Forge, Pennsylvania: Trinity Press International); Charlesworth sees the claim that the source was John as a western church counter to a Syrian provenance, Thomas the Twin.

7. This section is based on an address I gave at the first annual Sociology of Early Christianity Workshop, Latrobe, Pennsylvania, August 1992; a revised version has also appeared as "The More Basic Method in the Sociology of Early Christianity," Foundations & Facets Forum 9:1/2 (1993 [1996]): 7-18.

8. See Anthony J. Blasi, Early Christianity as a Social Movement (Bern and New York: Peter Lang, 1988), "Methodological Appendix."

9. Dieter Georgi, Theocracy in Paul's Praxis and Theology (Minneapolis: Fortress Press, 1991).

10. This has been most adequately explored in Georges Gurvitch, Dialectique et Sociologie (Paris: Flammarion, 1962).

11. Anthony J. Blasi, "Problematic of the sociologists and people under study in the sociology of religion," Ultimate Reality and Meaning 13:2 (1990): 145-156.

12. See Herbert Blumer, Symbolic Interactionism. Perspective and Method (Englewood Cliffs, New Jersey: Prentice-Hall, 1969), especially pp. 150ff.

13. In addition to any statistics text, one may also consult the essays on "radical empiricism" of William James.

14. I debate these issues, within a somewhat different context, elsewhere with the religious studies scholar, Robert Segal; see Anthony J. Blasi, "The Trouble with Religious Studies: Why Scientific Claims in the Study of Religions Should Be Left to Symbolic Interactionists and Other Scientists," Method & Theory in the Study of Religion 7:3 (1995): 251-258, followed by a stimulating response by Segal and by my rejoinder.

15. Georges Gurvitch, "Microsociologie." In Georges Gurvitch (ed.), Traité de sociologie, tome premier, seconde édition corrigée (Paris: Presses Universitaires de France, 1962), pp. 172-184.

16. Georges Gurvitch, "Sociologie en profondeur," in Gurvitch (ed.), Traité de sociologie, pp. 157-171.

17. Anthony J. Blasi, Making Charisma. The Social Construction of Paul's Public Image (New Brunswick, New Jersey: Transaction, 1991).

18. Anthony J. Blasi, Early Christianity as a Social Movement, pp. 51-76, esp. 74-76.

19. The term comes from C. Wright Mills, _The Sociological Imagination_ (New York: Oxford University Press, 1959); Mills added a critical objective to this kind of imagination.

20. See, for example, Blasi, _Early Christianity as a Social Movement_, pp. 5-8.

21. J. Louis Martyn, "Glimpses into the History of the Johannine Community," in M. de Jonge (ed.), _L'Évangile de Jean. Sources, Rédaction, Théologie_ (Leuven: leuven University Press, 1987), pp. 149-175, at p. 149, aptly refers to the fourth gospel as a "literary tel" having strata of evidence on the social history of a community.

22. This of course must be done with the Greek text; the _result_ is presented in translation in the Appendix for the convenience of a general readership. I have formulated my translation so as to highlight those features of the Greek text that affected my source critical decisions. That source criticism must be done in the redactor's language, in this case Greek, is a fundamental point that I would normally not mention, but a review of my _Early Christianity as a Social Movement_ (Bern and New York: Peter Lang, 1988) that appeared in the _Journal of the American Academy of Religion_ proved to be unaware of it, alleging that source critical decisions and subsequent sociological interpretations in the book were based on "idiosyncratic translations."

23. With some reluctance I need to introduce a critical note pertaining to the suggestion that the sources of the fourth gospel are not extant. A recent volume by Thomas L. Brodie, _The Quest for the Origin of John's Gospel. A Source-Oriented Approach_ (New York: Oxford University Press, 1993) asserts they are

extant. Brodie maintains that the gospel "systematically" used the "essence" of each of a vast array of Christian, Jewish, and other works, "transformed" their more superficial aspects, and produced a spiritual, unified statement. Less intelligent than most mortals, I have failed completely in my quest to comprehend the system that Brodie attributes to the (individual) author of the gospel. I attempted to align some of Brodie's proposed textual points of contact, in the manner of synoptic parallels, but found too little in the way of verbal agreements to suggest any direct literary dependencies. It turns out that where Brodie sees thematic parallels (rather subjective caption agreements between texts - e.g., "cost of discipleship") he proposes literary dependencies. Where rather major differences in material and message intrude, he speaks of "reworkings." Given this procedure of manufacturing "evidence" for textual dependencies in the form of caption parallels and dismissing evidence of independence with hypothetical reworkings, it becomes an extraordinary achievement to show any two generally Christian texts to be independent.

Brodie ignores altogether the gaps and jumps that characterize the gospel, taking it to be a polished unity. He therefore can consider and evaluate hypotheses about "the" purpose of the gospel. At one juncture, he baldly asserts the non sequitur that the gospel cannot be understood as a reflection of a conflict within a synagogue because it uses sources. One excursus (in a volume of excursuses) tries to minimize the independence of the fourth gospel by arguing that its specific community location does not exclude its community being the whole human race; clearly Brodie has not understood the basic social scientific insight that whole societies' (let alone races') cultures need be mediated to individuals through specific interactions in smaller groupings of people - precisely as one learns the human race's wondrous inheritance of speech in specific families and under the form of specific dialects. Toward the end of Brodie's book it becomes evident that his purpose is apologetical, that he is writing to further a theological stance that celebrates the development of doctrine within the Christian canon.

24. Anthony J. Blasi, Early Christianity as a Social Movement, specifically compares the early Christian movement to well-documented twentieth century ones, finding that the former contrasted the modern ones in significant ways.

25. See Blasi, Early Christianity as a Social Movement, pp. 199ff.

26. Within the canonical New Testament, the sayings of Jesus collected in a source conventionally labeled "Q" appear in Matthew and Luke. Outside the Bible, the Coptic Gospel of Thomas seems to have had such a collection as a source, and retains the collection character itself. See John S. Kloppenborg, "The Literary Genre of the Synoptic Sayings Source." Ph.D. dissertation, University of St. Michael's College, 1984; and David E. Aune, The New Testament in Its Literary Environment (Philadelphia: Westminster, 1987), pp. 71-72. While most materials in such collections consist of sayings, fragments of narrative also appear in them. Of course, not all collections of older material avoid major rewrites, but the fourth gospel seems to avoid such, given the seams it betrays.

27. On John of Ephesus as the principal author of the Gospel of John, see Martin Hengel, The Johannine Question (London: SCM Press; Philadelphia: Trinity Press International, 1989), especially p. 74.

28. See Raymond F. Collins, These Things Have Been Written. Studies on the Fourth Gospel (Louvain: Peeters Press; Grand Rapids: William B. Eerdmans, 1990), p. 6, who sees the redactor working with traditional, homiletical material, some of which had a basis in history.

29. Barnabas Lindars, "Traditions behind the Fourth Gospel." In M. de Jonge (ed.), L'Évangile de Jean. Sources, Rédaction, Théologie (Leuven: Leuven University Press, 1977, 1987), pp. 107-124, at p. 121, speaks of John having a "method of argument" in which a discourse proceeds "like a spiral staircase, continually returning to its point of entry, but always a stage higher until the top is reached." He argues that inconsistencies of thought, "such as the tension between consistent and realized eschatology, cannot be used as criteria for the separation of sources, because they belong to John's method of argument." I think it would be a flawed procedure to take what could be a result of multiple sources as a "method of argument" or an authorial style, without first showing cases of such a style at work in material which manifestly represents only one layer of tradition. We have known cases of works written in the gospel genre incorporating sources and cannot ignore this fact on the grounds of an hypothesized authorial propensity.

30. See James H. Charlesworth, Jesus Within Judaism. New Light from Exciting

Archaeological Discoveries (New York: Doubleday, 1988), pp. 117ff.

31. One commentator on a version of some of this material that was presented at a meeting insisted that the Greek term I translate as "Jews" should be "Judeans"; this seems only reasonable when the context suggests people from Judea. The term was used to refer to an ethnic group elsewhere in Palestine and elsewhere in the Roman Empire; "Judeans" conveys a geographical specificity that the Greek usage does not warrant in most instances.

32. Among those who have proposed separations into sources are Rudolf Bultmann, D. Moody Smith, J.M. Robinson, R. Kysar, R.T. Fortna, R.E. Brown, Urban C. von Wahlde, and A. Dauer. Others have thought in terms of oral rather than written sources. For a review of the history of these efforts, see D. Moody Smith, _Johannine Christianity. Essays on Its Setting, Sources, and Theology_ (Columbia: University of South Carolina Press, 1984).

33. Raymond E. Brown, _The Gospel According to John (i-xii)_ (New York: Doubleday, 1966), and _The Gospel According to John (xiii-xxi)_ (New York: Doubleday, 1970), gives extensive reviews of the discussions at appropriate junctures in his monumental commentary.

34. The original source may have spoken of an anonymous other disciple, as in Jn. 18.16-16, while "the one whom Jesus loved" may have been added by a redactor soon after the original source person died; see Charlesworth, _Beloved Disciple_, pp. 141ff.

35. See Charlesworth, _Beloved Disciple_, p. 19.

36. Rodney A. Whitacre, Johannine Polemic. The Role of Tradition and Theology (Chico, California: Scholars Press, 1982), pp. 1-4, reviews the literature on the relationship between the Gospel of John and the First Letter of John; the study as a whole argues that the gospel involved a controversy with people outside the Johannine community while the letter involved one with opponents inside it.

37. Interpreting repeated words or phrases as the basic narrative to be cueing in either narrative parallels or cueing in related sayings, is understanding them in quite a different way from M.-É. Boismard, "Un procédé rédactionnel dans le quatrième évangile: la Wiederaufnahme," in M. DeJonge (ed.), L'Évangile de Jean. Sources, Rédaction, Théologie (Leuven: Leuven University Press, 1987), pp. 235-241. Where an insertion interrupts a sentence, the resumptive repetition of a word or phrase in the manner suggested by Boismard is quite plausible; however, when the text separating such repetitions is too long to keep the original sentence in mind, or when the repetition is obviously part of different material, that kind of resumptive repetition is not plausible. Boismard himself would not have every repetition considered to be resumption; see the concluding paragraph in his article.

38. Nestle-Aland Novum Testamentum Graece, 26. neu bearbeitete Auflage, ed. by Kurt Aland, Matthew Black, Carlo M. Martini, Bruce M. Metzger, and Allen Wikgren (Stuttgart: Deutsche Bibelstiftung Stuttgart, 1979).

Ch. 2. Chronology of the Composition of the Fourth Gospel

Now that the identifiable source texts that were edited into the Gospel of John have been separated, as best as we can separate them, we can begin to locate them in time. This is essential to our study because social movements such as early Christianity have careers, so to speak, in which they develop and change; inferences that may be drawn about the movement at one point in its development may not hold for another point in time. Two general strategies for locating the texts in time will be used; in one, I will draw comparisons both **among** the three kinds of text and **between** these and non-johannine works, and in the other one I will search for clues from **within** each of the three Johannine sources. The first strategy will enable me to establish part of the sequence of the composing of the three source texts and of their being edited together into a unified gospel; the second strategy will enable me to relate the times of composition to known historical events.

A. **Comparisons among Johannine source texts and with non-johannine texts**

One feature of the text of the fourth gospel that stands out once one begins to separate the source material into separate columns is that the sayings and discourse material ("B") appear to be made up of disconnected statements that are cued in by important words in the other columns. For example, Jn. 3.20, which is "A" material, i.e., from the primitive narrative, reads as follows: "For everyone who practices evil hates the light and does not come to the light, lest his works be in evidence." The next verse in the gospel, which changes the framework of the discourse abruptly by changing the subject to "truth," was placed in the "B" column; it is a saying that seems to have been cued in by the word, "light," in the text of "A." The saying reads as follows: "But he who acts in truth comes to the light so that his works may be revealed to have been wrought in divinity" (Jn. 3.21). What is interesting is that the cue words sometimes come from the "A" column, the narrative of the anonymous disciple (later termed "beloved disciple") and sometimes from the "C" column, consisting of the narrative materials that seem to be socially distant from Palestinian Judaism. It can be inferred from this that the "A" and "C" material had been edited together beforehand, and that in a later redaction the "B" material was edited into the emergent joint text. Thus we have some elements of a chronology of the development of the Gospel of John: 1) separate compositions of the "A" and "C" materials, 2) editing together of the "A" and "C" materials, and 3) insertion of the "B" material into the edited product.

A consideration of the relationship between John and the two-part book, Gospel of Luke/Acts of the Apostles, can help us verify this chronology. I accept the majority opinion of contemporary New Testament scholars that if the authors of John knew the synoptic gospels they did not use them as sources.[1] Such synoptic material as the Transfiguration, the eucharistic formula, and, in the case of Matthew and Luke, the Q material (including the Beatitudes and the Lord's Prayer) do not appear in John, and no good reason would appear to have existed for these to be excluded if other materials from outside the Johannine community's tradition were to be used. However, there are some agreements of the Johannine and Lukan texts that together differ from both the Gospel of Matthew and the Gospel of Mark. If the Johannine authors did not use, or even studiously avoided using, one or more of the synoptics, how can these agreements of John and Luke against Matthew and Mark be explained? The question must be posed in the light of the widely-accepted theory that the authors of Matthew and Luke used in common two sources: Mark and a sayings source, "Q." This two-source theory explains the many agreements among the synoptics against John, but not the few agreements of one of them with John against the other two. The logical inference is that the author of Luke was familiar with at least some of the Johannine material.[2]

F. Lamar Cribbs has proposed a number of agreements of John and Luke against Mark and Matthew.[3] He infers from the agreements that the author of Luke may have been familiar with the developing Johannine tradition or with an early draft of John. Some of these proposed agreements are more persuasive than others; I limit the analysis here to those I find persuasive.[4] Many of these persuasive agreements pertain to narrative material, and hence do not include any of the sayings and discourse materials that appear in column "B" of my separated source texts of John (See Table I). This absence of material from column "B" does not tell us anything yet, but the presence of both "A" and "C" material suggests that if the author of Luke had known the Johannine material, he knew it after "A" and "C" sources had been joined together.

In addition to the narrative agreements of Luke and John against Mark and Matthew, I find eight verbal parallels persuasive enough to constitute additional agreements of this kind. These parallels are verbal formulae

Table I
Narrative Agreements of Jn. and Lk./Acts against Mt. and Mk.

Passage in Jn.	Lukan Passage	Column in Jn.
1.20 & 3.28	Lk. 3.15 & Acts 13.25	A & C
13.36-38	Lk. 22.31-34	A
19.1-3	Lk. 23.11	A
20.19-29	Acts 13.31	C

such parallel requires a little discussion: Cribbs proposed Jn. 1.14 as a parallel to Lk. rather than details of narrative. A ninth 9.32, which consists of "his glory" in the accusative (*ten doxan autou*). This is not a very remarkable parallel to begin with, but it could be important because it would be a lone agreement involving Johannine material from column "B." It turns out, however, that the same words appear in Jn. 2.11, which is from a "C" column passage. Since an examination of the other eight agreements turns up only material from "A" and "C," it cannot be assumed that Luke was familiar with anything from "B"; see Table II.

From these data one would infer the

Table II

Verbal Agreements of Jn. & Lk./Acts against Mk. & Mt.

Passage in Jn. Column	Passage in Lk./Acts	Text in Jn	
1.7	Acts 19.4	*hina...pisteusosin*	A*
2.11	Lk. 9.32	*ten doxan autou*	C§
10.23	Acts 3.11	*en te*$_i$ *stoa tou Solomonos*	A
10.24b	Lk. 22.67a	*ei su ei ho Christos*	C
10.25a	Lk. 22.67b	*eipon humin kai ou pisteuete*	C
12.36	Lk. 16.8b	*huioi photos*	C
18.37b	Lk. 22.70b	*su legeis hoti... eimi*	A
20.1	Lk. 24.1	*te de mia*$_i$ *ton sabbaton*	C
20.19c	Lk. 24.36	*este eis to meson kai legei autois, Eirene humin*	C

*Not proposed by Cribbs.

§Cribbs proposed Jn. 1.14, which would be B material.

following chronological sequence: 1) separate compositions of the "A" and "C" material found in John, 2) editing together of the "A" and "C" material, 3) composition of Luke/Acts, and 4) insertion of the "B" material into the emergent "A-C" text to form John.

Before turning to extra-biblical material, we should consider one more piece of evidence from the New Testament - Jn. 2.19 and its parallels:

Mk. 14.58b: *Ego kataluso ton naon touton ton cheiropoieton kai dia trion hemeron allon acheiropoieton oikodomeso*

I will destroy this shrine, which is made by hands, and in three days I will build another, which is not made by hands.

Mt. 26.61b: *dynamai katalusai ton naon tou theou kai dia trion hemeron oikoddomesai*

I can destroy the shrine of God and in three days build it.

Acts 6.14b: *Iesous ho Nazoraios houtos katalusei ton topon touton*

Jesus the Nazorean will destroy this place

Jn. 2.19: *Lusate ton naon touton kai en trisin hemerais egero auton ("C" material)*

Destroy this shrine and in three days I will raise it

The saying appears not only in different phraseology (with John sharing few words with any of the parallels - and those it does share it shares with Mark), but in different contexts. Mark and Matthew put it at the trial of Jesus; Luke deletes it from there because it already appears at the trial of Stephen in Acts. John is alone in putting it on the lips of Jesus and in the context of the Temple incident. His version seems to be independent of the others; the others phrase it as a misunderstanding on the part of Jerusalem authorities while the fourth gospel phrases it as Jesus would have meant it if he had had advance knowledge of a resurrection. Mark does not necessarily know about the historical destruction of the Temple; the accusation is vague and belies no knowledge of the fire that did destroy the Temple. Matthew appears to be dependent on Mark, deleting the latter's invidious comparison between a shrine made by hands and one not made by hands, a kind of comparison traditionally directed against idolatry. John is more concerned to present Jesus as the substitute for the Temple; that implies a knowledge of the absence of the Temple. This passage of "C" material would have been formulated after 70 C.E., when the Temple was destroyed by fire. The editing together of "A" and "C" material would also have been done after 70.

Now that we have made comparisons among the source texts of the fourth gospel and among the several canonical gospels, we can make similar comparisons with extra-canonical texts. There are quotations of the Gospel of John in some of the earliest examples of extra-biblical Christian literature. Clement of Rome, writing circa 95 C.E. to the Corinthian Christians (1 Clement 49.1) uses language that parallels Jn. 14.15. The Johannine text reads:

Ean agapate me, tas entolas tas emas teresete

If you love me, keep my commandments.

This is "B" column material in John; however we do not know that Clement knew of it from John. The "B" material may have had an independent existence and have been known to Clement in independent form. We can only conclude from Clement's allusion that this part of the "B" material had been composed before the mid nineties when Clement wrote.[5] However, eight convincing allusions to the fourth gospel are to be found in the letters of Bishop Ignatius of Antioch, writing circa 112 C.E.; see Table III. While Ignatius cites mostly "B" material, probably from memory, there is the reference to "living water." The author of John could not have been taking these expressions from Ignatius, since one of them had already been cited by Clement of

Table III

Allusions to the fourth gospel in the letters of Ignatius

Ignatius	John	John's text	Column
Eph. 5.2	6.33	ho...artos tou theou	B
Eph. 17.1	12.31 or 16.11	ho archon tou kosmou toutou	A or B
Tral. 4.2	12.31 or 16.31	ho archon tou kosmou toutou	A or B
Rom. 7.1	12.31 or 16.31	ho archon tou kosmou toutou	A or B
Rom. 7.2	4.10	hudor zon	C
Rom. 7.3	6.33 and	ho...artos tou theou	B
	6.51	ho artos...hon ego doso he sarx mou estin	B
Phil.2.1-2	10.11-12	(Good Shepherd discourse)	B

Rome. So they were already available by the time of Ignatius. Moreover, the hypothesis that all of this was contemporary Christian ritual language would not hold for the allusion from the Good Shepherd discourse. The simplest explanation appears to be that Ignatius knew of this material from one text, into which it had been edited.

With the benefit of all the above information, we can begin to put some dates in our chronology:

Composition of A (date unknown)
Composition of C (at least part of it after 70)
Editing together of A and C
Composition of Luke/Acts
Composition of B at least by this time, maybe earlier
Composition of First Clement (circa 95)
Editing of B material into the A-C text at least by this time
Letters of Ignatius of Antioch (circa 112)

B. Considerations based on the text of the fourth gospel

1. "A" material

There are no good clues in the "A" material indicating when it was written, but there are clues about the author, who is referred to as the "other disciple" and the "disciple whom Jesus loved." The author was known to the high priest, Caiaphas (Jn. 18.15) and was therefore sensitive about being suspected of betraying Jesus to the authorities. Hence he is emphatic that it was Judas Simon Iscariot who betrayed Jesus (6.70-71, 12.4, 13.2, 13.26-27, 18.2ff.). He was aware of people in Jerusalem who believed in Jesus, but he took a disparaging attitude toward rulers who believed in him but acquiesced to Jesus being condemned to death (7.31, 40, and 46; 8.30; 10.42; 12.42). Further, he was close to the family of Jesus (19.27). All this does not tell us precisely when this individual wrote, but it had to have been within the lifetime of someone who knew Jesus and the contemporaries of Jesus. Had he been a youth and lived a century, he could not have written after the year 110. Since the "A" material had been written down prior to Luke/Acts and First Clement, we already know it had been composed well before 110.

It should be noted that the "A" material is identified with the Jewish world. Jn. 4.22 says that salvation is from the Jews. We have already observed this writer's many references to believers in Jesus in Jerusalem. Jn. 12.23 observes that because of danger Jesus never conducted a mission to the Greeks. The association of the author with the family of

Jesus brings to mind the leadership of James the Brother of the Lord over the Jewish Christian church in Jerusalem until 62 C.E.[6] Nothing in the "A" material seems to insist upon Torah observance, however,[7] something James and his associates seemed to insist upon (see Gal. 2.12). This dispute between Pauline Christianity and Jewish Christianity over the imposition of some observances on gentile Christians seems to have left the Johannine world untouched. This absence of concern with observance, calendar, and related issues is surprising given the focus on these found in other first century Jewish religious materials. We can only speculate about this, but my guess is that the synagogue setting from which these materials emerged was located in a heavily Gentile setting that led the local Jewish population to unite as a minority group and avoid divisive issues.

2. **"B" material**

John 5.35 says, referring to John the Baptist, "He was the lamp, lit and shining; but you wished to rejoice in its light for a time." The next verse says that Jesus has a greater testimony than the baptizer's. Later on the same discourse adds, "You search the scriptures because you suppose you have eternal life in them...." The discourse seems to be criticizing followers of John the

Baptist who remained non-christian Jews. Since some of the earliest followers of Jesus had been followers of the baptizer, this kind of address appears to reflect a parting of the ways between Baptist Jews and Christian Jews. Significantly, Jn. 15.1-8, the "vine and branches" discourse, focuses on people leaving the Christian community: "If anyone not remain on me, he is thrown out as a branch and withers, and they gather them up and throw them into the fire, and it burns." At least this part of the "B" material seems to have been written after some followers of John the Baptist had parted ways with the Johannine Christians.[8]

The "B" material includes a number of doublets and near doublets. Their very existence raises the possibility that some of the material had been composed at one point in time and then revised later on. A particularly interesting doublet is to be found in chapter six. Jn. 6.58a reads, "This is the bread that has come down from heaven, such as the fathers did not eat and died." The reference to the fathers is to Exodus 16.13-35, itself a doublet recounting God supplying the Hebrews manna, bread from heaven, during their forty-year sojourn in the wilderness; all would die, according to the narrative, before entering the promised land. The verse in John makes an invidious comparison between the old bread that gave earthly life, and a new bread that is to give eternal life in heaven. What is interesting is the change that the parallel Johannine "B" verse adds to this: "I am the bread of life. Your fathers ate the manna in the wilderness and died. This is the bread that is coming down from heaven, so that anyone who would eat of it would also not die" (Jn. 6.48-50). It is not <u>the</u> fathers but <u>your</u> fathers. A change in identity has occurred, wherein the Johannine author and audience no longer consider themselves Jews. Again a parting of ways has occurred, this time between Christians and Jews.

If the Johannine Christians had parted ways with some Jews, did they identify themselves with Christians who retained some Jewish standing? Evidently not.[9] Jn. 8.31-37a seems to be addressed to such Jewish Christians; and while it affirms the authenticity of their Christianity, it criticizes them as being in some form of servitude.[10] "Then Jesus said to the Jews who had believed him, 'If you keep my word you are truly my disciples, and you will learn the truth, and the truth will free you'" (8.31-32). The Jewish believers are made to question any need to be made free. This seems to be an oblique reference to Torah observances, but at 8.34 the text turns to servitude as a metaphor for sin; however, the immediate context does not seem to call for a caution about sin. Evidently, there had been an insertion into this text; at first it meant to refer to Torah observance by the Jewish Christians. The parting of ways between Jewish and non-Jewish Christians may be what occasioned the several references to a desired Christian unity in the "B" material. Jn. 10.16 would have there be one flock and one shepherd, and in several places chapter seventeen would have the followers of Jesus be united.

The "B" material also speaks of an excommunication of Christians from the synagogue, and to the execution of Christians in the name of religion (Jn. 16.2). Exclusions of Christians from the synagogue may have occurred as early as 80 C.E.[11] Membership in a synagogue was not important for Jewish identity in Palestine before the destruction of the Temple in 70; one was a Jew by living as one in a Jewish community. Indeed, the synagogue was most characteristic of diaspora Judaism, where one had to maintain Jewish identity against a non-Jewish environment.[12] The "B" material is either from outside Palestine, or from after 80, or both. In contrast to an exclusion from the synagogue, Luke (12.11 and 21.12) speaks of the followers of Jesus being brought before synagogues, as would be miscreant members of the Jewish community, but members nonetheless. Luke's sources would appear to be pre-80, the fourth gospel's "B" material post-80.

Finally, Jn. 21.18 contains a legendary saying about the manner of Peter's death. We do not know for certain when Peter died, but Paul was still resisting his influence in the fifties when he wrote Galatians and First Corinthians.

3. "C" material

Some of the "C" texts (Jn. 9.22 and 12.42) reflect exclusions of Christians from synagogues. As noted above, this may have begun to happen as early as 80 C.E., but would not be as significant in Palestine before the destruction of the Temple as in the diaspora or in Palestine after 70. Another indicator of the date of composition is Jn. 2.19, which alludes to the destruction of the Temple. And quite in contrast to the "A" material, the "C" texts show hostility toward the family of Jesus (Jn. 7.5: "For his brothers did not believe in him"). Following John the Baptist, being Jewish, and following Jesus are seen as three distinct alternatives (Jn. 3.25). The people of Jerusalem are distrusted (2.25), as is Nicodemos, the Christian Pharisee (Jn. 3.3b-10). This material was evidently written in its present form after a parting of ways with the followers of the baptizer, with the Jewish community, and with the Jewish Christians and relatives of Jesus.

Martin Hengel presents an interesting thesis regarding the author of the Fourth Gospel and Johannine letters; he suggests that the author, John of Ephesus ("John the Elder"), was a member of a priestly family in Jerusalem and had been a young disciple of Jesus. As a Christian in Jerusalem, he had high regard for John Son of Zebedee, a leader of the Jerusalem Christians. He migrated to Ephesus and founded a school. There may have been, according to Hengel, some historical basis to the tradition given in the Revelation of John that John of Ephesus had been exiled at some time to the island of Patmos. When John wrote the materials that were to be published as his gospel, he allowed references to himself, "the disciple whom Jesus loved," to merge with references to John Son of Zebedee.[13] I would add the observation that Paul never mentions John of Ephesus, so that the latter's migration would have happened after Paul's time in Ephesus. If John of Ephesus had been punished by exile, he would have been cautious upon his return, especially as the persecution of Christians in Asia Minor became more serious. That would be why he does not identify himself in the gospel, except as the enigmatic "disciple whom Jesus loved," and why he allowed for a possible confusion between himself and John Son of Zebedee. This could be important for our chronology, insofar as it would place the beloved-disciple material (i.e., the "A" material) in Ephesus after the time of Paul there, after the mid-fifties, and perhaps after a period of exile on Patmos; we should think circa 65. The Hengel thesis depends, of course, on an association of the gospel with Ephesus, and that is something that many scholars question.

There is one more piece of evidence that in itself does not prove much but is consistent with the source-critical results that are presented in the Appendix. One set of parallels to the Fourth Gospel in early Christian literature appears in the Egerton or "Unknown" Gospel.[14] The parallels occur in a controversy narrative in which Jesus addresses some rulers of the people with words that resemble three verses in chapter five of the Gospel of John: 5.39, 45, and 46. Notably, all three of these verses in my source allocation (see Appendix) come from the same layer of tradition ("B_1"). A fourth, and more distant and doubtful parallel, in which Jesus is depicted as citing something his opponents had said beforehand, might correspond to Jn. 9.29; I allocated that verse to another layer of tradition ("C_1").[15] We have no solid evidence about the place or time of the Egerton Gospel in the trajectory of early Christian traditions and therefore cannot draw any inferences about the "B_1" layer, much less "C_1," from these parallels, except to suggest that "B_1" derived in part from some of the same traditional material from which part of the Egerton Gospel derived.

C. **Results**

If we add what we have learned from the texts of the fourth gospel to what we learned from comparisons among the texts and of the texts with extra-Johannine literature, we have a slightly more complete chronology of the composition of the Gospel of John. We still do not know exactly how early the "A" material is, and we do not know whether the "B" material was edited into the "A-C" text before or after the composition of First Clement. Nevertheless, we have the order in which the three bodies of material found in the gospel were composed, their temporal relationship to some important events within the Johannine community, and their temporal relationships to a few external events the dates of which are more or less precisely known; see Table IV.

Of course, mine is not the first attempt to construct a history of the composition of the fourth gospel. In a deservedly influential book, Raymond Brown presents a

Table IV
Composition Chronology of the Fourth Gospel

1. Johannine Christians consider themselves Jews; they are close to the Jerusalem church.

2. Migration of the source person out of Palestine

3. c. 65 Composition of "A" material.

4. Composition of early "B" material.

5. 70 Destruction of the Temple; flight of Jewish Christians from Jerusalem.

6. 80 Exclusion of Christians from synagogues begins.

7. Johannine Christians no longer consider themselves Jews; parting of ways with Jewish Christians.

8. Composition of "C" material.

9. Editing together of "A" and "C" material

10. Composition of Luke/Acts.

11. Parting of ways with followers of John the Baptist.

12. Composition of the later "B" material.

13. c. 95 Composition of First Clement.

14. Editing together of "B" material with the "A-C" text by this time.

15. c. 112 Letters of Ignatius of Antioch.

history that he worked out,[16] and he too constructs a history of the Johannine community on the basis of the composition history. Brown describes an "originating group" (50s to 80s C.E.) having relatively standard expectations and including followers of John the Baptizer. This much is consistent with my hypothesis, insofar as I identify "A" material written for a grouping about the year 65 C.E. However, Brown goes on to suggest that a second group joined this one in that early period, bringing with it an anti-Temple bias, converts from Samaria, and a high christology (Jesus as having a divine pre-existence). That there was some early literary material that had a high christology appears to be the case to me also; I labeled it **early "B" material**. However, I do not posit a second group but rather assume that some theological diversity was to be found in any proto-christian grouping from the beginning. This is largely an interpretive difference that is probably independent of different source-critical conclusions; Brown seems to find it necessary to explain theological diversity (in terms of the merger of different groups) while I find theological uniformity and crystallized positions to be the phenomena that call for explanation, taking diversity as the more natural situation.

In Brown's model, a high christology accounts for a rejection of the Christian trajectory, leading to a schism in which there is an expulsion from a synagogue. While some high christological elements are clearly early, the negative reaction to them would be immediate if it were a high christology alone that would spark such a reaction. That is to say, ejections from the synagogue would be immediate, before the earliest exponents of the Jesus tradition had gained any followers. I am inclined to suspect that the very fact that some new teachers attracted a following in a small ethnic community itself added to the problem; I will expand upon this in a later chapter where I speak of a jurisdictional dispute. I also suspect that the nationalist movement in the Jewish world, which reached its high point in Palestine in the 60s, would arrive in other localities at various points in time, and upon arrival lead to a desire for Jewish unity and relative uniformity. Brown and I both place the removal of the Johannines from a synagogue, which I will describe as a schism, in the decade of the 80s.

From the period of the 90s, Brown and I both see the emergence of more high christological materials, defensive discourses against the non-christian Jews, and texts that refer to other Christian groupings. Brown does not find a layering of these literary materials as do I, with "B" passages being edited into both "A" and "C" passages. Rather, he focuses on a different phenomenon, the secession of docetists from the adherents of the author of the Epistles of John. I do not offer an alternative to this aspect of Brown's analysis; it is well supported by the literary material found in the epistles. Rather, I have limited myself to the fourth gospel, which admittedly has a few anti-docetist verses, and to that gospel's principal concerns, which do not include, as far as I can ascertain, a conflict with docetists.

NOTES

1. For a history of the scholarly study of the relationship between the Gospel of John and the synoptic gospels, see D. Moody Smith, _John Among the Gospels. The Relationship in Twentieth Century Research_ (Minneapolis: Fortress, 1992).

2. Raymond E. Brown, _The Gospel According to John (i-xii)_ (New York: Doubleday, 1966), p. xlvii, sees the influence of Johannine material on Luke as an open question.

3. F. Lamar Cribbs, "St. Luke and the Johannine tradition," _Journal of Biblical Literature_ 90 (1971): 422-450.

4. Ones I do not find persuasive are Jn. 1.20/Acts 13.25a; Jn. 1.26/Acts 13.25b; Jn. 1.29-34/Lk. 3.18-22; Jn. 2.1-11/Lk. 4.14-16; Jn. 6.1-4/Lk. 9.10-17; Jn. 7.50-51/Acts 5.34-39; Jn. 10.24, 36/Lk. 22.67, 70; Jn. 12.13/Lk. 19.38; Jn. 18.38-19.6/Lk. 23.4, 13-22; Jn. 20.11/Lk. 24.13; Jn. 20.31/Acts 17.3.

5. Other Johannine allusions for 1 Clement have been proposed, but this is the only one I find persuasive.

6. The term, "Jewish Christian," is used here to refer to adherents of the Jesus tradition who also maintained the customs of the Jewish ethnic group. Smaller categories within that one would be 1) Judean Christians, 2) ethnically Jewish Christians who believed Torah observances should be normative for all Christians, and 3) Christians whose oral or written traditions were those of such writings as the Gospel of the Hebrews. These smaller categories are perfectly interesting topics for inquiry, but not the ones in question in the present study.

7. This is also noted by J. Louis Martyn, "Glimpses into the History of the Johannine Community," in M. de Jonge (ed.), <u>L'Évangile de Jean. Sources, Rédaction, Théologie</u> (Leuven: Leuven University Press, 1987), pp. 149-175, at p. 158.

8. Raymond E. Brown, <u>The Community of the Beloved Disciple</u> (New York: Paulist, 1979), pp. 29-30 and 69-71 sees similar implications, but does not speak of a parting of the ways.

9. Jack T. Sanders, <u>Schismatics, Sectarians, Dissidents, Deviants. The First One Hundred Years of Jewish-Christian Relations</u> (Valley Forge, Pennsylvania: Trinity Press International, 1993) finds more evidence of

tension between Jewish and Gentile Christians than between non-Christian Jews and Christians.

10. Brown, Community of the Beloved Disciple, p. 77, follows the discourse further, as it is arranged in the final version of the fourth gospel, until it reaches a declaration of a higher christology; this enables Brown to conclude that the dispute was between Samaritan Johannine Christians and Jewish Johannine Christians who parted ways over the high christology of the former. If my separation of source texts is correct at this juncture, one would not be able to reach that conclusion.

11. Fréderic Manns, John and Jamnia: How the Break Occurred Between Jews and Christians c. 80-100 A.D. (Jerusalem: Franciscan, 1988), p. 26. There is much discussion over whether the birkath ha-minim, a curse in the synagogue prayer, was meant to be directed at Christians; Rodney A. Whitacre, Johannine Polemic. The Role of Tradition and Theology (Chico California: Scholars Press, 1982), p. 8, notes astutely that it need not have been intended at first as a step against Christians for it to soon acquire such a purpose or to have the effect of excluding Christians from the synagogues.

12. Anthony J. Saldarini, Pharisees, Scribes and Sadducees in Palestinian Society. A Sociological Approach (Wilmington, Delaware: Michael Glazier, 1988), pp. 194-195.

13. Martin Hengel, The Johannine Question (London: SCM Press; Philadelphia: Trinity Press International, 1989), esp. p.132.

14. A modern translation is provided in Jon B. Daniels, "The Egerton Gospel," The Fourth R 4:5 (1991): 9-13.

15. Egerton 1.2/Jn. 5.39; Egerton 1.3/Jn. 5.45; Egerton 1.4/Jn. 9.28; and Egerton 1.6/Jn. 5.46. I do not find a proposed parallel of Egerton 3.2 with Jn. 3.2 at all persuasive because the relevant Egerton material is comprised of too few, very common words.

16. Brown, Community of the Beloved Disciple.

Ch. 3 "Forum" as a Generic Social Category

Though placed third in sequence, this is not the third chapter of the present study, in order of composition. Chapters One and Two were indeed written first and second, independently of anything to follow, because methodological principles require that the source criticism and dating of the texts precede any interpretation of them. It would have been a case of circular reasoning to interpret a text first, then base a source criticism on the interpretation, and finally elaborate the interpretation on the basis of the source critical conclusions. So only after having isolated the three layers of literary tradition that appear in the Appendix, was any attempt made to develop the sociological interpretation. That sociological work, reported below, followed a "grounded theory" problematic, wherein the qualitative data (in the present case, the three textual layers) were approached in the first instance with only the most generic and vaguely defined concepts. In the course of engrossing oneself in each text, the evidence was itself to suggest any further conceptual precision. The procedure was intended to be as inductive as humanly possible, within the unavoidable constraints of the hermeneutic circle, so that the concepts with which we regard the social world of the Johannine Christians would reflect their understandings rather than our own presuppositions. Many sociologists maintain that this approach is preferable even in the study of our own modern society;[1] it would appear to be even more important in the study of a social world that is as removed in time from the contemporary world as early Christianity. So I engrossed myself in the three textual layers, one at a time, and drafted Chapters Four, Five, and Six, before writing this one. What follows here is an exposition of the sociological concepts that came to mind as a result of writing those three chapters. Naturally, these concepts will reflect both the modern and the ancient worlds insofar as the ancient data led me to highlight aspects of the modern sociological repertory of concepts while at the same time my modern repertory led me to highlight selected features of the ancient texts. This is simply to say that the present conceptual discussion embodies a necessary dialectic of new and old.

Mainstream sociological theory has long recognized that the discipline is a science rather than a philosophical exercise only to the extent that it encompasses social worlds on those worlds' own terms, and hence that it is a science to the extent that it is interpretive. The subtitle of **Wirtschaft und**

Gesellschaft, Max Weber's famous general sociological treatise, **Grundriss der verstehenden Soziologie**, "Outline of Interpretive Sociology,"[2] reflected this concern. Unfortunately, the philosophy of science that is usually taught in the English-speaking world focuses more on propositional theories than on social worlds, and speaks of "testing," or more subtly, of "falsifying" social theories. The situation has not been helped by the necessity of applying the experimental design logic in introductory methodology courses in sociology departments in order to keep questionnaire and quantitative data enthusiasts from going on "fishing expeditions" for randomly-occurring correlations among "variables." Nevertheless, for purposes of concept formation the interpretive problematic is widely accepted, and it is the result of a process of concept formation that is reported here.

The significance of this basic decision to pursue a "grounded theory" problematic can be seen when contrasted with the alternative. That alternative is to seize upon some favored theory first and proceed to apply it to every possible object of inquiry. Hence one would "be" a marxist and look for "class" conflicts in the ancient world in a manner that Karl Marx himself would have been too intelligent to entertain. Or one would become obsessed with the rather arbitrary "grid/group" typology of Mary Douglas and impose that on ancient texts. Or again one would insist that ancients had "dyadic" personalities and could have had no other kind. No more than one would in everyday life limit one's consociates to being caricatures of philosophical positions and refuse to accept them as meaning-creating persons, should one proceed in such a manner in a sociological study. The goal is not to use concepts as blinders, to see less because of them, but to open up the possibility of seeing as much as possible. Competent social scientists know this, even if certain philosophers do not.

A useful kind of concept for interpreting social worlds is one that denotes a "form of sociation." "Sociation" simply refers to a pattern of interpersonal interaction, and a form of sociation denotes a particular one such pattern. The classical sociologist, Georg Simmel, thought of such a form as having similarities from one case to the next, irrespective of the "content" of the interactions in question; hence superordination/subordination would be similar in essential respects whether in a government bureaucracy or in a gang.[3] The coalition of two against one could occur in a threesome of siblings, a competition among three unions at an industrial site, or in the foreign relations of three nation states - each of these representing the "triad" form of sociation. Understanding the form of sociation present in any given historical situation helps one identify the possible lines of activity that may take place in it; one would not look for a coalition in a two-party conflict but would be on the lookout for one in a triad. This kind of analysis obviously does not yield causal explanations for social conduct; the social actors themselves are the causes of their conduct. Rather the analysis leads one to see the potential lines of conduct that inhere in a social situation and enables one to interpret people's actions in the light of those potentialities.

Nature of concept needed

The array of sociological conceptualizations available for use in inquiry presents us with some general alternatives. For example, some concepts are macro-sociological; they pertain to whole societies. Others are micro-sociological; they pertain to small groups. Then there are levels of inclusiveness between these - the organizational and community levels, for example. The "data" in the Gospel of John do not lead us to the macro-sociological level; we do not see the formation of status groups, power blocs, or class systems characteristic of the roman Empire. Rather, here and there, we see some local effect of such macro-structures - references to persecution. It is possible to make a macro-level interpretation of a text that responds for the most part to persecution - as one might, for example, with the Revelation of John and with other apocalyptic works. However, the fourth gospel does not read like a response to official Rome or to some other large political entity. Neither does it articulate a class perspective or a society-wide system of status group stratification. There does appear within it a great deal of local status group concern, especially in regard to local Jewish ethnic identity. So we are led by the text away from macro-sociological conceptualizations, away from such concerns as tributary systems and imperial elites - not at all because these are unworthy of our concern but because the focus of the text in hand is more local in <u>its</u> orientation.

On the other hand, the focus of the text, while not macro, is not individual. An individual conceptual framework such as, for example, cognitive dissonance theory, may apply well to the biography of a person such as Paul of Tarsus.[4] The fourth gospel, however, does not have the individual mentality of one person as its theme.

Cognitive dissonance may also be used to characterize **typical** individual responses to **typical** situations, such as how people respond when their heart-felt expectations are disconfirmed. However, this is still quite different from what is there to be found in the fourth gospel, where we find that some members in a local community, some among the synagogue, respond one way to the Jesus tradition and others quite another way. Again, it is not that cognitive dissonance theory or any other individually-focused theories are flawed or that they cannot provide an insight here and there, but rather the focus of the gospel is other than individual.

If the appropriate conceptualizations are not to come from macro-sociological theoretical traditions such as structural functionalism or marxian theory, and not from individually-focused social psychology, the remaining level is to be found in the intermediate level of groups, organizations, and communities. Groups, when they acquire more or less formalized roles and rules ("structure"), become organizations. When they set up boundaries around themselves, holding themselves apart in contradistinction to other groups, they become communities. Specifically organization-centered and community-centered sociological conceptualizations may apply in such cases. However, as later chapters will reveal, the world of the fourth gospel does not seem to have been so crystallized as either organizations or communities - at least not at the outset. The Christians will be seen to develop a group identity, but there are no references to a local formal organization with officers and norms, as one finds in the various letters of Ignatius. And while the later passages of the fourth gospel seem to reflect separate Jewish and Christian communities, that is not the case with the earlier passages. As conceptualizations, organization theory and community theory presuppose established social patterns, circumstances for better or for worse already in place. The fourth gospel, in contrast, will be seen in the later chapters to present us with a trajectory in which an organization and a community might **develop**.

I went looking for a theoretical perspective that would give me some working concepts, even a vocabulary, for what seems to come to the fore in the Gospel of John by way of social formations. Something processual seemed necessary, given the presence of a trajectory in the gospel, but the neo-marxian notion of a **project** implied a greater political concern than can be found in the text, and contemporary structuration theory seems too macro-sociological. The dramaturgical concepts seem more relevant for observational data than textual, while communication theory would center more on the nature of the text itself than its social environs. In my search I happened upon the rather antiquated collective behavior approach, which at least applied to **localized processes**. What Robert Park did with it, in his dissertation on the crowd and the public,[5] suggested a way to render it useful for understanding the kind of social processes that seem to be in evidence in the fourth gospel. The concept I think is most useful is not quite the fully developed "public" of which Park wrote, but it bears some resemblance to it.

Naturally, while the focus of the fourth gospel and, hence, of our conceptual apparatus may be local, we are not entitled to ignore and contradict what we know about other levels. We know, for example, that the macro-level political apparatus of the Roman Empire was socially artificial in the sense that people identified themselves in ethnic and local terms. We know that many people spoke Greek and Aramaic, among other languages, not Latin. We know that many religions were local in nature. It would be a major distortion to depict the whole Empire or the whole of the Mediterranean Basin as a singular cultural area, while such local and ethnic differences thrived. What happened among Christians and Jews in one place cannot be assumed to be a simple example or case in point of something happening throughout the first century Mediterranean world, nor can we explain the local community events in terms of some sweeping, regional pattern.

Forum

Now the concept that came to my mind in the course of occupying myself with the texts was "forum." This is not a pre-existing technical term in sociology, but a variation on some disciplinary concepts with which it bears some resemblance. So I will review those other concepts in order to approximate what I have in mind when I refer to the "forum" form of social interaction, and add further precision where I think it should be helpful. The broadest of these concepts is **collective behavior**, the phenomenon of gathered people engaging in one or more lines of action that they would not have pursued alone. In the nineteenth century collective behavior had been associated with analyses of revolutions that were fought out in the streets of the European capitals, especially the 1789 revolution in Paris. Gustave Le Bon, who had first-hand experience with the Franco-Prussian War and the Paris Commune, spoke of "organized" or "psychological" crowds in this context, referring in a rather polemical fashion to a kind of behavior that formed a unity among a number of people on the basis of a contagion that represents a lower level of civilization than do the minds of the individuals composing that unity. He focused on the presence of irrational crowd behavior in political life and elsewhere. When speaking of religious or political sects, he had in mind a subset of this kind of crowd phenomenon.[6]

Le Bon's "crowd psychology" approach to collective behavior, apt perhaps for the study of modern riots and sports crowds, differs from what I have in mind in several important respects: It limits the focus to what happens spontaneously at moments of collective excitation, thereby excluding developmental processes that take place over extended periods of time. Specifically, it excludes any consideration of people taking impressions from crowd experiences, pondering them, and conducting themselves in subsequent gatherings in reasoned and planned courses of activity. It also fails to appreciate collective settings as theatre, as occasions in which various aspects of daily life can be symbolically recapitulated and placed in a wider social context in a nondiscursive manner. Moreover, it de-emphasizes the extent to which subworlds that are defined by group identities are reinforced rather than suspended in crowd situations. Nevertheless, the collective behavior approach does bring to the fore the fact that spontaneity amidst gatherings can be an important social force.

In the same scholarly tradition we find Scipio Sighele's concept of the **secte**.[7] As was Le Bon, Sighele was describing a social phenomenon that he considered to be negative in character; specifically he was developing a conceptual framework for criminology in order to comprehend crimes that are collective rather than individual in nature. He did not limit his focus to street phenomena, usually the resort of poor or otherwise powerless people, but included as well the political chicanery of legislators and factional conspiracies of modern business tycoons and political players.

> On the one hand, we have the rich, the bourgeois, the cultivated people, who in politics and business sell their vote, their influence, and, by using intrigue, the ruse, and the lie, steal the public's money; on the other hand we have the poor, the mean, the ignorant, who by the conspiracies of anarchists, by demonstrations and riots attempt to revolt against the condition that is imposed on them and protest against

> the immorality that comes from high.[8]

There is more sympathy for the commoner to be found here than in the writings of Le Bon, but in the context of the times Sighele was referring to lower class actions that would be termed "terrorism" eight or nine decades later - assassination, dynamiting buildings, looting, and the like. He went on to speak of different kinds of crowd. As did Le Bon, he spoke of an event unifying associable people into an association having ephemeral goals, but sometimes the crowd that is thusly unified is composed of heterogeneous people who have nothing in common to keep them together. Other crowds have more stability insofar as they can periodically gather on repeated occasions. Other crowds, such as the parliament, may be divided. Different from all these is what he called the **secte**, a unity of otherwise diverse people who share a common faith or ideal.

> The **secte** is a chosen and permanent crowd; the crowd is a transitory **secte** and one that does not choose its members. The **secte** is the chronic form of the crowd; the crowd is the acute form of the **secte**.[9]

Sighele was obviously articulating an important insight, but his conceptual apparatus was self-contradictory insofar as a crowd is inherently ephemeral and cannot be "permanent" or "chronic." We might think of a **secte** representing a continuity among a number of related crowd phenomena. The **secte** would be a form of sociation having crowd behavior as a potential activity inherent within it.

In describing the psychology of the **secte**, Sighele provided us with a number of important insights. He noted that a person's actions are not isolated and atomistic but in fact are shaped by a veritable interior multitude of ancestors, contemporaries, and educators within one's mind. Such factors have their impact in crowd situations insofar as crowds act in many cases with some implicit idea of a goal. The members of the **secte** have a specific ideal goal in mind, and they may at first have to enter into a destructive line of action in order to clear the way for their ideal, and act more as a party than as a **secte** at a later stage of their group development. Thereby they would develop into something they had not thought of at the inception of the **secte**'s history. Nevertheless, according to Sighele, the members of a legitimate association such as a party may often be dispersed and hence not act as a crowd while the members of a **secte** are almost always gathered.[10]

In a dissertation that sought to highlight the essential character of sociology's matter of inquiry, Robert Park, later to become a highly influential sociologist at the University of Chicago, reviewed the literature in which the "collective behavior" tradition of sociology had been articulated.[11] In so doing, he was particularly concerned that a scientific approach be respected, wherein the unity and connectedness of the discipline would be founded on the basis of a fundamental social unit. He came to the conclusion that since the relationships among people were not physical observables, the social psychological processes by which people came to be oriented toward one another should be central to the discipline. Specifically, he spoke of **collective attention**, "...a process in which the group acts upon itself; that is, the group takes a stand on something in its environment."[12] Rather than the mere passing down of customs and traditions from one generation to the next, customs and stable forms of social interaction are suspended and even dissolved when a collective attention unifies a group. More or less intense social interaction defines a problem and response, as well as the membership of those for whom it was a problem and who would respond.

Fundamental to all this is interaction, wherein one experiences oneself making another's intent an object of attention.[13] This was a distinctive sociological approach in which Park highlighted social interaction and its attendant collective attention as an occasion of social innovation, quite in contrast to the sociology of Max Weber, for example, wherein innovation is explained in terms of the "charisma" attached to some striking personage. What I have in mind when I refer to a "forum" differs from Robert Park's "collective attention" insofar as the latter is what happens in a forum while the forum itself is a social framework or situation that occasions collective attending-to.

Another analogous concept that it is helpful to consider is the **social world**, as described by Tamotsu Shibutani. A social world is a culture area bounded not by territorial borders or organizational rosters but by communications channels. It is a "place" within a larger societal context that one inhabits, along with others who share one's own special pursuit.[14] What I have in mind differs from the social world insofar as I hope to highlight the interactive process that suspends the customs and forms of everyday life and thereby increases the likelihood of social innovation. I am concerned less with a static symbol system within which one find a "place" and more with the processes in which such systems are engendered and changed.

Finally, I would call attention to what Robert Park called the "public." A public forms when a number of people need confront an issue of some kind. Rather than share identical emotions, as would occur in a crowd, members of a public typically disagree with each other, hold rather different stances, experience divergent feelings, and engage in discussion over the matter at hand.[15] The public is capable of innovation precisely because of the discussions that take place in it. What I have in mind when I speak of the "forum" has some obvious analogies with this, but there are two important differences. The forum is a customary, re-occurring event in which discussion takes place because an issue seems relevant; the public comes into being only when the issue requires some imminent response. Thus while the public develops precisely because tradition has not provided a resolution to some issue, a forum develops because tradition or custom leads people to gather and at the gathering the issue can arise. Secondly, while the public occasions discussion of a rational nature, the forum can occasion discussions that have expressive content, especially evocative of identities, as their theme. Nevertheless, the sociological literature on the public offers us some important insights. In writing of the implications of the public, Herbert Blumer notes that the public's members interact on the basis of interpretations, enter into disputes, and sometimes maintain conflict relationships. He notes that "individuals in the public are likely to have their self-consciousness intensified and their critical powers heightened instead of losing self-awareness and critical ability...."[16] It is the formation of new group identities that will prove to be important in analyzing the social situation of the Johannine Christians and their non-Christian Jewish associates.

The forum, then, is a form of social interaction that draws individuals into lines of activity that they would not pursue alone, that occasions spontaneous responses that constitute departures from received tradition and normalcy, that receives a coherence out of a shared faith or ideal, and in which the participants position themselves with respect to some matter and develop new group identities. This is the social form that seems to be suggested by the Gospel of John as the circumstance of its intended audience. Within such a social formation, any number of social processes can occur. I will review a few of them that seem pertinent to the present study - i.e., which various passages in the fourth gospel suggested to me as I examined them.

Jurisdictional dispute

We can speak of the jurisdictional dispute by analogy from the "system of professions" in the modern world.[17] Professions, each having its respective cognitive and organizational apparatus, compete with each other over the right to monopolize expert work. Library science competes with computerized information science, for example, and tax attorneys with accountants. The medical profession has gained dominance over nursing and pharmacology. Jurisdiction over the care of the disturbed has shifted about, as has the right to perform various legal services in nations such as Britain and France. What is particularly interesting is the fact that the identities and number of professions in competition vary from one nation to another, as does which one profession gains jurisdiction over any given activity. In the case of the social setting of early Christianity, it is not, of course, a matter of any system of professions, but of a jurisdictional dispute within first century Judaism over influence and leadership. Several social movements within a vaguely-defined Jewish world seemed to be in competition over the exercise of religious authority. This is to suggest that the conflict that is apparent in the text of the fourth gospel was not only over alternative theologies and religious symbols but also over what constituted a proper religious career. If it had been a question of alternative theologies, there need not have been any conflict; the east Asian experience teaches us that people are perfectly capable of participating in more than one religious tradition at a time. A jurisdictional dispute implies an exclusivity that is necessarily occasioned by more than a mere plurality of theologies.

Schism

"Schism is the process by which a religious body divides to become two or more distinct, independent bodies."[18] This obviously presupposes an existent organizational framework in which there is a "religious body" that has an identity. We are dealing in this instance with more than a terminological nicety since the existence of an organization to which people devote labor and time and with which they identify creates an interest on the part of the active participants in fashioning that organization into something acceptable and in keeping it so. It is that kind of interest that can lead to disputes that become schisms. Such disputes may focus on issues of belief and practice, wherein one or more parties accuses others of heresy or heteropraxy; the great schism between the Roman Catholic and the Reformation churches exemplifies this kind of schism. However, it is also the case that a jurisdictional dispute can occasion a schism; in the Great Western Schism (1378-1417) in medieval Catholicism, a college of cardinals had elected rival popes amidst much confusion, and these popes in turn appointed rival sets of church officials who made often overlapping jurisdictional claims; there was no particular matter of doctrine or practice that was at issue.[19] Inherent in the schism process is a tendency toward reunion; the participants would have preferred that the split had never occurred and that their opponents would reconsider matters and stop being so obstinate. Once the dispute has receded into history, however, this kind of desire will have receded with it; the likelihood of any reunion would then depend both on the two resultant organizations having not come to differ from one another in any essential way, and on the emergence of some ecumenical or unity movement.

Ambivalence

As a social phenomenon, "ambivalence" is the public process of defining feelings in such a way that the object of those feelings is regarded as having both a positive and a negative aspect. Interactions among people, especially people who are in some manner unlike one's own identity group ("us") become objects of conflicting feelings, especially when one's own group ("we") interacts with "them." Such a situation is inherently unstable:

> In interaction with persons who are not like us, there is some evidence that ambivalent attitudes lead to over-reactions. It is as though persons seek to resolve ambivalence by overly embracing one of their emotional tendencies.[20]

Such ambivalence is likely to accompany organizational schism, but it is able to arise from various sources. Consider the situation of the early Christians, who adhered to a religious tradition and subcommunity that were largely Jewish and yet had societal, communal, and often family ties to the world of the Roman Empire; the Empire had gone to war against militant Jews in Palestine, and Judaism had increasingly come to emphasize purity codes that were separatist in nature. This ready source of ambivalence was likely complicated by generational effects, in which an older generation had known a Jewish community that was less at odds with the gentile world than that known to a younger generation.

> In a sense...old and young live in different worlds with specific languages, life experiences, and societal imperatives. The greater the social differences between self and other, the less self-knowledge and self-experience help in understanding others. Yet, society takes these opposites and makes them the building blocks of that most intimate group to which many of us will ever belong.[21]

We cannot automatically take such insights that are derived from the modern condition and retroject them back into the first century, since there was no delayed adulthood with a concomitant youth culture in the ancient world. However, in instances in which social changes (such as the rapid decline in status of Judaism in the Roman world, as well as the internal changes in Judaism brought about by the destruction of the Temple and the dispersion and dissolution of the Jerusalem authorities) impinge upon the everyday world, a comparable ambivalence may well have occurred.

*　　　*　　　*

So we have three textual layers in the Gospel of John, each edited for use by people at a different point in time. I have found that I might think of these people as participating in a kind of social situation that I am calling a "forum," a situation in which individuals are drawn into courses of conduct that are collective in nature and which those people would not have pursued were they not interacting with one another. These courses of conduct include, I am proposing, jurisdictional disputes, schism, and the experience of ambivalence, though not all these occurred all at once; some might occur during the time period corresponding to one of the Johannine textual layers and some at a time period corresponding to another layer. These processes involve spontaneous responses and planned actions both, and they resulted in suspensions of normalcy and departures from received custom. In the accompanying ambivalence, some shared ideals united the opposed factions, thereby lending pathos to their dispute, while other ideals provided an internal unity for each faction over against the other one. The participants in all this had to define their own individual and group positions on the matters in dispute. I propose these general concepts **after** having occupied myself with the separate textual layers, and I invite the reader to examine the same evidence in the next three chapters with these same general concepts in mind. I will return to the concepts themselves and the implications that they help us draw, in Chapter Seven.

NOTES

1. See especially Herbert Blumer, Symbolic Interactionism. Perspective and Method (Englewood Cliffs, New Jersey: Prentice-Hall, 1969).

2. Max Weber, Wirtschaft und Gesellschaft. Grundriss der verstehenden Soziologie, ed. by Johannes Winckelmann (Köln and Berlin: Kiepenheurer and Witch, 1964). First published posthumously in German in the 1920's; the standard English translation (Economy and Society. An Outline of Interpretive Sociology, ed. by Guenther Roth and Claus Wittich. Berkeley: University of California Press, 1978. Two Volumes) is based on the 1964 paperback edition.

3. Georg Simmel, "The study of societal forms," in Kurt H. Wolff (ed.), The Sociology of Georg Simmel (New York: Free Press, 1950), pp. 21-23, and "Contents (materials) vs. forms of social life," ibid., pp. 40-41.

4. Nicholas Taylor has a forthcoming article on this, "Paul, Pharisee and Christian. The Law and the Salvation of Israel in Light of Cognitive Disonance Theory."

5. Robert E. Park, Masse und Publikum (Bern: Lack und Grunau, 1904); see Anthony J. Blasi, "Science, Social Relations, and the Human Subject. The Sociology of Robert E. Park," in Renzo Gubert and Luigi Tomasi (eds.), Robert E. Park e la Teoria del "Melting Pot"/Robert E. Park and the "Melting Pot" Theory (Trento, Italy: Reverdito Edizioni, 1994), pp. 43-53.

6. Gustave Le Bon, Psychologie des Foules (Paris: F. Alcan, 1895).

7. Scipio Sighele, Psychologie des Sectes, translated from Italian by Louis Brandin (Paris: V. Giard and E. Brière, 1898). I will use the French spelling of Sighele's translator rather than the English because the English cognate refers to something quite different.

8. Ibid., pp. 16-17.

9. Ibid., p. 46.

10. Ibid., Ch. 2.

11. Robert E. Park, Masse und Publikum; citations are from the English translation by Charlotte Elsner, The Crowd and the Public and Other Essays (Chicago: University of Chicago Press, 1972).

12. Ibid., p. 46.

13. Park seems to have taken this suggestion from Theodor Kistiakowski as much as from anyone else; see Theodor Kistiakowski, Gesellschaft und Einzelwesen. Ein methodologische Studie (Berlin: Verlag von Otto Liebmann, 1899), pp. 51-52.

14. Tamotsu Shibutani, *Society and Personalty. An Interactionist Approach to Social Psychology* (Englewood Cliffs, New Jersey: Prentice-Hall, 1961), p. 130.

15. Park, *Crowd and the Public*.

16. Herbert Blumer, "Collective Behavior." In Alfred McClung Lee (ed.), *Principles of Sociology*, third edition (New York: Barnes & Noble Books, 1969), pp. 67-121, at p. 90.

17. Andrew D. Abbott, *The System of Professions. An Essay on the Division of Expert Labor* (Chicago: University of Chicago Press, 1988).

18. Nancy T. Ammerman, "Schism: An Overview." In Mircea Eliade (ed.), *The Encyclopedia of Religion*, Vol. 13 (New York: Macmillan, 1987), p. 99.

19. Anthony J. Blasi, "Sociological Implications of the Great Western Schism," *Social Compass* 36:3 (1989): 311-325.

20. Andrew J. Weigert, *Mixed Emotions. Certain Steps Toward Understanding Ambivalence* (Albany, New York: State University of New York Press, 1991), p. 23.

21. Ibid., p. 94.

Ch. 4. The Christianity of the Beloved Disciple Literary Stratum[1]

The purpose of the present chapter is to develop a sociological model of the early Christian community for which the "Beloved Disciple" texts (Column A of the Appendix) in the Gospel of John were written. My source-critical analysis of the complete gospel shows that it was the product of an editing together of texts that had been composed separately for different audiences; at least one audience, for example, was expected to distinguish among the different factions that flourished in the Palestinian Jewish world before the fall of Jerusalem in 70, while other audiences could only be spoken to about "the Jews" of the time of Jesus. The "Beloved Disciple" texts are the ones that were addressed to an audience that could distinguish among the Palestinian Jewish factions. These texts often give accurate information about sites in Jerusalem,[2] and they contain reminiscences about named disciples of Jesus, as well as about an un-named "disciple whom Jesus loved." Moreover, they provide the basic narrative structure of the Gospel of John as a whole. They do not constitute a complete story, however, insofar as they presuppose on the part of the audience a general knowledge of the career of Jesus of Nazareth and of the early religious movement that developed after his death.

Internal evidence in the Beloved Disciple texts reveals that the author had been a disciple of Jesus and had been thought to be a favorite of Jesus. If he were personally responsible for most of the editing of the fourth gospel, we could speak of the youth of this person because the long life he would have lived would have extended into the reign of Trajan (98-117), some sixty-five years after the death of Jesus.[3] Moreover, this source person was known to the household of the high priest in Jerusalem, and was therefore probably a Judean; hence he was quite different from the Galileans who claimed Jesus as one of their own. Though the world this anonymous disciple knew best was that of Jerusalem, he had gone to beyond the Jordan to learn from a religious teacher there, John the Baptist. It was also beyond the Jordan that he first made the acquaintance of Jesus and his disciples. The writings of this Jerusalemite do not stem from before he met Jesus but later; they take the form of reminiscences about Jesus and his major disciples. According to one tradition, these reminiscences were written for the benefit of the church in Ephesus; Irenaeus speaks of the author as "John, the disciple of the Lord, who also had leaned upon his breast," and says that he "did himself publish a Gospel during his residence at Ephesus in Asia."[4] What was published, wherever it was published, was the final edition of the Gospel of John, of which the Beloved Disciple texts were a part. (We can speak, then, of this author, whom some say was "John of Ephesus" - to distinguish him from the Galilean, John Son of Zebedee, one of the twelve - as having had migrated from Jerusalem. We see no mention of John of Ephesus in the authentic Pauline writings or in the account of Paul's career in Ephesus in the Acts of the Apostles; thus, we may conclude that any migration, to Ephesus according to some, would occur after Paul's time.) Still, the Beloved Disciple texts do not come too late in the history of the early Christian movement; they do not suggest that the destruction of the Temple in Jerusalem had occurred yet, and unlike other Johannine material they do not mention an exclusion of Christians from synagogues. They do not even really speak of a non-Jewish Christian identity - again, unlike some other Johannine material. It seems reasonable to think of the Beloved Disciple texts as written for the Christians, most of whom were ethnic and religious Jews, after the year 65 but before 70. This would be over three decades after the time of Jesus when John begins providing "roots" for some Jewish Christians ("Luke" would do that for the Gentile Christians there some twenty-five or so years later).

The basic narrative.

The content of the basic narrative presented in the earliest layer of the text of the fourth gospel consists of recollections that seem prompted by questions. The first of these questions concerns John the Baptizer and his status in relation to Jesus. The beginning of the narrative introduces the Baptist as a witness rather than as a messiah. Traditional Christian citations from the prophetic literature identify the Baptist as a voice crying in the wilderness straightening the way of a lord. The Baptist is portrayed as speaking of a greater one whom his hearers did not know. Then the Baptist points Jesus out to two of his disciples as the "lamb of God," and they follow Jesus. These disciples bring more, so that Jesus acquires a small following. What they find intriguing about Jesus is that he has insight into individuals, so much so that they are ready to proclaim someone from lowly Nazareth the Son of God and king of Israel. Jesus does not seem to believe they had seen enough yet to arrive at such conclusions.

The second question concerns how different Palestinian groups responded to

Jesus. The Pharisee Nicodemos comes to him secretly in the night. The Pharisees in Judea actually posed a threat to Jesus, so that he left Judea by way of Samaria, en route to Galilee. In a dialogue with a Samaritan woman Jesus teaches that God is spiritual and not limited by the geographical distinction between Judea and Samaria. He identifies himself as the Messiah, and proves to be eager to develop a following among the Samaritans. Further along in the journey to Galilee, an officer from the Herodian government, asking Jesus for a miraculous cure of his dying son, believes Jesus when Jesus simply says it is done. The official's whole household comes to believe. The scene changes to Jerusalem, where a cure of a disabled man is done on the Sabbath.

At the Sea of Galilee Jesus has attracted a large crowd. The multiplication of loaves and sardines is accomplished to accommodate the crowd, but Jesus flees when the crowd wants to form a kingdom for him. Jesus joins the smaller group of his disciples after a storm at night, by walking on or near) the sea to their boat, just before they arrived at he shore. In Capernaum Jesus speaks of the Father sending him, but much of the crowd and some of the disciples find that to be a hard teaching, and abandon him. Judas Iscariot begins to have doubts. The question of the divine origin of Jesus appears to have occasioned controversy from the beginning. Jesus' brothers leave Galilee for a feast in Jerusalem, but Jesus does not accompany them.

Jesus goes to Jerusalem in secret and proceeds to teach inside the Temple. Some want to kill him, and the high priests and Pharisees try to arrest him, despite protests from Nicodemos. But the presence of crowds and Jesus' impact on some of those sent to apprehend him make any arrest impossible. At most, Pharisees succeed in debating Jesus in the treasury of the Temple. Jesus cures a blind man on the Sabbath, leading to rejection by Pharisees and Jesus' criticism of them for their own kind of blindness. After further controversy and attempted arrests, Jesus leaves Jerusalem, going beyond the Jordan. All this establishes why at least some authorities in Jerusalem wanted Jesus killed, presumably a matter of interest later in the Johannines' community.

Personal obligation brings Jesus back to Judean territory when Lazarus dies. The astonishing miracle of reviving Lazarus magnifies the whole controversy over Jesus; the Sanhedrin decides Jesus must die. Jesus and his disciples flee to the wilderness, but return to the house of Martha, Mary, and Lazarus in Bethany. Mary anoints Jesus with expensive perfume, Judas Iscariot protests, but Jesus speaks of his own impending funeral. Riding a donkey, he leads a palm branch parade into Jerusalem; his hour is near. Then be hides in the city. The author seems very interested in explaining how it came about that Jesus is eventually arrested.

A three-fold drama develops. Jesus has no illusions about escaping, and speaks about loving his own to the end. He insists on washing the feet of the disciples. Judas Iscariot, meanwhile, decides to betray Jesus, and Jesus knows as much. Simon Peter protests Jesus doing the menial work of washing feet, but acquiesces when Jesus insists; Peter also nods to the Beloved Disciple to find out who it is who will betray Jesus, when Jesus mentions it. But Jesus is more concerned about final instructions - that he is to be glorified, that the disciples cannot go with him yet, that Peter (who would be so hard on the betrayer) would disown him, and that Jesus would return to bring the disciples to the Father. The teaching takes place when Jesus responds to questions from Thomas, Philip, and Judas (not Iscariot): "I am in the Father and the Father is in me." They leave for a garden.

Further discourse reiterates the same points, and the disciples begin to understand both the situation and the teachings. Jesus predicts that they will scatter, and says that his discourse was intended to put them in peace. Judas Iscariot arrives with officers to arrest Jesus, as Peter tries to resist with a sword. Jesus is brought to Annas, then to Caiaphas the high priest. The "other disciple," known to the high priest, gets Peter into the courtyard of Caiaphas, where Peter denies being a follower of Jesus. Jesus is brought to Pilate at dawn; Pilate wants to know whether Jesus is a king while Jesus prefers to talk about truth. After Pilate's soldiers scourge and mock Jesus, Pilate brings him in mock crown and robe before the high priests and constables: "Crucify!" "We have no king but Caesar."

The narrative leaves out much of the Jesus tradition - the Last Supper and the details of the execution. It adds some of the author's personal observations - that Jesus asked the Beloved Disciple to care for his mother, and that a physical death occurred, with blood and water coming out of a spear wound when a soldier made sure Jesus was dead. There was a hurried, temporary burial, but the author and Peter found the tomb empty after the Sabbath. Jesus appears to some disciples at the Sea of Tiberias, where Peter had proposed returning to the fishing trade. Jesus asks if Peter loves him more than he loves fish, and when Peter says he does Jesus tells him to "Feed my sheep." The author denies a rumor that Jesus promised at this juncture that he, the Beloved Disciple, would never die.

The fact that the narrative seems to respond to controversies or questions suggests that such matters were under discussion in the Johannines' community ("forum"). I will focus on specific sections of the Beloved Disciple texts that hint at the nature of the Christianity of his local community at that time.

There came to be a human, sent from divinity, named John. (Jn. 1.6)[5]

The anonymous disciple ("Beloved Disciple") speaks here of John the Baptist without going out of his way to make it clear that he was not writing about himself. He may have intended to have what is said about the Baptist to apply to himself as well - that he was not the light but would testify about the light. This may strike one as a mere literary device or the author's merely personal means of expression, but I would propose that there is more to it than that. Here and throughout the Beloved Disciple texts the author undermines the importance of anyone but Jesus himself. Religious authority seems to be an issue for this writer; he seems to go out of his way to establish that John the Baptist and even he himself are merely people who testify about Jesus. The anonymous disciple has a relatively anti-authoritarian stance that he will not risk undermining by claiming to be an authority himself. The nature of his anti-authoritarianism should be observed, however; he is not denying the validity of some authorities in religious matters, but subordinates authority to the purpose of making Jesus known to others. We might think of him as something of an ecclesiastical minimalist.

With the verse cited above we also see the Beloved Disciple stratum of the gospel taking up the matter of the Baptist's status in general, not merely his status as an authority.[6] It does this a second time, having John the Baptist confess, "I am not the Christ" (Jn. 1.20) and "I am baptizing with water. Among you stands someone whom you do not know, who is coming after me, the thong of whose sandal I am not worthy to loose." (Jn. 1.26-27) This, of course, is also found in non-Johannine texts, though in different phraseology; it is a common part of the early Christian tradition. However, the anonymous disciple passes over much of the Christians' tradition, and reproduces largely what suits his own purposes. He does not offer a compendium of traditional material but a peculiarly Johannine testimony. It was evidently important to him to establish the secondary role of the Baptist and primary role of Jesus. However, it does not seem to have been the case that some other church in the local community had a cultus of John the Baptist and his a cultus of Jesus; he establishes no opposition between the Baptist and Jesus. He has John the Baptist initiate the following of Jesus: "...John was standing as well as two of his disciples, and looking at Jesus walking by he said, 'Look! The lamb of God.'" (Jn. 1.35-36) The followers of John the Baptist and Jesus in the local community seemed to be the same social entity, but they had not yet settled upon the substance of their theology. They had an identity - Christian, or Messian - but they were not certain whether it would be John-the-Baptist Christianity or a Jesus Christianity. "Then why do you baptize if you are not the Christ or Elias or the prophet?" (Jn. 1.25) In this context it is useful to recall that the Acts of the Apostles speaks of a wandering Christian teacher from Alexandria named Apollos who "taught accurately the things concerning Jesus, though he knew only the baptism of John." (Acts 18.25) Similarly Acts speaks of Paul finding disciples, in Ephesus, who never heard of a Holy Spirit but who had been baptized into John's baptism. (Acts 19.1-3)[7] So the Christian movement had an existence as a social reality in Ephesus and probably elsewhere before it had a theology, or had even identified its central religious figure. Thus, we can see the Beloved Disciple literary stratum as a part of the negotiation of what was to become the religious content of early Christianity.

And the two disciples listened to him talking and followed Jesus. (Jn. 1.37)

John recounts the collecting of the first followers of Jesus, some of whom became well-known figures in early Christian history. The two who heard John the Baptist speak of Jesus as the lamb of God and followed Jesus were Andrew and an unnamed other, presumably the author or source of the fourth gospel. Andrew then brings his brother Simon to Jesus, and Jesus says, "You are Simon Johnson; you will be called 'Kephas,'" (Jn. 1.42); then "Kephas" is translated as "Peter." Unlike the other traditions, the naming of Peter has no conferral of authority tied to it, but seems to acknowledge that Peter will some day have authority. Peter finds his fellow townsman, Philip, who in turn finds Nathaniel, into whose character Jesus immediately has insight. The series of episodes in which this nucleus of a discipleship is collected is presented by John as a matter of the Galileans finding Jesus a striking and fascinating person who has a wondrous insight into people and who must therefore be the Messiah.

If Jesus was already behaving as a seer, these episodes do not, and were not intended to, represent the beginning of Jesus' ministry. The moment when John the Baptist celebrates Jesus as the lamb of God and the moment in which the Baptist speaks of someone standing among his hearers whom they did not know, should not be conflated. The text says they occurred a day apart. On one day Jesus - evidently already a religious teacher, perhaps having addressed gatherings elsewhere - assumes anonymity in the audience of John the Baptist. On the next day, the Baptist identifies him as a religious figure worthy of attention, the "lamb of God." Jesus honored the Baptist by coming to learn from him. The Baptist, depicted as having as much prophetic insight as Jesus, knows Jesus for what he is. And what is a "lamb of God"? Presumably a disarming figure who enjoys the protection of a divine shepherd, but whose earthly tragedy, like those in Jewish legend that were slaughtered to ward off divine wrath, would become a symbol of election. Andrew, Peter, Philip, Nathaniel, and the source for the fourth gospel are fascinated by a simple man who sees into the character of each and speaks of what he sees, after that man had been called to their attention by John the Baptist. They learn from him, much to their fascination, to ignore matters of estate and reputation - "Can anything good be from Nazareth?" - and to focus on personal qualities, especially sincerity.

It is possible to build a theology or morality around the foregoing, but that is not why I am singling it out for attention here. Sociologically, this is a very important feature of the Beloved Disciple material that its author deemed particularly relevant to his listeners/readers. To the way of thinking of the migrant anonymous disciple, the social categories employed in the local society were not legitimate. It was not as if there were a fixed and firm community structure that enjoyed the consensual support of all and to which a powerless immigrant had to conform but rather that society would be in doubt and an immigrant could say not to worry about social estate and reputation but to take each person as an individual. For this immigrant writer there were face-to-face interactions from which social dynamics emerged - voice alternating with voice, listener's glance punctuating speaker's discourse. What is said and how it is said exert their force, irrespective of the status of the speaker. The world of the Beloved Disciple is a religious crowd phenomenon that has placed the quasi-totemic Pantheon in abeyance, stopped the music, so to speak.[8] Even the ancient traditions of the Jews, and certainly the newer Pharisaic practices, were to be held in suspension. This local Christian community had to define itself anew, and for the time being one could only place faith in each individual's manifest character.

There was a man of the Pharisees named Nicodemos. (Jn. 3.1)

This sentence introduced a brief pericope in the Beloved Disciple layer of tradition, into which much further discourse was introduced in the final edition of the gospel. All that the Beloved Disciple material says about Nicodemos the Pharisee at this juncture is that he came at night and addressed Jesus respectfully. Jesus is depicted as dwelling on Nicodemos coming at night, evidently in secret. "The light has come into the world, and humans prefer the darkness over the light, since their works were evil." (Jn. 3.19) This does not accuse Nicodemos of cowardice but of evil works. The evil work is maintaining the social divide between Pharisee and non-Pharisee. The anonymous disciple understood the relevance of Jesus to reside in a critique of religious categories. If one were to come to the religion of Jesus in the Beloved Disciple's new community, he would have it be a matter of a personal quest, not a matter of hiding behind a received factional category.

He would have the Nicodemoses of the world shed their religious identities and openly inquire into something new. This seems as well to be something of a criticism of secret followers of Jesus in the local Jewish community.

Madam believe me, an hour is coming when you people will worship the Father neither on this mountain nor in Jerusalem. (Jn. 4.21)

The conversation Jesus has at Jacob's Well with a Samaritan woman in the Beloved Disciple material is one of the most revealing passages in the New Testament. At stake is the Jewish identity of Christianity. It was obvious that the Jewish religion would soon be turned upside down; the Roman legions would surely overcome the revolt in Palestine and take over, if not defile, the Temple. The hour was coming when everything religious would change. And what would this do to any distinction between Jew and Samaritan? John has the eccentric Jesus break a taboo against Jewish men conversing with Samaritan women, and as usual has Jesus prophet-like reading his interlocutor's character. It would be impossible to undergo a religious revolution without also undergoing a social one. Customs of all kinds would be broken, and John presents this incident to the Christians of his community by way of an endorsement of all this. He does not stop at an endorsement, however; Jesus' preaching to the Samaritan woman was the sort of endeavor to be promoted: "Do you not say 'Four months yet and the harvest comes'? Look, I tell you, 'Lift your eyes and see the fields,' for they are already white for the harvest." (Jn. 4.35) The time of social confusion was, to John's way of thinking, an opportunity. He could evidently draw a parallel between Jesus' eccentricity and the eccentricities of the times in his own new community. As for Jewish tradition, it would serve largely an intellectual function: "You worship what you do not know; we worship what we know...." (Jn. 4.22)

The man believed what Jesus told him and went. (Jn. 4.50)

The focus of the Beloved Disciple layer of the gospel changes at a point in chapter four, where it ceases to be a matter of Jesus having insight into others and begins to be a matter of others having insight into Jesus. The first pericope marking this change is a miracle narrative in which a "royal officer" who wants Jesus to cure his sick son back home, believes Jesus' assertion out on a wilderness road that the cure has taken place. That is followed by another cure story, this time of a disabled man by the pool called Bethzatha in Jerusalem; the Beloved Disciple fragments of the narrative (Jn. 5.2-3, 5-9, 13-14) emphasizes that the healed man did not know who had cured him and that Jesus talked to him about the cure later in the Temple. These miracles resulted in a crowd following Jesus up to the shore of the Sea of Galilee (Jn. 6.1-2), where the multiplication of the loaves and fish takes place. "Then, seeing what sign he had worked, the people were saying, 'Truly this is the prophet who is coming into the world.' Then Jesus, knowing that they were about to come and seize him to make a kingdom, withdraws again by himself to the mountain." (Jn. 6.14-15) After that the disciples go off in a boat, and Jesus joins them, walking on the sea, and then the boat lands immediately.

There is a progression in this sequence of miracle accounts - from getting a benefit from Jesus, to receiving a benefit and then hearing Jesus, to being fed and wanting a kingdom, and finally to having Jesus join a little band in a symbolic boat. One may understand the progression in purely theological or spiritual terms, but I would suggest a sociological reading as quite plausible as well. The early Christian movement was internally differentiated, with some participants being little more than fellow travelers who find solutions to certain problems. They may have sought actual magical cures from Christianity, or they may have had a more spiritualized notion of healing from a Christianity that came to them unsought for. Others, more closely identified with the movement, found religious sustenance and a spiritual world in the movement; these can be said to have lived as Christians. Then there was a small number who saw Jesus in a special way - saw the "risen Lord," to use traditional terminology. All four kinds of participation in the Christian movement were evidently known in the anonymous disicple's new community, but judging from Jn. 6.60ff., the suggestion of a risen Lord who had seen God and spoken to a few people about it, was met with some skepticism and was, unfortunately from the disciple's perspective, received as a "hard saying."

For he did not wish to move about in Judea because the Judeans sought to kill him. (Jn. 7.1)

Chapter 7 begins an account of a confrontation between Jesus and the Jerusalem authorities. While the later layers of tradition in the Gospel of John heighten the confrontation considerably, it is a fact that Jesus and the Jerusalem authorities had been opponents, and that the followers of Jesus and later Jerusalem authorities were also opponents, as the experiences of Paul in

Jerusalem showed, both early in his career and late. For Christians in the Johannines' community this contributed to a crisis of legitimacy - not of their own legitimacy in particular but of legitimacy in general. Judaism was not a monolith, and factions such as the Christians could at one time be accommodated. But the nagging fact that the high priests persuaded the Romans to crucify Jesus on the pretext that he wanted to be a king, that they authorized the persecution of the followers of Jesus by Pharisees such as the young Paul, that the Judeans later sought the life of the converted Paul, that James was executed in Jerusalem - all this made the Christians a persecuted sect. Under conditions of persecution, one at least had the honor of a sectarian legitimacy, made visible by a record of arrests and punishments.

The time of the Beloved Disciple literary material, however, was unique. The Jewish War was in progress. The Jewish community of Jerusalem had been taken over by a faction of radicals who rose up in revolt against the Romans. The Temple itself was doomed. The Christians thus had not only lost any legitimate place in the Jewish world they may have once had, ever so briefly, but they also lost the honor of being persecuted by the Jerusalem authorities, since these were soon losing the ability to persecute. Would Rome step in to take Jerusalem's place? This was not altogether clear. "Some of them wanted to arrest him (Jesus), but no one laid a hand on him." (Jn. 7.44) The problematic relationship with Judaism arose not only in terms of hostility between the high priests and Jesus, but also of an opposition between Pharisees and Jesus. In Chapter 9 the Beloved Disciple material presents a miracle narrative in which Jesus elicits criticism from Pharisees by curing a blind man on the Sabbath, and in turn Jesus criticizes the Pharisees for their own kind of blindness. Implicit in this is a solution to the problem of legitimacy; the Christians were claiming a special kind of insight, or at least a special kind of freedom from ideological blindness. The Christians' freedom was to entail their own claim to rightness.

Sir, if you would have been here my brother would not have died. (Jn. 11.21)

The narrative of Jesus' raising Lazarus from the dead is a most puzzling one. The Beloved Disciple material is not, as we have noted, a compendium of Christian tradition; it leaves important, even central elements out. Even greatly expanded by other Johannine material, the Gospel of John does not have a complete Last Supper, for example. So there would seem to have been no imperative to devote a special pericope to the doctrine of the resurrection of the dead, especially one out of sequence, as the Lazarus story would have been if it were a simple theological affirmation of that doctrine. So why did John include this account in this layer of material? In what way was it germane to the life of the anonymous disciple's Christian neighbors in the late sixties?

I think the point of the narrative is contained in the verse cited above. It is spoken in the narrative by Martha, the sister of Lazarus; and it is repeated by his other sister, Mary (Jn. 11.32). The two sisters speak in the role of a dramatic chorus, verbalizing the author's own commentary. "Sir, if you would have been here...." The point is not the miracle; it never is in the Gospel of John. The point is that Jesus, according to the source, **is** with the Marthas and Marys of the world. And this presence is not the normal presence of a human individual, bound within the limits of an historical biography, but a presence that survives spatial and temporal remoteness. Lazarus, after all, arises. I suggest that this narrative should be considered in the light of the legitimacy crisis of the local Christian community. The Jewish world in which Christianity had found an uneasy place, the

Temple-centered Jewish world, was passing from the scene, writhing in a death agony. Would Christianity disappear along with it? A subtle analogy with the miserable death of Jesus, and his presence, according to Christian belief, despite it, provides an answer to the legitimacy problem. The social relevance of Jesus survived the crucifixion; after all, the followers of Jesus had still been persecuted long after Jesus was gone. So according to a certain social logic - as well as according to Christian theology - Jesus was not gone at all. Because of its peculiar social circumstance of experiencing persecution long after the execution of its central figure, Christianity had already in place a symbolic plausibility structure for a resolution to a problem comparable to the problem that the wider Jewish world would have. The Beloved Disciple text in fact associates the Lazarus narrative with the attempt by the Jerusalem authorities to arrest Jesus (see Jn. 11.47ff.), before recounting premonitions of the crucifixion (see Jn. 12.1ff.).

Then he poured water into a basin and began to wash the feet of the disciples.... (Jn. 13.5)

This appears to be an act of deliberately transparent symbolism on the anonymous disciple's part. All symbolism is transparent insofar as the audience for whom an act is symbolic has its attention transported to something beyond the symbol itself, but here the Beloved Disciple text calls attention to the present "transporting" action by making it jar. Where one would expect to find a narrative of Jesus beginning the meal with a blessing, culminating in the command to do that in commemoration of him, the disciple writes of Jesus washing his disciples' feet and culminating with, "...I have given you an example so that as I did to you, you also should do." (Jn. 13.15) The local community's Christians, by the sixties of the first century, would have been accustomed to the ceremonial breaking of the bread and its connection with the Last Supper, as recounted in 1 Cor. 11.23-25 (which presents itself as a received tradition). What the disciple writes here must have been jarring indeed, calling attention to itself. How are we to understand this?

In theological terms, the point of the passage is not difficult to understand - Christians are called upon to serve each other in practical, this-worldly ways. The message parallels Mt. 25.40 - "...as you did it to one of the least of these my brothers, you did it to me." But why did the disciple reiterate this moral point at this juncture in his text and in such a jarring way? We must remember that the Temple-centered Jewish world was about to undergo a cataclysm, that this was a cataclysm for Christianity as well, and that everyone in the disciple's world would have known it. The embodiment of the sacred in this world was in jeopardy; the threat to the life of Jesus seems to have called this to mind by analogy. To contemplate an absence of the sacred may well have fit the times well. Every narrative is built upon an opportune tension between a then and a now, and the anonymous disciple's jarring device reaches into the now in order to grasp some presence with which to make the then live. In so doing he intimates to us, modern readers that we are, the psychology of his "now." It too would have an "absence" that would be as short-lived as the one that followed the crucifixion.

...One of you will betray me. (Jn. 13.21)

Once again the disciple portrays Jesus as one who posses a remarkable intuition for the minds and hearts of others. Jesus is "troubled in spirit," the disciples are "at a loss over whom he was talking about." One can easily imagine Peter's nervous body language to the youngster who was reclined near Jesus, as if to say, "Find out who it is!" "So leaning thus near Jesus' chest he said to him, 'Sir, who is it?' Jesus answered, 'That is he, to whom I will give this piece of bread when I dunk it.'" Is this merely good drama? No. There is no reason to doubt the report of a betrayal by Judas, and as someone known to the high priests (Jn. 18.15) the Beloved Disciple would, as a chief suspect himself, have reason to set the record straight with exact detail, even years later. Moreover, anyone who has ever been betrayed knows that it comes at the hand of someone accustomed to receiving small deeds of graciousness from one, such as a piece of dipped bread. After Judas leaves, there is a brief discourse in which every word speaks of eternity, and then an abrupt, "Arise, let's go out." (Jn. 14.31) But the little band hasn't a real chance to elude its pursuers; Judas can accurately predict where it will go. And all along Jesus seems to know that he will soon be caught.

What importance does this have for the disciple's Christian neighbors? Betrayal as a phenomenon requires a social complexity, wherein people are engaged in more than one social circle at a time. To find it worth mentioning, the people to whom the disciple addressed he gospel would have to have known such a society. And betrayal also reflects ambivalence - people having trouble being singularly committed. This would be particularly true amidst a legitimation crisis, when the vicissitudes of individuals' personalities and interpersonal dynamics count for more than is the case amidst the stable patterns of legitimated institutions.

Sheathe the sword. Am I not to drink the cup that my Father has given me? (Jn. 18.11)

There is an easy temptation to read a pacifism into this verse. Yet we should remember that the narrative has Peter with his sword facing "the cohort as well as the constables." (Jn. 18.3) Jesus suggests that his own arrest accords with the will of God, while a fight to the death by Peter would not. For the authorities to kill Peter in open combat would have been perfectly justified on their part, while for them to execute Jesus seemed, even to the administrator Pilate, completely lacking in justification. As portrayed by the anonymous disciple, Jesus does not seem to want to allow any side skirmishes to obscure the situation. Once arrested, he knew what would happen, and he wanted it to be obvious why it was happening. Unlike John the Baptist, the Jerusalem authorities could not celebrate any moral authority that was not their own, and in pursuing their monopoly over such authority they would appear to undermine what credible claim they may have had to moral authority at all.

What meaning could this have in the

Beloved Disciple's new community? That city, unlike Jerusalem, had no single unifying moral culture. The situation in which Christians could feel morally secure despite disapproval by officialdom seems to be reinforced by the Johannine arrest scene, which highlights the a-morality of officials. Moreover, the conclusion that some kind of armed resistance on the part of the Christians was unrealistic seems to receive reinforcement from this passage. The Christians in the disciple's new community, though probably not a down-and-out lot, were not in command of armed forces. They were also probably not a likely sort of people to behave like saboteurs, highwaymen, or guerrillas. Jesus' caution to Peter would make sense to these people.

Your nation and high priests handed you over to me. (Jn. 18.35)

This verse is pure dramatization; it has no parallel in the synoptics and it makes no claim to be based on an eye-witness account. The ancients readily reconstructed situations by supplying dialogues like this one. Here the anonymous disciple depicts Pilate, the Roman authority, as indifferent to the fate of Jesus and willing to execute an innocent person to placate the high priests. His principal concern turns out to be that of making the high priests know that he was doing them a favor: "Look, I am leading him out to you, that you may know that I find no guilt in him." (Jn. 19.4) This is presented without explanation, as something already familiar to the audience; the same Roman authority that had power but not legitimacy in the Palestine of the time of Jesus had a similar power in the migrant disciple's new city. Such a power does not prevail without being acknowledged: "Pilate said to them, 'Shall I crucify your king?' The high priests answered, 'We have no king but Caesar.' Then he handed him over to them to be crucified." (Jn. 19.15-16)

Simon Johnson, do you love me more, or these? ...Feed my lambs. (Jn. 21.15)

The appendix to the primitive narrative has Jesus saying this to Peter in a post-resurrection narrative, after Peter had proposed going back into the fishing business. Jesus has Peter give him some fish, which he proceeds to cook over a fire, and then he asks Peter whether he prefers Jesus more, or the fish. Peter protests that he loves Jesus; so Jesus tells him, in effect, to be a shepherd, or pastor. The account gives Christian religious legitimation to a full time ecclesiastical role, as symbolized in Peter. The passage does not speak of an organization of people who hold such an occupational status, but it does suggest a distinction between shepherd and shepherded. Evidently, the local Christians had an elemental ecclesiastical structure that was centered around a leadership role, but no elaborate organization.

Summary

The religious world known to the migrant Beloved Disciple in his local Christian community of the later 60's was a social reality whose symbol system was still being negotiated. Jesus of Nazareth was still being affirmed as the principal messianic figure, as opposed to John the Baptist; the priority of Jesus was not yet simply taken for granted. The Christian social reality had guiding personages said to have been designated by Jesus - e.g., Peter. However, there does not seem to have been any firm organization, and no orderly succession after the time of Peter, James, and Paul appears to have been established. The social reality of Christianity thus experienced something of an internal legitimacy deficit, as well as an external one, and seemed ready for the anonymous disciple's reminiscences in order to find its roots. What the Beloved Disciple remembered from his earlier years was a Jesus who appraised situations and evaluated persons well; this would be an appealing portrait in a community that was undergoing a general legitimation crisis and ready to value individual persons.[9] It was a world in which people set out on personal quests - and hence were ripe for conversion, even if it meant constructing in part that to which one would be converting.

The Jewish world had had a crisis in legitimacy for quite some time. It was itself pluralist and faction-ridden. The young who were destined to become Jewish intellectuals were evidently expected to sample a variety of traditions before they set the courses of their own lives. We know that Flavius Josephus did this as a youth, and Paul seems to have experimented with Phariseeism before becoming a Christian. The anonymous disciple was apparently doing this when he came to John the Baptist, and then to Jesus. The kinds of commitment that could be made in that world are the product of the individual's personal pursuit, not a simple conformism. They could be carried about with one through tumultuous times as a personal philosophy of life. They could survive export from Palestine in a time of war, and they could appeal to a community like that of the migrant disciple, which knew Roman government but not authority, Jewish antiquities but not a solid Jewish cosmos. The Roman government was on the verge of storming and taking the Temple of Jerusalem, a temple that it saw as a mere means of keeping a conquered people under control. If one was to find the sacred in such times, one would find it within, with the help perhaps of a striking individual who seemed to have something to say about life.

NOTES

1. An earlier version of this chapter was presented at the 1991 meeting of the Society for the Scientific Study of Religion in Pittsburgh, Pennsylvania.

2. Contrary to the contentions of scholars earlier in the twentieth century, the Beloved Disciple materials and other Johannine texts have been found to be in accord with archaeological evidence; see James H. Charlesworth, Jesus Within Judaism. New Light from Exciting Archaeological Discoveries (New York: Doubleday, 1988), pp. 119ff. On the Beloved Disciple as a real person rather than a literary symbol, see James H. Charlesworth, The Beloved Disciple. Whose Witness Validates the Gospel of John? (Valley Forge, Pennsylvania: Trinity International Press, 1995).

3. See Martin Hengel, The Johannine Question (London: SCM; Philadelphia: Trinity Press International, 1989), p. 3, who cites Irenaeus.

4. Irenaeus, Against Heresies Book 3, Ch. 1, verse 1; in Alexander Roberts and James Donaldson (eds.), The Ante-Nicene Fathers Volume I (Grand Rapids, Michigan: Eerdmans, 1987), pp. 315-567, at p. 414. On the authorship of the Gospel of John, see Hengel, Johannine Question, pp. 2-3, 33, 74, and 132,

and from a different perspective, Charlesworth, Beloved Disciple.

5. Quotations from the Gospel of John are from my own translation, which is based on Novum Testamentum Graece, post Eberhard Nestle et Erwin Nestle, 26. neu bearbeitete Auflage, ed. by Kurt Aland, Matthew Black, Carlo M. Martini, Bruce M. Metzger, and Allen Wikgren (Stuttgart: Deutsche Bibelstiftung, 1979). The translation attempts to capture nuances of meaning, sacrificing when necessary the ease of literary elegance in the process.

6. By "stratum" I am speaking here of a literary layer of tradition, not a social stratum.

7. See C.K. Barrett, "Apollos and the Twelve Disciples of Ephesus." In William C. Weinrich (ed.), The New Testament Age. Essays in Honor of Bo Reicke, Volume I (Macon, Georgia: Mercer University Press, 1984), pp. 29-39, at p. 37.

8. On the crowd as a social form which suspends old structures and engenders new ones, see Robert E. Park, "The crowd and the public," in Robert E. Park, The Crowd and the Public and Other Essays, edited by Henry Elsner, Jr. (Chicago: University of Chicago Press, 1972), pp. 5-81.

9. I find no evidence whatsoever for the "Mediterranean" approach to personal identity alleged by Malina: Individuals in the Mediterranean society are, he claims, "anti-introspective, not psychologically minded at all. Consequently, persons are known according to stereotyping in terms of locale, trade or class, but especially according to the family, clan or faction in which they are embedded." Bruce J. Malina and Jerome H. Neyrey, Calling Jesus Names. The Social Value

of Labels in Matthew (Sonoma, California: Polebridge, 1988), p. 15. Frankly I find an assertion of "embeddedness" not itself grounded in evidence, and indeed to be founded on dogmatism, not science. Specifically, Malina derives it deductively from the writings of Mary Douglas; see Bruce J. Malina, Christian Origins and Cultural Anthropology. Practical Models for Biblical Interpretation (Atlanta: John Knox, 1986), pp. 38-39; and Mary Douglas, Natural Symbols. Explorations in Cosmology (London: Barrie and Jenkins, 1973).

Ch. 5. A Divided World[1]

The narrative that is associated with the "Beloved Disciple" and provides reminiscences about named disciples of Jesus is not the only narrative source to be found in the Gospel of John. There are numerous narrative interpolations, placed in column "C" in the appendix to this study, that cause awkward beaks and repetitions in the fourth gospel. These narrative interpolations use the expression, "the Jews" (hoi Iudaioi), to refer to the Jerusalem authorities. Put together, the interpolated passages would not constitute a complete narrative of the career of Jesus. Because they sometimes seem to be inconsistent with one another, I have labeled their spaces in the appendix "C_1," "C_2," etc. These fragments may have been taken from some larger works, or they may have been separate literary or oral products that were not united with one another in most cases until placed into the fourth gospel. Because they reflect a time after the destruction of the Temple in the year 70 and after an exclusion of at least some Christians from some synagogues, I concluded in Chapter Two above that they must have been written after the year 80. And because Luke seems to have known of some of this material, they were probably written before the year 90.

"The Jews"

The most striking feature of this material is its use of the expression, "the Jews." While the author of the "Beloved Disciple" text assumed that the reader knew who Pharisees and high priests were, the person responsible for these interpolations - perhaps the same person as the author of the Beloved Disciple text, with a somewhat changed audience in mind - calls the Jerusalem authorities as well as inhabitants of Judea "the Jews." The more precise labels in the "Beloved Disciple" text suggest some minimal familiarity with Palestinian Judaism on the part of the audience, while the vague expression in these interpolations suggests some distance from Palestinian Judaism. The expression itself, "Jews" (*Iudaioi*), is both a geographical and ethnic designation, given in a short form. In that sense it is similar to the way "Arab" is used in twentieth century English to refer to a native of Arabia (making the term a synonym of "Arabian") and to someone whose culture is linguistically, legally, and religiously the one that Arabians also share. To speak of the Arab forces involved in the 1991 liberation of Kuwait may be to speak either of the Saudi Arabian military personnel who were involved, or to speak of some other national units as well. Such an expression would be directed to an audience for whom the particulars bear no immediate relevance. Similarly, precisely who is said to have done what to Jesus in Jerusalem does not seem to have been expected to be of much importance to the audience of these narrative fragments.

In reading, translating, and interpreting the Gospel of John, one faces the difficulty of deciding if and when *Iudaioi* should be understood in a narrow, geographical sense ("Judeans") or a wider ethnic one ("Jews"). Robert Fortna points to clues in the fourth gospel itself: the Samaritan woman at Jacob's well identifying Jesus as a Jew (Jn. 4.9), Pilate identifying Jesus as a Jew (18.35), and Jesus' own people not accepting him (1.11).[2] Jn. 4.9 is from the "Beloved Disciple" text, suggesting that a Galilean such as Jesus would be called a *Iudaios*. Jn. 18.35 is similarly from the primitive narrative. The usage of the word shows no distance between Christians and Jews here, since both passages in the "Beloved Disciple" text refer to Jesus as a Jew. Ironically, that same usage in the discourse material (column B in my appendix) shows such a distance, since it refers to Jesus not being accepted by his own (Jn. 4.9). So both before and after the time of the narrative insertions under consideration in this chapter, *hoi Iudaioi* refers to a category of people encompassing more than residents of Judea. The modern English term, "Jews," is in most contexts a closer translation of what the Greek denotes than "Judeans" would be.

Early Christian literary evidence, especially in the fourth gospel, evinces controversy between the early followers of Jesus, who deemed him to be the Messiah or Christ, and other Jews. An early term for the post-crucifixion followers of Jesus is commonly translated as "Christian." A term for the cultural identity of ethnic Jews who were uniting in a national expression under the observances of the Pharisee party is "Judaism." Of course, first century "Christianity" is not the same thing as the civilizational complex of later times, and first century "Judaism" is not identical to the fully developed rabbinic tradition. That does not mean that the use of the words is anachronistic or, as some even suggest, prejudicial. I disagree with Prof. Richard Horsley,[3] who advocates avoiding the terms out of a fear of modern anti-Judaism. I think we should encourage our readers to be intelligent ones; the point of a sociological analysis is to highlight contextual structures that differ from one setting to another, despite similarities in wording, ritual, and identity. It seems to me that there is a danger that a failure to use such terms would result in a failure to recognize real social entities and thereby delete them from one's comprehension of humanity. While the suggestion to abandon the terms "Christian" and "Jewish" is designed to avoid any implicit modern antimony between the two, it hardly seems sensitive to verbally deny religious identity trajectories their ancient roots.

"And this is John's testimony when the Jews sent priests and Levites from Jerusalem to ask him, 'Who are you?'" (Jn. 1.19) The event behind this narrative would have been a trip by some "priests and Levites" from Jerusalem to the desert place where John the Baptist conducted his ministry. The original tradition may have been referring obliquely to different factions having claims to priestly status in Palestinian Judaism. As understood by the narrator, however, there was a relatively organized and unified Jewish authority that would be investigating and evaluating new religious personages such as John the Baptizer. Moreover, the tradition of the Baptist is presumed to be something other than Jewish; that is to say, it is not a matter of some religious figures going to hear a new teacher - something common enough in the Jewish world - but "the Jews" delegating functionaries to investigate the founder of the Baptists. The connotations are sectarian; the Baptists and the Jews will have parted ways by the time the narrative was formulated. More important yet, finding out whether an unknown teacher is "one of us" is a significant concern that is sufficiently self-explanatory as not to require further elaboration. The sectarian situation is not merely one of denominational label but of group identity; one was not a teacher or clergyman first and a teacher or clerical representative **of** some system second, but a representative of some religious identity first and a specialist in it second. Membership in one sect or another appears to be a master status.

"Then the Jews answered him, 'What signs do you show us for you to do such things?'" (Jn. 2.18) This appears in the fourth gospel's version of the Temple incident. In the synoptics the incident, in which Jesus rides a donkey colt ahead of a parade up to the Temple and then stops the ritual activities, appears to have provoked the Jerusalem authorities to seek his execution. In the Gospel of John the events in the Temple itself appear out of context, separated from any parade, and inserted at an early point of the narrative of the ministry of Jesus. When Jesus demands that the sale of sacrificial animals cease, the above quoted demand for a sign is attributed to "the Jews." There are several features of the narrative that seem important, but here I want to point out that a challenge from "the Jews" occasions the resort to a theological tenet: "Jesus answered, 'Destroy this shrine and I will raise it in three days.'" (Jn. 2.19) By "shrine" he was referring to his body. The significance of the Resurrection tradition as a sign of divine authorization for the cessation of the Temple cultus seems to have been articulated in the context of an exchange with "the Jews." The legends of early Christianity in Jerusalem contained in the Acts of the Apostles betray no such dissociation of Christians from the Temple, but this inserted narrative asserts such a dissociation. Unlike what was to become mainstream Judaism, with fragments of the Temple cultus transported into a diaspora ritual system, the Christians addressed by this text saw a divinely authorized imperative to dispense with at least some Jewish ways. The text construes the Resurrection tenet as precisely such an authorized imperative. The significance of this is not only to be found in the result and content of the tenet but also in the fact that a controversy exchange - a particular kind of interaction - plays an important role in the articulation of doctrine. The Christian-Jew relationship seems to have been the social context for this kind of articulation for the narrative's author and audience. By way of contrast, any controversy with the Greek and Roman religious and philosophical worlds seems irrelevant or absent altogether.

John 8.21-26, 28b-29 is a dialogue between Jesus and "the Jews" in which the status of non-christian Jews is spoken of as being "of the world." Jesus says where he is going, they cannot follow. The Jews correctly understand him to be speaking of his death, though nothing in the text had prepared the reader for that interpretation. Then Jesus says, "You are from below, I am from above. You are of this world, I am not of this world." From there the discourse proceeds to Jesus' divinity and the matter of the judgment against those who could have believed but would not. In one sense, one could simply see this textual material as an articulation of a "high christology," a theological tenet that the messiah, Jesus, is divine; the reflection on the non-believing Jews would be a secondary matter following upon that. An examination of the text, however, reveals the reverse sequence; "the Jews" are associated with "the world" first, and then mention is made of the high christological material. In fact, the discussion proceeds from the observation that where Jesus was going they could not follow, not that Jesus had been sent from God. The terms of the issue were set by the fact that "the Jews" could not follow. In what sense could "the Jews" be associated with this-worldly powers after the destruction of the Temple, evacuation of Jerusalem, and further scattering of the Jewish people? Why could they not follow? There were still ethnically Jewish Christians. So what could this be saying? By "world" the author seems to mean something quite different from the Roman political system. "The Jews" had all the more to consolidate their existence as an ethnic entity once their institutional system had been disestablished, and this very consolidation kept them from pursuing a kind of religiosity that transcended ethnic lines. It is this that the writer seems to have sensed, and the development of a high christology seems to be the theological counterpart of the supra-ethnic or cross-ethnic extension of the early Christian movement.

John 8.37b-46, 49-59 presents another dispute between Jesus and "the Jews." As with most speech and dialogue material in ancient literature, this passage should be understood as historical drama, dialogue written well after the fact to present a situation **as understood well after the fact**. Jesus is made to say, "But you want to kill me because my word finds no place in you." (Jn. 8.37b) Even though the Romans executed Jesus, the writer accords the responsibility for the execution to "the Jews." This allocation of blame did not originate with the author of this Johannine material; Paul had already written something like this in his earliest letter (1 Thess. 2.14-15). There are several historical possibilities that can explain such texts: 1) The Jerusalem authorities were actually responsible for Pilate having Jesus executed. 2) The Jerusalem authorities were not primarily responsible for the execution of Jesus, but later ethnic Jews in the Roman world were so opposed to Christianity that they associated themselves with that execution. 3) The Christians unilaterally blamed the ethnic Jews for the crucifixion. 4) Some combination of separable elements from the foregoing. The dispute material does not contain denials of a desire to kill Jesus; indeed it leads up to an attempt to stone him after he says what Jews would understand to be blasphemy (Jn. 8.58-59). More tellingly, the dialogue reproduces reasons why Jews **should** want to kill Jesus and then essays retorts on the part of Jesus. Jesus, they suggested, meddled with Jewish tradition even though he was not legitimately Jewish but rather was a Samaritan; Jesus speaks of his truth proceeding from God. They accuse Jesus of having a devil (being out of his mind); Jesus says they speak from the devil, the father of lies. From the vantage of the author of the dialogue, "the Jews" did not deny being responsible in some way for the death of Jesus but rather associated themselves with it. The result is not a mere cultic or theological difference between the Christians on the one hand, many of whom were ethnically Jewish, and the Jews on the other, who considered themselves legitimately Jewish; rather, there was an adversarial relationship. The existence of one of the two groups was a sore point for the other. From this dialogue, it appears that the existence of Jews who associated themselves with the execution of Jesus was a sore point for the Christians.

John 9.18-33 is an extensive controversy passage in which "the Jews" have an exchange with a blind man whom Jesus had cured. The passage seems to have been inserted into a parallel passage in the Beloved Disciple text (Jn. 9.1-17, 34-41) that has a shorter controversy between "the Pharisees" and the formerly blind man. In the inserted controversy involving "the Jews," the latter are feared authorities before whom the cured man's parents are reluctant to testify. Moreover, these authorities had "decided that if anyone confessed the Christ, that person would be put out of the synagogue." (Jn. 9.22)

This would not reflect the situation in Judea since the synagogue was an important institution in the diaspora, not in Judea. It also reflects a time in which Christians had in fact been excluded from synagogue life. But perhaps the most striking feature of this controversy passage is the fact that the cured man, not Jesus, is depicted as arguing with "the Jews."

A controversy with Jesus comes soon after in John 10.24-38, where Jesus speaks of God as his father and thereby provokes "the Jews," who had surrounded him, to threaten to stone him. In the midst of the controversy dialogue is a reference by Jesus to those who are of his sheep and those who do not recognize his voice. This, of course, is metaphoric language for a schism that has progressed to the point of an irreversible parting of ways. A schism implies some mutual velleity for an eventual reunion,[4] but once it has developed into a permanent separation it has become a rather different social phenomenon. The point at issue - the belief by Christians that Jesus was the son of God - had precipitated such a permanent separation. Thus while the schism may have required such a theological ground for its justification, the theology in turn transformed the division into a more permanent separation and led to the formation of separate religious identities.

John 11.4-5, 6-11a is a later version of part of the narrative of Jesus raising Lazarus from the grave. Jesus has been told that Lazarus is ill, and he resolves to return to Judea. The text appears to have been written with a serious Jewish persecution of Christians in mind. The connection between death and the glory of God is placed at the beginning as a theme: "This illness is leading to death, but is also for the glory of God - that the son of God may be glorified through it." (11.4) Jesus then tells the disciples they are going into Judea, and they protest that the Jews will kill them. He answers with a saying about walking in the daylight so as not to stumble. The intent of the passage seems to be that of instilling courage among the Christians. What is of interest to us is the possibility that Jews in the community of the gospel's redactor were feared as people who were willing and able to persecute the Christians.

We know of persecution outside Judea from other sources. Writing in the mid-fifties, for example, Paul speaks of his mission in Ephesus, the city many would associate with the fourth gospel. Paul says that at first his mission had both great prospects and great opponents: "But I will stay in Ephesus until Pentecost, for a wide door for effective work has opened to me, and there are many opponents." (1 Cor. 16.8) He eventually met with calamity: "For I do not want you to be uninformed, brothers, about our travail that arose in Asia, that we were burdened utterly beyond strength, so as to be in doubt about ourselves and life." (2 Cor. 1.8) Paul goes on to speak about being delivered from peril. However, Paul does not speak of this peril as coming from the Jewish community. The narrative of the events formulated some thirty-five years later by the author of the Acts of the Apostles speaks of a riot against the Christians stirred up by silversmiths who made shrines to Artemis (Acts 19.23-41), and in the middle of that narrative is found this curious passage: "And some from the crowd joined Alexander, the Jews having put him forward; and having motioned with the hand Alexander wished to address the people in defense." (Acts 19.33) What persecution there may have been in Ephesus was perpetrated by followers of Artemis, not by Jews; indeed Jews were ready to defend Paul in Ephesus, and Christians were aware of this as late as the time of the composition the Acts of the Apostles.

Since the Johannine material under consideration here predates Acts, we have two logical possibilities: 1) Jews in Ephesus and other places where the fourth gospel may have been edited persecuted Christians, having begun to do so after Paul's time, or 2) Jews did not persecute Christians, but some other group was doing so in the redactor's city. If the first alternative were true, something about the change in circumstances would have been noted in Acts - e.g., "for Jews were not persecuting followers of the way yet." If the second alternative were true, then the Johannine Christians were having difficulties with their non-Jewish neighbors. The danger to Jesus from the Judean Jews would serve as a parallel to danger from non-Jewish persecutors. This is not to say that relations between Jews and Christians in the local community of the redactor were still friendly, but that either because of a lack of ability or because of a reluctance to set any persecution at all into motion, Jews there were not persecuting Christians.

In fact, John 11.18-19, 31-42, 44b-45, fragments of a parallel to the narrative of the raising of Lazarus from the grave, speaks of Jews in Palestine who believed in Jesus. These references would have been lost in history if they were not significant to the Johannine community in some way, since they do not advance the narrative in any way. The fact that Jews in Palestine, in the homeland of Judaism itself and even in the environs of Jerusalem, believed in Jesus could only have stood in contrast to the situation in the redactor's community. It no doubt served the apologetic purposes of the Johannine community well to point out that belief by Jews was possible in the era of the Temple and in the authentic Jewish setting, even if it was becoming impossible for them in their community after the era of the Temple. This tells us that the standing of Christianity in the Jewish world was still very important to the Christians and was indeed a sore point.[5]

A number of texts suggest that Jesus and his followers remained a matter of interest in the Jewish world. John 11.55-56 depicts Jews gathered at the Temple for a feast and speculating whether Jesus would show up. Though this is presented as a depiction of the situation at the time of Jesus, it probably reflects Christians' supposition about Jews' interest at a later point in time as well. Jesus, of course, shows up, as noted in John 12.9-11; that implies a Christian claim to Jewish tradition. The passage recalls the raising of Lazarus by saying that a crowd came out to see both him and Jesus, and it immediately speaks of the high priests plotting to kill Lazarus because he occasioned people converting to Jesus. The burden of all this is symbolic: Where Jesus gave life, the high priests wanted to take it away again. This probably does not reflect current persecution and execution but rather a battle over the hearts of converts to Christianity. Some important figures in the Jewish officialdom of Jerusalem had apparently been close to the author or the Johannine community, had believed in Jesus, but later had been converted back to a non-Christian Judaism when Christians were put out of the synagogues:

> Still many of the rulers also believed in him, but they did not confess it lest they be put out of the synagogue. For they loved the glory of humans more than the glory of God. (Jn. 12.42-43)

The interest in Jesus on the part of members of the Jewish community was reciprocated by the Johannine Christians' having an active interest in at least some Jews. The excommunication of the Christians caused a crisis in the relationship that had given historical form to this mutual interest. For the Christians, the appropriate response to the crisis was an act of faith in Jesus, the Christ; for the non-Christian Jews, it was an act of faith in a chosen people who needed to unite under the Covenant in a time in which the destruction of the Temple had created a national crisis. What to the Jews was a matter of preserving the coherence of the Covenant people under the Torah was seen by the separating Christians as a love for "the glory of humans." What to the Christians was a preservation of their faith was undoubtedly seen by the non-Christian Jews as sectarianism. The centrality of faith in the Christians' response to the crisis can be seen in John 12.34-36a, where Jesus is made to urge in a dispute that the Jews "believe in the light" while it is there to be had.

The Fourth Gospel contains some inserted fragments in the passion narrative that appear to parallel and add detail to the principal narrative (Jn. 18.12, 19-23, 31a). There are places where "the Jews" is used to refer to the Jerusalem authorities in these passages, but they seem to be added to the texts. For example, Jesus says at his hearing before the high priest, "I have spoken openly to the world. I always taught at synagogue and in the Temple...," and the apparent addition clarifies by continuing, "where all the Jews gathered." (Jn. 18.20) The text may be relatively primitive; it speaks of Jesus having taught at synagogue (presumably in Galilee) and in the Temple. The clarification explains for people unfamiliar with Palestinian Judaism that all Jews would gather at one time or another in the Temple. Parts of this material are evidently older than most of the gospel's passages that speak of "the Jews," but it is interesting to see what kind of old parallels have been edited into the text. John 8.12 speaks of Roman soldiers and Jewish constables collaborating in the arrest of Jesus. John 18.19-23 is an interrogation before the high priest, at which a constable strikes Jesus. John 18.31 is a fragment of Pilate's exchange with the Jerusalem authorities in which Pilate tells "the Jews" to proceed under their own Law. All three passages preserve the tradition that the Jerusalem officials proceeded against Jesus as prosecutors, not as impartial judges, and that they did so in their official capacity, not as private parties. If at the time of the separation of Christianity and Judaism some who had been well disposed toward the Christian tradition but who had stayed in the Jewish community tried to deny having decided against Jesus and his followers, this kind of text could be cited to argue that their conciliatory position was untenable. The context seems to be one of people being forced to decide between the two communities.

High Christology

The first chapter of the Gospel of John contains a number of fragments embodying the legend of John the Baptizer and paralleling the beginning of the Beloved Disciple narrative. Much of this parallel material may have quite early origins; what is of interest in the present context is the selectivity at work in culling the material out of tradition and inserting it into the gospel. The operative principle of selectivity seems to be that of high christology; sayings attributed to John the Baptizer that speak of Jesus as divine seem to have been selected out of tradition. Consequently the basic message is not so much Jesus, as opposed to John the Baptizer, being the Messiah, but Jesus' being a **divine** Messiah. For example, the Baptist is presented as saying, "He who is coming after me is created prior to me because he has priority over me" (Jn. 1.15). The play on the after/prior contrast is to lead the reader to infer an eternal existence for the Person of Jesus. It would be incorrect to assume that this high christological material is necessarily late; it is reminiscent of the tradition Paul included in Philippians 2.6-11, where Christ Jesus is said to have been in the form of God and to have taken the form of a slave. Rather, an increasing pertinence of such material can be seen in its insertion into the Fourth Gospel.

There were apparently more than one such text available to the gospel's redactor. A parallel to John 1.15 is found at 1.30, preceded by "Look! The lamb of God who is taking away the sin of the world." (Jn. 1.29) The "lamb of God" saying in turn has a parallel in the Beloved Disciple narrative, and that may have served as a cue telling the redactor where to insert the material. It is useful to compare the parallel texts to see what the insertion adds:

> The next day John was standing as well as two of his disciples, and looking at Jesus walking by he said, "Look! The lamb of God." (Jn. 1.35-36, Beloved Disciple narrative)
>
> The next day he saw Jesus coming to him and said, "Look! The lamb of God who is taking away the sin of the world. This is the one I talked about: a man is coming after me who is created prior to me because he has priority over me. (Jn. 1.29-30, inserted material)

The insertion added an affirmation of a Christian theology of redemption ("taking away the sin of the world") and the statement suggestive of a prior divine existence on the part of the Person of Jesus. The passage goes on to invoke language and symbols reminiscent of the synoptics' accounts of the baptizing of Jesus by John the Baptizer, and it concludes, "...I have seen and testified that this is the son of God." (Jn. 1.34) The insertion of this material, with its distinctively Christian statements of salvation theology, symbolism and high christology, serves to emphasize the developed state of the Christian community's tradition, including the very features that non-Christian Jews may have found objectionable. A high christological statement inserted farther on in the gospel almost says as much:

> Jesus answered them, "My Father is still working now, and I am working." Because of this, the Jews then wanted even more to kill, because he not only broke the Sabbath, but he was also calling God his own father, making himself equal to divinity. (Jn. 5.17-18)

From the earliest days of the Christian movement, at least some Christians held Jesus to be equal to the God of Jewish tradition. That no doubt antagonized some non-Christian Jews, and perhaps even some Christian ones. The resultant separation of Judaism from its Christian faction not only concentrated those who held the controversial high christology into the separate Christian community, but it set the stage for them to highlight the doctrine that had made them distinctive. In an inserted disputation passage farther on in the gospel, Jesus is made to find fault with those who do not adhere to the high christological position, suggesting that they are too much a part of the world, weighted down with sin, and subject to final judgment (Jn. 8.21-26, 28).[6]

The Spirit

This "C" material that was inserted into the Gospel of John has a theology of the Spirit. John 1.32-33, an insertion made up of traditional material about John the Baptizer, associates this theology with baptism:

> And John testified, "I have seen the spirit descend from heaven as a dove and remain over him. And I did not know him, but he who had sent me to baptize with water - it was he who said to me, 'Over whomever you see the spirit descend and remain, it is he who baptizes with a holy spirit.'"

As noted above, this material is reminiscent of the synoptics' narrative of John baptizing Jesus (see Mark 1.10). However, a more interesting parallel is to be found in the Acts of the Apostles 19.1-6, a narrative of Paul's happening upon some dozen Christians in Ephesus who, it is to be inferred, had been converted by Apollos. Paul discovers that they had never heard of the Holy Spirit, and explains to them before rebaptizing them and laying hands on them to impart the Spirit: "John baptized the baptism of repentance, telling the people that they should believe in him who is to come after him, that is, in Jesus." (Acts 19.4) The narrative found in Acts evidently preserved a correction of ritual and theology that had been made in Ephesus; those people who had been corrected had only known of the baptism of John. The Johannine text reflects a similar situation in which two baptisms had existed, one of John the Baptizer, and one of Jesus in which the Spirit is imparted. The ritual practice of John the Baptizer and his followers was not an unusual one in the Jewish world; in distinguishing between such and the Christian one in which the Spirit is imparted, the Johannine community was ritualizing its existence apart from the Jewish religious community. The Spirit was tantamount to a theophany marking a new covenant.

Evidently there was a sense in the Johannine community of an inevitable change. In one passage, John the Baptizer is depicted as in a dialogue, reviewing a series of traditional sayings about himself and concluding that he must diminish (Jn. 3.27-30). Once the divide between Judaism and Christianity had occurred and each community had begun to regard the other as outsiders, holding onto a Jewish tradition such as the baptist one (albeit a marginal, factional tradition) within a Christian context would be more and more difficult. John the Baptizer now came to occasion questions rather than repentance - who was he, why did he baptize? In the end, the Baptizer cult became untenable: "You yourselves bear me witness that I said, 'I am not the Christ,' but that I am sent before him." (Jn. 3.28) How could one cultivate a figure who was to serve largely as a forerunner? "He must grow, and I diminish." (Jn. 3.30)

The theology of the Spirit was associated with a certain other-worldliness, whereby a sharp divide separated the Christian life and the world of everyday affairs. The divide invoked the language of the spirit/flesh contrast:

> What is born from the flesh is flesh, and what is born from the spirit is spirit. Do not wonder that I told you that it is necessary for you to be born anew. The spirit blows where it wills and you hear its sound, but you do not know from where it comes and where it goes; so is everyone born of the spirit. (Jn. 3.6-8)

Such language is suggestive of a communal inner life that is relatively inscrutable from an outside perspective. The theology of the spirit would be an insider's theology, a universe of discourse unfamiliar to non-Christians, including the non-Christian Jews who formerly had at least inhabited the same symbolic world as the Christians.

Ritual

One of the distinctive features of the Fourth Gospel is the placement of the Temple incident, in which Jesus causes the ceremonies to stop for a time, early in the narrative. In the synoptic gospels this incident follows a Galilean ministry and occurs soon after Jesus makes a triumphal entry into Jerusalem; but in the Gospel of John Jesus gathers a small number of disciples, works a miracle of turning water into wine at a wedding party in Cana in Galilee, and then in not many days goes to Jerusalem for Passover and creates the Temple incident. Once John the Baptizer has called Jesus the "lamb of God" (Jn. 1.29) and once the topic of wine has been highlighted by the miracle at Cana (Jn. 2.1-11), the reference to Passover in the introduction to the Temple incident pericope (Jn. 2.13) can be seen to have symbolic significance. As the Jewish ritual recalled the escape from death when the angel passed over, the Christian ritual was to recall a different kind of escape, symbolized in the Resurrection imagery. Thus when Jesus stops the Temple ceremonies (Jn. 2.14-16) and is challenged to show by what sign he should do such a thing, he answers, "Destroy this shrine (his body) and I will raise it in three days." (Jn. 2.19) The Jewish ritual at the Temple had been stopped by the Romans, and the new rabbinical tradition had not substituted for it yet; the Christians sensed their Jesus-centered commemorative ritual as their substitute. The fact that these passages are juxtaposed in the Fourth Gospel does not necessarily mean that they were associated prior to their insertion into that gospel; but given the separatist theme found in the other texts at the same level of tradition, their prior association with one another to symbolically create this kind of meaning system seems quite likely.

We have already mentioned that the Johannine Christians had a baptism that they saw as being a different one from the baptism of repentance used by John the Baptizer's followers and by others in the Jewish world. This Christian baptism is the subject of a number of inserted, "C" material, texts. One of these texts turns up in a dialogue that Jesus has with a woman and that the redactor inserted into the dialogue between Jesus and a Samaritan woman. In all likelihood the redactor created or refashioned the inserted dialogue (Jn. 4.10-12) in order to create a space for the pre-existent saying about baptism:

> Everyone who drinks from this water will thirst again. But whoever would drink from the water that I will give will never thirst, but the

> water that I will give will well up within with water leaping up to eternal life. (Jn. 4.13-14)

The text is not without difficulty; it refers to the drinking of water rather than the immersing of oneself (**baptizein**) in water. The symbolic weight is not carried by the water per se - in a cleansing function - but by the drinking of the water to give life. The Johannine Christians may well have had a ritual drinking of water, in contrast to an immersion ritual. A similar text is to be found later on in the gospel:

> On the last day, the great one of the feast, Jesus stood up and called out, "If anyone thirsts who believes in me, let him come to me and drink. As the scripture said, 'Rivers of living water flow from within him.'" (Jn. 7.37-38)

To what scripture the text refers is unclear. There is Proverbs 18.4: "The words of a man's mouth are deep waters; the fountain of wisdom is a gushing stream." And there is Zechariah 14.8: "On that day living waters shall flow out from Jerusalem, half of them to the eastern sea and half of them to the western sea...." The latter image is given in more elaborate form in Ezekiel 47.1-12.[7] River waters coming from a source are available for watering; the suggestion seems to be that one would go to Jesus, from whom rivers would come, as the scriptural imagery had them coming from the Temple in Jerusalem. Drinking water seems again to be the ritual action in question. If the Johannine Christians had a unique ritual involving the drinking of water, that fact would suggest that they existed for at least a time apart from the broader Christian movement.

The Family of Jesus

One of the early Christian communities had been organized around James the Brother of the Lord in Jerusalem. Paul reports that very early in his career, after three years in Damascus, he went up to Jerusalem to visit Kephas (Peter) for fifteen days and met no other "apostles" except James the Lord's Brother (Gal. 1.18-19). He names James as the leader of the "circumcision party," the Christian faction that wanted Christians to observe the Jewish circumcision as well as priestly dietary and purification practices (see Gal. 2.12). In a recitation of the resurrection appearance traditions, he speaks first of an appearance to Kephas, then to the twelve, then to more than five hundred, then to James, then to all the apostles, and finally to himself (1 Cor. 15.5-7). In one of the Jerusalem traditions preserved in the Acts of the Apostles, Peter escapes from prison and is left standing outside the Christians' door as they debate whether it is really he; after they let him in he tells how he escaped, concluding, "Tell this to James and to the brethren." (Acts 12.17) James is also described as a major participant in the debate over minimal Torah observances required of Gentile Christians (Acts 15.13ff.). According to Acts, Paul reports the success of his mission among the Gentiles to James and "all the presbyters" in Jerusalem, toward the end of his career (Acts 21.18ff.).

We know that there was tension between the Gentile Christians associated with Paul and these Jerusalem-centered Jewish Christians led by James the Brother; the dispute over Torah observance as recounted in Paul's Letter to the Galatians suggests that no special observances were required of Gentile Christians until the Pharisee movement had gained some ascendancy in Palestine, resulting in a great deal of pressure being put on the Jerusalem Christians (see Gal. 6.12). The Gospel of Mark, which seems to reflect something of an underground Christianity from Galilee, seems to slight the family of Jesus; in one scene Jesus does not answer a call from his mother and brothers but identifies those he was teaching as his true family (Mk. 3.31-35). We have already seen that the Beloved

Disciple texts of the Fourth Gospel associate themselves with the Jerusalem Judaism of the time of Jesus, and with the mother of Jesus. With that in mind, how the layer of inserted Johannine narratives regard the family of Jesus takes on a particular interest for us.

A passage that is relevant in this respect focuses on Jesus' deciding whether or not to go up to Jerusalem from Galilee for a feast. The passage is a parallel to a part of the basic narrative (Beloved Disciple level of tradition) of the gospel. The latter noted the danger Jesus could face in Judea and says Jesus followed his brothers up to Jerusalem, but in secret (Jn. 7.1, 10). The inserted material has the brothers of Jesus trying to persuade him, even daring him, to go up. Then a verse offers an explanation: "For his brothers did not believe in him." (Jn. 7.5) This material would seem to have little to do with the community of Jerusalem Christians that was led by James the Brother of the Lord. However, another passage leaves a contrary impression; one of the resurrection appearance traditions has Jesus saying to Mary Magdalene, "But go to my brothers and tell them, 'I am ascending to my Father and your Father, my divinity and your divinity.'" (Jn. 20.17) From the next verse, one would believe that "brothers" referred not to relations of Jesus but his associates: "Mary Magdalene went announcing to the disciples, 'I have seen the Lord,' and the things he said to her." (Jn. 20.18) It is quite possible that these verses came from different origins and had been edited together into the narrative, or that it means to say that Mary was to have gone to Jesus' brothers and went to the disciples too, or instead. In any event, the fact that the text uses the term *adelphous* shows no desire to distance the tradition from the Christian community of the relatives of Jesus. This confirms for us that the various narrative insertions, located in the "C" columns in the Appendix, do not all reflect one source, and that they were severally edited into the gospel by a redactor for whom the status of the Christians of the James tradition was not an issue. The salience of previous divisions in the Christian movement may have been weakening as the division between Christianity and Judaism was becoming increasingly salient, and as migrations caused by war and commerce were dispersing and mixing into new combinations the second and third generations of Christians.

Roman Authority

The Fourth Gospel is not an overtly political document, in contrast, for example, to the Revelation of John, which expresses resentment against the Roman government for persecution (see Rev. 17.1-6). The narrative insertions in fact seem more neutral in the few references to representatives of Roman authority. Pilate finds no guilt in Jesus (Jn. 18.36b) and tries to negotiate an agreement to have Jesus released. When he finally permits the crucifixion, Pilate orders that it be at the hands of the Jerusalem authorities themselves (Jn. 19.6b; see also 9.12). Jesus is made to say in a dialogue with Pilate that Pilate's authority is from God and that the greater guilt in the affair is not Pilate's but theirs who handed Jesus over to him (Jn. 19.11). The Christians associated with these texts had not yet become bitter over any official Roman persecution.

The redactive activity responsible for the insertion of these narrative passages, probably reflecting circumstances somewhere outside Palestine in the eighties, shows us the group psychology of a schism in progress. The other side of the schism, "the Jews," represents a sore point, and there is a belief that they are ill-treating the Johannine community. The issue is not persecution but the schism itself, the fact that at least some people who could have been Christians chose instead to be Jews. The schism was not merely a dissociating from Christianity of Jews who were never interested in the Jesus tradition but an abandoning of that tradition by Jews who had formerly shared the faith. That can only have been very threatening to the Christians.

The Johannine Christians' response was to assert precisely what the non-christian Jews would have found unacceptable - a high christology. Moreover, the inferences that were drawn from that high christology were that God was being revealed anew in a manner comparable to the Mosaic theophany, as a Holy Spirit, and that the Christians' rituals were therefore more authentic than the Torah observances. The Johannine community may have elaborated further rituals that differed from Christianity elsewhere but copied Jewish ceremony in the course of supplanting it; there may have been a eucharist meal in which lamb was shared, for example. Other Jewish imagery, that of waters flowing from Jerusalem, may have also been appropriated ritually.[8]

NOTES

1. An earlier version of this chapter was presented at the 1992 meeting of the North Central Sociological Association in Fort Wayne, Indiana.

2. Robert T. Fortna, The Fourth Gospel and Its Predecessor. From Narrative Source to Present Gospel (Edinburgh: T. & T. Clark, 1989), pp. 312-13.

3. Richard A. Horsley, "Social Conflict in the Synoptic Sayings Source Q," in John S. Kloppenborg (ed.), Conflict and Invention. Literary, Rhetorical, and Social Studies on the Sayings Gospel Q (Valley Forge, Pennsylvania: Trinity Press International, 1995), pp. 37-52, at p. 37. I have no problem with Horsley's central thesis that the Q texts do not proclaim a judgement against Israel.

4. See Anthony J. Blasi, "Sociological implications of the Great Western Schism," Social Compass 36:3 (1989): 311-325, for the characterization of "schism" as a division which retains an imperative to reunite.

5. The passage also tells us that when this layer of tradition speaks of "the Jews," it does not have Christian Jews principally in mind; it makes a special note to indicate when Jewish believers in Jesus are being spoken of. For example, there is Jn. 11.45: "Then many of the Jews...believed" (*Polloi oun ek ton Ioudaion...episteusan*); literally this speaks of many "out of the Jews."

6. See also Jn. 8.37b-46, 48-59.

7. See Raymond E. Brown, The Gospel According to John (i-xii) (New York: Doubleday, 1966), pp. 320-323.

8. The gospel may have once included a "last supper" that had significant departures from those in the synoptic accounts and from the ritual practices of Christians elsewhere; the final redactor may have suppressed this to

help bring about a conformity to wider Christian cultus.

Ch. 6. An Era of Religious Competition[1]

The latest layer of texts in the fourth gospel, which was inserted into the largely narrative gospel that had been composed of the two earlier layers, seems preoccupied with the status of Jesus as a Christ who supplants the Jewish Law. By the time these latest texts took form Judaism had in fact the status of a religio-ethnic legal system; the Jewish world had lost its cultic focus (the Temple). Messianic Judaism had taken the form, at least for the time being, of a trans-ethnic movement (early Christianity) that was incompatible with both the dominant Jewish religious tradition (Pharisaic observance) and the ethnic identity-maintaining function the Jewish religion had come to perform. So a messianic Judaism came to counterpose itself to an observance centered Judaism, and in the process transformed itself into Christianity. It is this transformation that is evident in the third layer of Johannine texts.

The fact that the writings contained in this layer focus on a messiah who pre-exists his human history, comes down from heaven, returns thereto, and sends a comforting spirit to his own, until such time as they join him in heaven, has led many to associate the gospel with gnosticism. This was a reasonable link to make in the past when the gospel had been thought to have been written well into the second century, but now that scholars are confident the fourth Gospel is older than that it seems more likely that the known Christian gnostic works were dependent on John and other Christian sources rather than vice versa. The debate over whether the Gospel of John incorporated gnostic themes is beside the point in the present inquiry, in one sense, since we would want to know why the themes appealed to the writer and the intended readership, irrespective of whether they came from Jesus and the Christian communities or whether they diffused to them from Mandaeans or others. Yet we will follow the prevalent view on the matter and assume that there was no gnostic influence at work in the composition of the gospel, including the later layers; the argument against gnostic influences that seems most persuasive is the absence of gnostic influences in the Qumran texts, which share some of the terminology of the later Johannine material and thereby allow us to associate the material with a non-gnostic Jewish universe of discourse.[2]

Jesus and the books of the Law

The most famous of these texts stands at the beginning of the Gospel of John as it is found in modern Christian Bibles:

> There was a speech in genesis, and the speech was to God, and the speech was divinity. In genesis this was to God. All things came to be through this one, and apart from him nothing came to be that had come to be. In him was life, and the life was the light of humans. And the light shines in the darkness, and the darkness has not caught it. (Jn. 1.1-5)

Writers of a speculative bent have found important metaphysical principles resident in these words. The writer may indeed have intended to hint at such, but the clearest allusion to any outside writings is to the Greek translation of the Jewish Book of Genesis. Not only does the Johannine text begin with the same words as does the Greek Genesis - *en arche*, in the beginning - but repeats those words lest the reader miss the citation; that is why I have translated *en arche ho logos* as, "There was a speech in genesis." And since the opening lines of Genesis recount creation, this text too speaks of all things coming to be. What the writer does here is draw a parallel between heavenly and earthly events, a practice justified in Genesis itself by a reference to humanity being created in the image and likeness of God. Hence the earthly creation - all things coming to be - is but an earthly parallel to a heavenly creation. Genesis has God speaking in the beginning, and the writer of the Johannine text would have us think of the word that God spoke - *ho logos* - when God said to himself the words of creation. Hence, says the author, "All things came to be through this one." The claim that the author would impress upon us is that this Word, spoken by God to God and which was God, had not been heard by humanity: "In him was life, and the life was the light of humans. And the light shines in the darkness, and the darkness has not caught it." Thus is set forth at the outset the basis for a drama of a Jewish missed opportunity. What was becoming official Judaism, at least as known by the author, had not accepted a theology of a divine Word, and the author is using this missed opportunity as a precedent for and characterization of a non-reception of the messiah in an earthly drama.

While seeing the tandem development of early Christianity and formative Judaism as related oppositional developments helps us appreciate both traditions as social products, we cannot explain every belief held in the two traditions as a mere product of religious competition. The Christians needed a legitimating personage comparable to Moses, but they did not need a divine Christ since

Moses was not believed to be divine in Judaism. Nevertheless, the fact that the Christians could believe in a divine Christ apart from any invidious comparison with Moses does not prevent our seeing their holding him to be a source of revelation comparable to Moses as an aspect of the competition between the two religions.

> ...for the Law was given through Moses, grace and truth came to be through Jesus Christ. No one has ever seen divinity; the only son of divinity, who is near the bosom of the Father - it was he who drew revelation forth. (John 1.17-18)

Moreover, the Jewish revelation is not nullified in the Johannine perspective, since the Law is conceded to have been given by God. Rather, the author's claim is that Christian tradition comes from a source that is closer to God than Moses had been. The result is expressed in terms of two intangibles - grace and truth. Almost by default, such language must refer to an experiential aspect of religiosity that a person can only know from within the tradition in which the experiences had been elicited. The association of the purely personal and individual experience of religiosity with one religion encourages an invidious comparison with other religions - even if one of those other religions is conceded to be valid.

"Amen amen I say to you, you will see heaven opened and the angels of God ascending and descending over the son of humanity." (Jn. 1.51) In Genesis 28.12 Jacob sees angels ascending and descending on a ladder. This text seems to be alluding to that, with the Christian (Nathanael, in the context into which the text had been inserted) taking the role of Jacob and Jesus ("the son of humanity") being prefigured by Jacob's ladder. This seems to see the Christian movement as a social entity comparable to the Hebrew nation (=Jacob). Angels had an ambiguous status in both Jewish and Christian traditions. The author of this Johannine text seems ready to dispense with them, making Jesus the angel: "And no one has ascended into heaven except he who had descended from heaven - the son of humanity." (Jn. 3.13) This, of course, is meant as an affirmation of the authenticity of Christian tradition, an affirmation made in the face of an older and authentically Jewish tradition.

These inserted texts that comprise the third Johannine layer seem to be the product of the author's contemplation on the five books of the Jewish Law. The Jewish tradition is not only accepted as valid, but is used by the writer, so that the competitor to the early Christian movement stays present in mind. The result is a series of allusions that, as we have seen, present Christianity as superior to Judaism or in some other way seeks to impress upon the reader the excellence of Christianity.

> And as Moses lifted up the serpent in the wilderness, so it is necessary for the son of humanity to be lifted up, so that everyone who believes in him may have eternal life. (Jn. 3.14-15)

Even the scandal of the cross is asserted to have been prefigured in the Hebrew Bible, for even Moses lifted up a snake, a sign of evil since the Garden of Eden. "You search the scriptures because you suppose you have eternal life in them; and they are what testify about me." (Jn. 5.39) In the strife of the religious competition, the claims the writer makes on the basis of Jewish scripture becomes pointed (see also Jn. 8.55):

> Do not suppose that I will accuse you before the Father. He accusing you is Moses - he in whom you have hoped. For if you believed Moses, you believed me also, for he wrote about me. (Jn. 5.45-46)

Christianity is sometimes said to have originated as a spiritualization of Pharisaic

Judaism. If by "spiritualization" it is meant that it directed its followers' focus to other worldly concerns, this would be only partly true since there is a clear concern with this-worldly morality in early Christianity. If it is meant, however, that early Christianity de-emphasized received religious practices and referred to the deity more directly, it is true that the early Christians attempted that. The belief that Jesus descended from heaven, expressed so frequently in this third Johannine layer, has the effect of relativizing the received Jewish traditions, and thereby serves an argumentative purpose in the Jewish/Christian competitive setting.

> Then they said to him, "Then what sign do you perform, that we may see and believe you? What do you work? Our fathers ate manna in the wilderness. As it is written, 'He has given them bread from heaven to eat.'" Then Jesus said to him, "Amen amen I say to you, it was not Moses who has given you bread from heaven, but my Father gives you the true bread from heaven." (Jn. 6.30-32)

The symbolic significance of bread, of course, ties in with the Christian ritual: "I am the living bread that has come down from heaven." (Jn. 6.51)

Much of this literary material takes the

form of a disputation, wherein an objection to Christianity is formulated on the basis of the Hebrew scriptures, and a reply is placed into the mouth of Jesus. It may well have been the case that Jewish intellectuals had begun to subject Christianity to a critique, and that these texts represent answers that the members of the Johannine community found useful. For example, Jewish intellectuals may have pointed out that there is no second witness confirming the claim of Jesus to have been God's son; the Johannine author turns the traditional Jewish legal requirement of two witnesses around:

> And it is also written in your Law that the testimony of two people is true. I am one testifying about myself and the Father who sent me testifies about me. (Jn. 8.17-18)

This duality of witnessing persons depends, of course, on accepting the contention that Jesus worked miracles (and hence enjoyed divine endorsement) or the contention that the Hebrew scriptures talk about Jesus. The non-christian would hardly accept either contention; hence the Christian answer seems to have met the needs of the Christians themselves and was likely formulated for their benefit. This suggests that the fourth gospel, comprised of all three textual layers, was the work of one or more intellectuals serving the Christian community, not a missionary tract intended to convert people from outside the Christian community. This indicates that by the point in time that these third layer texts were formulated, the Christian church had already become a separate entity, set apart from other social entities that may have emerged in the Jewish world.

Concern with Jews not accepting Jesus

In the local competitive situation that appears to have existed between Johannine Christians and synagogue Jews, the fact that the Jewish contemporaries of Jesus in Palestine had not generally accepted Jesus as the Messiah continued to be of interest to the Johannine community. The author of the third textual layer of the fourth gospel refers to it a number of times, including one time in the gospel's Prologue: "He came to his own, and his own did not accept him." (Jn. 1.11; also see 4.44, and 6.36). This non-acceptance was seen to extend to the textual tradition that had begun with Jesus' utterances: "Amen amen I say to you that what we know we pronounce, and to what we see we testify, and our testimony is not accepted." (Jn. 3.11) The Christians, who conceived of themselves as preaching the same as Jesus had taught, took this personally; the rejection of what Jesus said ("I say to you") was a rejection of what they too were saying ("our testimony").

The author of the tertiary Johannine text sees the non-acceptance of Jesus by Jews as a religious defect in them (see Jn. 8.47). The text implies that the Jews' status system prevented them from appreciating the divine origin of Jesus' teaching: "Then the Jews wondered, 'How does this uneducated man know letters?' Then Jesus answered them, 'My teaching is not my own but that of Him who sent me." (Jn. 7.15-16) By extension, the same implication is applied to the rejection of Jesus himself: "'But we know where this man is from. When he comes, no one knows where the Christ is from.'" (Jn. 7.27) Another passage presents a similar rejection, this one of the Christian ritual meal, but because the meal is associated with the commemoration of the Passover and exodus into the desert, the text refers to "grumbling," which tradition reports occurring among the Hebrews in the desert:

> Then the Jews grumbled about him because he said, "I am the bread coming down from heaven," and they were saying, "Isn't this Jesus, Joseph's son, whose father and mother we know? Now how does he say, 'I have come down from heaven?'" (Jn. 6.40-42)

Reading this as a misunderstanding on the part

of the Palestinian Jews makes an unlikely story out of the passage; the non-Christian Jews had no more difficulty distinguishing human parentage from divine procession than did the Christians. They understood the claim, and rejected what it claimed. Whether the claim itself went back to Jesus, and the rejection of it back to the time of Jesus, is hard to ascertain, but the problem, whenever it arose, was not an intellectual one. The passage rather proposes the humdrum earthly parentage of Jesus as a problem. There seems to have been a status differential between synagogue Jew and Christian in the community, with the lower status of the Christians going back to the low status of Jesus himself.

Jews in the tradition of John the Baptist

Among the Christians' Jewish competitors at the time of the third layer of Johannine textual material were followers of John the Baptist. These were adherents of a messianic Judaism who evidently made sure that it was clearly a Judaism.

> You have sent to John, and he has given testimony to the truth. But I do not accept testimony from humanity.... He was the lamp, lit and shining; but you wished to rejoice in its light for a time. But I have a greater testimony than John's; for the works that the

> Father has handed over to me for me to complete...testify about me.... You search the scriptures because you suppose you have eternal life in them; and they are what testify about me. (Jn. 5.33-34a, 35-36a, 39)

The passage goes on to make it clear that Moses is the significant symbolic personage for the addressees of this discourse (see Jn. 5.45-46). It is evident that at the author's point in time the Baptists were a group quite separate from the Christians. This seems to be a result of the Christians distinguishing themselves from them: "...I do not accept testimony from humanity...."

This situation, as embodied in the text, tells us something about the basis of the religious competition in the local community. It was not a competition among separate leaders principally and among religions secondarily; both John the Baptist and Jesus of Nazareth had long before passed from the scene, and it is unlikely that either had ever visited the locale of the gospel's intended audience. No leader of the non-Baptist Jews is even named. It was not a competition between those prone toward messianic movements and those not; both the Christian and the Baptist movements were messianic, and no controversy over messianism is reflected in the texts. Though the Baptists are distinguished from other Jews, and hence are addressed by a specific passage, there is no evidence of conflict between those two religious entities. The controversy seems to be over the Christians' claim to an unmediated divine endorsement of Jesus. This is suggestive of a Christian religiosity that is un-communal, in the sense of not being totally derived from and subordinate to the ethnic community. One would expect this Christianity to have an element of an individual experiential foundation.

Transcendent eternity

One of the kinds of text in the third Johannine layer that points to how crucial the role of multi-ethnicity was becoming in Johannine Christianity is the kind that speaks of the universal significance of the Christ. "The true light that enlightens every human was coming into the world." (Jn. 1.9) Such universalism was, of course, not original with Christianity; such a universality is to be found in the Hebrew prophetic tradition. When it is given enough emphasis, however, it stands in contrast to another theme of Jewish tradition, that of a special relationship between God and the chosen nation. As emphasized by the Johannine author, universality does indeed stand in contrast.

> But whoever received him, he gave to them power to become children of God - to those who believed in his name; they were born not from blood or from the will of flesh or from the will of a man but from divinity. (Jn. 1.12-13)

The language of rebirth, wherein one becomes a child of God, is a birth that, according to the author, supersedes a first birth into a nation.

In one passage, the issue of bringing the religion to non-Jews is taken up explicitly, and the fact that the evangelization of the Greeks might be contemplated is presented as unthinkable to Jesus' Jewish interlocutors.

> Then Jesus said, "I am with you a little time yet, and I am heading to him who sent me. You will seek me and not find me, and where I am you cannot come." So the Jews said to themselves, "Where is he about to go that we will not find him? Is he about to go to the diaspora of the Greeks and teach the Greeks?" (Jn. 7.33-35)

This is probably anachronistic since there is no evidence that there was any widespread avoidance of Greek places by Jews in Jesus' time, but a movement to do precisely that developed in Palestine soon after. The text does not necessarily testify to such avoidance behavior existing in the locale of the Johannine Christians because the text attempts to portray a Palestinian setting. Nevertheless, the status of Greeks in a Jewish religious movement seems to have been at issue, and texts like this purportedly relating to Palestine take up a particular relevance to this issue.

The transcending of ethnicity takes the religious form of a universal salvation, a delivering over of all humans to God in an earth-transcending and time-transcending life.

> Father, the hour has come. Glorify your son, so that the son may glorify you, since you have given him power over all flesh, so that he may give to them all you have given him - eternal life. (Jn. 17.1b-2)

> I showed your name to the people of the world whom you gave me. (Jn. 17.6)

However, this universal salvation was to be a contingent one, since those who rejected its bringer could not be thought of as receiving it: "I do not pray for the world but for them whom you gave me, since they are yours." (Jn. 17.9) So while nationality per se is transcended in the third Johannine layer, the conflict over the issue of nationality is not completely so; there remains a concern over whether people believe in the savior or not, and this focus becomes a new basis for a collective identity. These new lines replace the old ethnic or national lines. Thus, a new worry enters the picture, a worry over "the world" not accepting the Messiah.

> I have come into the world as light, so that everyone who believes in me would not stay in the dark. And if anyone should hear my words and not keep them, it is not I who judges him, for I did not come to judge the world but to save the world. (Jn. 12.46-47)

Thus the lines of group identity were drawn for the Johannine Christians not only between them and non-believing Jews but also between them and non-believing Greeks.

> I will ask the father and he will give you another advocate to be with you forever, the spirit of truth that the world cannot accept, because it does not see or know it. (Jn. 14.16-17a)

This seems to be reinforced by hostility, and perhaps persecution, from non-believing Gentiles:

> If the world hates you, know it has hated me, the first of you. If you are of the world, the world would befriend its own; but because you

> are not of the world, but I chose you out of the world, the world therefore hates you. (Jn. 15.18-19)

The passage goes on to draw a parallel between the treatment Jesus himself received and the treatment that the addressees of the discourse can expect to receive.

At this juncture it might be useful to call to mind some similar phenomena in more contemporary settings. In twentieth century American race relations traditional status inequality relations have been replaced by a system of a legal equality of rights within which material inequalities are allowed to obtain; the situation of the individual became more significant than status group membership. Meanwhile, those of both black and white races who promoted the new framework of legal equality distinguished between themselves and those who seemed content with the prior system. The passing of status group identity systems did not prevent a new basis for group identities from forming. The era seemed characterized by large scale movements of populations, with an attendant loss of some traditions and revival of others. Early Christianity might be regarded as a kind of social movement that can evolve when received status group lines break down and new cognitively identified grounds of distinction are being formulated.

Christian identity

Some of the textual material at this third Johannine layer of tradition emphasizes the importance of Christianity itself as a religious identity. In the Good Shepherd discourse, this identity is expressed in terms of sheep knowing their shepherd. The discourse begins with a contrast between the manner in which some alternate religious figure is presented, and the coming of Jesus the good shepherd. The good shepherd comes through a gate that a gate keeper opens. "The gate" may have been a tentative reference to Judaism and the "gate keeper" a similarly tentative reference to John the Baptist; but a later portion of the discourse identifies both gate and shepherd with Jesus. Any other figure would be a Greek, Roman, or some other deity.

> Amen amen I say to you, that person who does not enter the sheep yard by the gate but climbs over another place, is a thief and guerilla. But he who enters through the gate is a shepherd of the sheep. The gate keeper opens for him.... (Jn. 10.1-3a)

The passage suggests that the Johannine community recognized other Christian groupings as authentically Christian:

> And I have other sheep that are not from this yard; it is necessary for me to bring them, and for them to listen to my call, and become one flock, one shepherd. (Jn. 10.16)

Competition and conflict with non-Christian Jews and with the adherents of other religions that were older and more established than Christianity ("All who came before me were thieves and guerillas...." - Jn. 10.8) made it important for the Christians to identify with one another, even though they may have first organized themselves in separate, independently founded communities in Ephesus.

This third Johannine layer contains the famous passages where the "love command" is found. That command should be understood not only as a recommendation about the excellence of mutual charity and respect, but also as an encouragement of a common Christian society in the face of relatively hostile non-Christians.

> I am giving you a new command, that you love one another; as I loved you, you should also love one another. By this all will know that you are my disciples, if you have love for one another. (Jn. 13.34-35)

The competitive situation called for not only different individual Christians to unite in an accord, but also for different Christian communities to do so. The Johannine community, which heretofore seems to have had a tradition that was independent of those of other Christian communities, seems ready under pressure (and perhaps persecution) to make common cause with other Christian communities. In one passage Jesus is depicted as praying not for the non-Christians but for emphatically all Christians. (Jn. 17.9-10) The Christians are to be united:

> Father, keep them in your name that you have given me, so that they may be one, as we. When I was with them, I kept them in your name that you had given me, and I guarded them, and none of them perished.... (Jn. 17.11b-12a)

The sense of danger from outside the Christian community is as evident as the quest for unity in the face of it. (See also Jn. 17.20-21, and 22.) A particular overture to Peter, the leader of another Christian community, that was located in Antioch on the Orontes, might be understood in the light of this quest for unity (see Jn. 21.18).

The extent of the Christian community

The author of these third layer texts seems quite concerned lest something less than the whole Christian community be included in the young religion's identity.

> Everyone whom my Father is giving me will come to me, and I will not cast out him coming to me, because I have come down from heaven not so that I would do my will but the will of Him who sent me. This is the will of Him who sent me, that I not lose any from His whom He has given me, but raise every one of them up on the last day. (Jn. 6.37-39)

This phraseology is very curious; the inclusion of all Christians is presented as part of a divine plan that stands in contrast to some other preference. Some Christians had evidently preferred to "cast out" one or more Christian groupings, but the author would have all included on the grounds that all who followed Jesus ("coming to me") conformed to the plan of salvation. We have already seen this reflected in the Good Shepherd discourse (Jn. 10.16). The author is not, however, ready to include any faction within the early Christian movement indiscriminately:

> I am the true vine, and my Father is the gardener. He removes every branch on me that does not bear fruit, and clears each that does bear fruit, so that it would bear much fruit. You are already cleared by the word that I have spoken to you. (Jn. 15.1-3)

It would seem that not every breakaway Jewish movement and that not every new religious movement that shared the Christians' social space was to be included in Christianity; but all those that preserved the Jesus traditions ("the word that I have spoken to you") were to be included. It is unclear whether Jesus' "word" refers to the wider body of Jesus logia or, more likely, to the specific ones contained in the Johannine trajectory. One reference in the texts suggests that one other group of Jewish Christians had been welcome (Jn. 8.31) but had been more concerned about being Jewish than concerned with Christian redemption. (Jn. 8.33-37a) There seems to be some ambivalence, to say the least, about the wider Christian world.

Ritual

The third layer of Johannine texts continues to refer to religious rituals. An insistence on a baptism not only like that of John the Baptist but also in the "spirit" remains: "Amen amen I say to you, unless someone is born of water and spirit, one cannot enter into the kingdom of God." (Jn. 3.5b) There is also a mention of the bread that is from Jesus and is Jesus himself:

> Work not for the food that perishes
> but for the food that lasts into

> eternal life, which the son of humanity will give you. (Jn. 6.27a)

> I am the bread of life. He who comes to me will not hunger, and he who believes in me will never thirst. (Jn. 6.35b)

The import of the references to the ritual bread is that something transcending earthly realities is in question. There may have been a concern on the part of the author that the performance of the rituals had become something of an end in itself and that the audience of the texts needed to have more profound quests brought to mind.

Persecution

As in much early Christian literature, persecution of the Christians lends an urgency to the appeals to think of transcendent values. In the case of the third Johannine layer, there is an added emphasis upon the appeal for Christian unity and, presumably, mutual assistance. One consequence of persecution seems to have been a cessation, for the time being, of public evangelization.

> It is necessary that we work the works of him who sent me during the day; night is coming, when no one can work. (Jn. 9.4)

This likely led the local Johannine community toward internal Christian affairs. In any case, the gospel tradition ended up presenting the fate of Jesus as a precedent, under such circumstances:

> Recall the saying that I told you, "No servant is greater than his master." If they persecuted me, they will persecute you also.... (Jn. 15.20a)

The persecution seemed to have been feared to come at the hands of both Jews and Gentiles, and this fact seemed to scandalize at least some of the Christians:

> I have spoken these things to you that you not be scandalized. They will excommunicate you from the synagogue. Indeed an hour is coming when everyone who has killed you will think that he is carrying out a worship service to God. (Jn. 16.1-2)

Matters seemed to have been serious enough to give the Christians no choice but to bring at least some good out of adversity - perhaps a sense of fellowship under adversities, a fellowship that had not been present beforehand.

> Amen amen I say to you, you will weep and mourn, but the world will

> rejoice. You will grieve, but your grief will become joy. (Jn. 16.20)

The newly solidified Christian movement is like a new person.

> The woman has grief when with child because her hour comes. But when she gives birth to the child she no longer remembers the distress because of the joy that a human has come into the world. (Jn. 16.21)

Social roles within Johannine Christianity

By the time of the third literary stratum, there seems to have been some specialized roles in Johannine Christianity. One verse (Jn. 12.26) speaks of serving Jesus as an option that a believer might make (see also Jn. 14.12). Another seems to refer to missionary apostles, people who were in some way sent by Jesus; a problem had evidently arisen insofar as these missionaries were not always well received (Jn. 13.20). Jesus himself was considered the model for the Christian religious specialists; he was sent, according to one saying, to do the work of God. (Jn. 9.4) The doctrine of God sending a Holy Spirit to inspire the Christians legitimated the continuation of Jesus' work long after he had been gone (Jn. 14.25-26). The result was held to be testimony about

Jesus. (Jn. 15.26-27).

NOTES

1. An earlier version of this chapter was presented at the 1992 meeting of the Association for the Sociology of Religion in Pittsburgh, Pennsylvania.

2. See Raymond E. Brown, The Gospel According to John (i-xii) (New York: Doubleday, 1966), pp. LII-LVI, for an overview of the question. On the milieu common to the Qumran materials and the Gospel of John, see the "Foreword" and two essays by James H. Charlesworth, and the essays by Raymond E. Brown and Annie Jaubert, in James H. Charlesworth (ed.), John and the Dead Sea Scrolls (New York: Crossroad, 1991).

Ch. 7 Interpreting the Evidence

It is routine in sociology to distinguish among three fundamental categories: social structures, social processes, and cultures. Structures are patterns of social interaction, such as rank, division of labor, and organization. Social processes are event-like occurrences within the framework of the structures. Cultures are symbol systems that emerge as people make their thoughts and feelings public to each other as they live in the structures and live through the processes. For purposes of interpreting the several textual layers of the Gospel of John, the social forum is the concept that seems most useful as a structural - or at least quasi-structural - concept. The jurisdictional dispute and schism are useful processual concepts for our purposes, and ambivalence is a useful culture-like concept.

Forum as an interpretive concept

Back in Chapter Three social forum was shown to be analogous to but still distinct from some other kinds of collective behavior - the crowd, the **secte**, collective attention, and the social world. I characterized the forum as a form of social interaction that draws individuals into lines of activity that they would not pursue alone, that occasions spontaneous responses that in turn constitute departures from received tradition and normalcy, that receives a coherence out of a shared faith or ideal, and in which the participants position themselves with respect to some matter. It differs from the crowd in that it is not an ephemeral enthusiasm of the moment, from the <u>secte</u> in that it is not necessarily criminal or deviant, from collective attention in that it is a social framework in which such collective attention could occur, and from the social world in that it is an interaction process rather than a cultural subsystem. Now on the basis of our readings of the texts of the Gospel of John, let us see what more we can say about the social forum and about the Johannine Christians in their social existence as a forum.

The concept of forum seems to be most relevant to the Beloved Disciple textual layer of the gospel, the early narrative into which other materials were inserted. First, we can speak of the Johannine Christians who were addressed by the Beloved Disciple text as being in interaction with one another in the first place; they were being addressed by a text, and that alone constitutes an interaction in some minimal sense. Moreover, the text presents them with reminiscences about legendary people who had been among the early followers of Jesus, and these reminiscences serve to provide a traditional anchor in an earlier time for the audience of the text. The text also highlights the giving of testimony as an archetypical activity manifested by both John the Baptist and the anonymous disciple. Testimony as a form of speech goes beyond mere exposition; it is not a matter of one person telling another person about something but of one person placing a statement into evidence for an unspecified other. It is more like writing than talking, in the sense that persons beyond those immediately present are potential beneficiaries of testimony. Giving testimony memorializes, makes a record. It implies an audience that is composed of more than a few individuals and likely to be reconstituted at one or more future occasions. The nature of the text in question, highlighting as it does a testimony motif, suggests that its author was anticipating a continued form of interaction among those addressed by the text.

Does the text similarly presuppose that the readers would be drawn into lines of activity that they would not pursue alone? In this context it is useful to recall the author's ecclesiastical minimalism, in which little or nothing was made of church-like offices and hierarchy, yet the expectation of a functioning pastoral activity was insisted upon. The imperative "Feed my sheep" comes to mind. The ecclesiastical minimalism (absence of hierarchy and named offices and their attendant prerogatives) cannot be attributed simply to the early point in Christian history reflected by the text; earlier yet, Paul had written of apostles and had cited quasi-codified Jesus logia. Exactly what was entailed in a line of pastoral activity at the time of the Beloved Disciple text is never spelled out, but it is evidently done amidst a plurality of people. The giving of testimony is also a group-based activity. The Beloved Disciple text does not seem in the least interested in a hermetical lifestyle; the Jesus of this gospel attends wedding celebrations and feeds crowds. The gospel is not one of an individual contemplative life; rather it presupposes a christian (messian) movement.

The forum, as suggested above, occasions spontaneous responses that constitute departures from received tradition and normalcy. The idealized personages in the narrative - John the Baptist and Jesus - characteristically have on-the-spot insights into people; they do not allow religion to remain a matter of various social strata enacting traditionally accorded roles. Neither the Baptist nor Jesus is presented a an inheritor of any priestly status, and their followers similarly act out of caste, so to speak; people who fished for a living took up religion as a specialization. People mentioned in the narrative, as was seen in Chapter Four, were placed into types for the reader not on the basis of their estate or position but on the basis of their insight into Jesus. The received tradition - Temple-centered Judaism - is given little prominence; indeed the claim of Temple Judaism over the reader is neutralized by the narrated role of the Temple authorities in opposing Jesus and in demanding his execution. The messian context of the narrative would have the reader seek a new cosmological center to replace the Temple, seek a living Messiah.

The texts present a shared ideal that is to give coherence to the readership. Jesus, who reads people's hearts, is presented as the ideal. When John the Baptist gives testimony about him, two of the Baptist's own disciples begin to follow Jesus, and this is undoubtedly narrated for the reader's edification. In fact, this is the kind of spontaneous response the narrative seems intent upon eliciting, and the qualities that make this kind of response more likely - openness to spontaneity itself, suspicion toward the fixedness of social categories, a more or less person-centered approach to religious and ethical matters -

comprise the content of the shared ideal that is to be cultivated on the part of the Johannine Christian.

The readers are to position themselves on the question of the Messiah. Within the social forum the Johannine audience is to be the one that takes Jesus rather than the Baptist to be "the one." A central theme of the Beloved Disciple text is the defining of Jesus as the Messiah, described as a recognition of who Jesus was. They are to recapitulate the experience of the sacred being absent from life, by finding that experience in the narrative of the execution of the Messiah. One might speak of a **habitus**, a behavioral logic of these people's religious activity, according to which the disappointed seek the sacred in the persecuted. "Recognizing" Jesus as sacred in this disposition in turn provides them a certain stance toward the Baptist, toward the Jewish authorities of Jerusalem, and perhaps even toward the Roman government.

When the Johannine Christians are thought of as being in a forum in this way, these motifs in the Beloved Disciple text cohere; they make sense as a unit. If the Johannine Christian community were to be thought of as a more institutionalized church, the ecclesiastical minimalism would seem out of place. If they were thought of as a Jewish sect, the motif of setting aside inherited status and ethnic categories would seem out of place. And if they were thought of as existing as one of the other forms of collective behavior (crowd, **secte**, collective attention, social world), there would be similar lacks of fit between concept and evidence. For example, if the Johannine Christians were thought of as something of a revival crowd, the motif of pastoral care would seem out of place. If they were to be thought of as a **secte**, more condemnation of the Roman government would be expected, and Jesus would seize upon rather than flee the occasion of being made a king. If it were a matter of collective attention, the protracted existence of the social phenomenon implicit in the giving of testimony would not fit the context. If it were a matter of a social world, the received categories of the Jewish subculture would have been sufficient for the participants. It is the social forum as a genre of human organization that best fits the totality of this evidence.

Jurisdictional dispute in the narrative insertions

"Jurisdiction" implies the existence of specialists who claim a right to exercise an expertise over some matter or activity. In Max Weber's sociology this kind of right could be founded on a traditional division of labor, on the charisma of a great personage, or on an acquired system of knowledge. The traditional division of labor in Jewish religion that had existed under the form of priestly familial lineages had been more pertinent to the Temple cultus in Jerusalem and does not seem to have had a counterpart in the readers' local community at the time of Johannine Christianity. Diaspora Judaism would have known jurisdiction as a claim to knowledge about the religion and customs of the Jewish people. The followers of Jesus in the Johannines' local community had Jesus preached to them as a significant personage and evidently responded to traditions about Jewish customs as to something too narrowly ethnic to function as a religion in a multi-ethnic world.

In the kind of jurisdictional dispute most familiar to us, different professions compete with each other over recognition as the appropriate specialization for some matter over which people are concerned. But there is another kind of jurisdictional dispute in which the specialists compete with amateurs;[1] for example, professional musicians in the modern world do not compete with some other profession as much as with part-time improvisers and people who have little formal musical training. The disputes occur when the question arises over who should be allowed to record music for pay, who should be allowed to teach music, and who should be allowed to perform in entertainment business establishments. In the world of contemporary religion, the jurisdictional dispute between formally credentialed specialists and part-time improvisers having little formal training usually involves a more cosmopolitan credentialed body of specialists and a more localistic type of improviser. Usually a denominationally organized mainstream body of specialists is competing with local individual religious entrepreneurs, or a body of international missionaries representing a formal doctrinal and ritual complex competes with local traditional practitioners of a syncretic popular religion.

In the setting that is reflected in the inserted narrative texts of the Gospel of John (the "C" columns in the Appendix to this study), the situation is quite different. It is the amateurs, the formally unrecognized followers of Jesus, who are the more cosmopolitan; and it is the beneficiaries of the more systematic training in Jewish customs and law who are the more "local" in the sense of being ethnicity-specific. The Christian amateurs inhabited a wider social circle, at least when it came to religious matters, and the Jewish specialists who inhabited a narrower social circle. Consequently the dispute is not like those that had occurred in Palestine among traditional Jewish factions; in fact the Johannine Christians had ceased even referring to such factions and had begun to speak of "the Jews."

The textual evidence that we reviewed in Chapter Five suggested that there were more than one dividing line in the world of local Jewish life. One dividing line separated the messian Jews (including followers of John the Baptist and followers of Jesus) from non-messian ones; another line separated the followers of Jesus (both Jewish and non-Jewish) from Jews who were not followers of Jesus. People who were neither Jewish nor followers of Jesus do not appear to have been in the social forum under consideration. No evidence exists in the texts that there was any serious dispute between messian followers of John the Baptizer and Jewish intellectuals of the proto-rabbinical world, but that may be simply because our evidence comes from followers of Jesus, people who would have no direct participation in such a dispute. There is some evidence of a lingering dispute between the Baptists and the followers of Jesus, but this does not appear to be a jurisdictional dispute. In fact, the Jesus Christians appear to have been co-opting the Baptist tradition on the one hand, by depicting John the Baptizer as testifying to the divinity of Jesus, and sharply distinguishing themselves from the Baptists on the other, by emphasizing a "baptism in the spirit" that was different from that of the Baptist.

What the evidence of the inserted narrative texts points to is a jurisdictional dispute between specialists of proto-rabbinic Judaism and amateurs from the Christian movement. It is necessary to use the terms "specialist" and "amateur" (not to mention "rabbinic") in rather qualified senses since we do not know that intellectuals who had studied somewhat formally in Palestine (as had Flavius Josephus and Paul of Tarsus) took part in the local dispute against the Christians or that the Johannine Christians lacked a full-time intellectual. What we can say is that Palestinian Judaism had had specialists in the past and that the Jews in the Johannines' local community would have known of them; more to the point, the local Jews would have known that the Christians were not theologically or ritually in accord with the known traditions of Jewish Palestinian specialists. Moreover, the evidence from the earlier, Beloved Disciple layer of the fourth gospel was characterized by an ecclesiastical minimalism, in which no offices were ever named; this does not mean that the Christians did not have officers but that legitimacy was neither given to or based upon such specialized office holding. The Christian faction took the form of a folk or "little tradition" movement that was, ironically, more cosmopolitan in content than was the Jewish, and the non-christian Jewish faction took the form of an appeal to a more specialized "great tradition" that was more ethnic in content.

From the perspective of the Christians, the non-christian Jews were "of the world" and hence could not follow Jesus. We need to recall that "cosmopolitan" and "worldly" are <u>our</u> terms for people who are ethnically pluralist in outlook as well as sophisticated in the pleasures of the material and cultural realms. For purposes of the present discussion, only the sense "ethnically pluralist" should be read into the term "cosmopolitan." When the text speaks of the Jews (Jerusalem authorities) as being "of the world," it means that their rejection of Jesus and local Jews' rejection of his Johannine followers was based on a social distinction, virtually an occupational one, not some theological or spiritual rationale. More specifically, the rejection was based on the fact that he and they were not among those who could exert jurisdiction because they did not represent ethnic learnedness. From the Jewish perspective, such a criticism would be placing an intellectual preference for a non-ethnic religiosity ahead of a divinely-mandated duty toward one's nation, a nation favored by God. Placed in these terms, the jurisdictional dispute could be a more serious question than one of quasi-professional or quasi-disciplinary prerogatives.

That there was an adversarial relationship between a Christian faction and one that associated itself with the tradition of Temple Judaism can be seen from the textually evident willingness of the non-christians to associate themselves with the execution of Jesus. The texts do not argue for making such an association, as if it were a point at issue. Rather the point at issue is whether Jesus should have been executed, not whether the Jerusalem authorities and their successors favored the execution. That they did is taken as given. The Christian faction saw this as a disability on the part of the Jewish religious authority; their "this-worldly" desire to be associated with the Jerusalem authorities of the recent past meant that they could not follow Jesus. The association between the participants in the social forum and the Jerusalem of the recent past seems to have been a natural one; the Johannine Christian faction seemed to have some purpose served by the reference to Jews in Jerusalem during the Temple era who followed Jesus; as noted in Chapter Five, the fact that there was such a following in the authentic and undisputed center of the Jewish world served an apologetical purpose against those in the Johannines' local community who honored a jurisdictional claim against the Christians.

Something that often happens in disputes is that both sides unify into disputant camps against each other. Two group identities, each corresponding to a side, develop in the course of the dispute. One of the aspects of such an identity is the development of an inner life in the group, a subculture of sorts, that is fashioned in the context of the conflict. The peculiar rituals - e.g., a drinking of water - of the Johannine Christians can be understood as a manifestation of such an inner group life. Once separate identities emerge in this fashion, a schism becomes thinkable.

Schism in the narrative insertions

It is not possible to discover whether some of the texts from the layer of narrative insertions of the fourth gospel reflect an earlier point in time than others, or whether they all reflect one point in time at which they were inserted. In any event some of them reflect a jurisdictional dispute while others reflect a schism, and it seems reasonable that the former would precede and precipitate the latter. A schism has the consequence of breaking up a social forum so that a jurisdictional dispute that corresponds to the two factions could no longer take place; the disputants would no longer be co-present in the same set of social interactions. There seem to be several logical possibilities. First texts reflecting the jurisdictional dispute were collected earlier than those reflecting a schism, and both sets were edited into the gospel together. Second the rhetoric from the jurisdictional dispute served the purpose of legitimating the stand taken by one of the groups that had been newly formed by the schism and was given literary form at the time of a post-schism re-editing of the gospel. Third two separate editions - one during the jurisdictional dispute and one after the schism - occurred, and the Appendix to the present study should show four columns rather than three. I am not prepared to choose among these alternatives, but it is worthwhile making analyses using both the concept of jurisdictional dispute and that of schism.

The texts that use pastoral figures to distinguish between the sheep of Jesus and those who do not recognize his voice imply an existence of two separate entities. The very figure of a shepherd suggests the existence of some office, and hence of an organization having offices. Other references to Christians being put out of the synagogues also lead us to believe that by the time of some of the Johannine narrative insertions, a schism within Judaism in the Johannines' community had to have taken place. The action of putting followers of Jesus out of the synagogue was itself a defining one; people who had been favorably disposed to the Jesus traditions had to choose sides at that point, had to decide whether they adhered to the group that was being put out or to the group that was putting out. Indecision or not speaking out grouped one by default with the latter.

The language that speaks of "putting out" implies that the initiative for the schism came from the critics of the Jesus-following rather than from the following itself. The party that thus takes the initiative will have to have organized first, and the people who were put out will have been less organized at the time and would after the fact become more organized than beforehand. Thus we should not think of two organized parties opposing each other within the synagogue context but of one organized entity acting, as it saw matters, to keep order in the synagogue, and a looser collection of people who had been expelled developing an organization after the expulsion. This can explain why the Johannine Christians had ritual and literary traditions that differed in significant ways from the rest of early Christianity; they were not initially part of a wider Christian world sharing in some real though elemental organizational and symbolic apparatus of that world, but were instead a grouping of "fellow travellers" within a local synagogue who suddenly found themselves outside that synagogue and not yet inside a Christian counterpart.

Once the schism had taken place, once the Johannine Christians found themselves outside the synagogue of their community and had organized themselves, the question of persecution can arise logically. One opposes one's fellow member who thinks differently than oneself but does not persecute; however, one can logically persecute as well when it is a matter of someone who is an "other," someone whose organizational identity is found from outside one's own group. "Persecution" maximally entails using one's organizational apparatus and public standing against a category of non-members, and minimally withholding such an apparatus and standing, in situations in which they would have been used in the past for defensive purposes against outside enemies. Of course, any given ancient city had many non-jews, who were not subject to this persecution. To be an object of persecution, one had not only to be a non-member but an irritant. The synagogue was an ethnic institution, and one could not be "put out" of an ethnic status. Hence those who had been expelled became a public problem in identity management, being both associated with and dissociated from local Jewish life at the same time. This alone does not mean that Jews from the local community's synagogue persecuted the Christians, but it does mean that when persecution or even disputes arose from other quarters the synagogue Jews would not be defending the Christians any more.

As was noted in Chapter Five, we can learn from a persecution that is known to have taken place in Ephesus; it had been led by people who worshiped Artemis, not by Jews. It would appear unlikely that Jews would rouse these people up against the Christians because the devotees of Artemis could turn against the Jews as well as against the Christians. It is quite conceivable, however, that community disputes between Christians and others occurred, as they would also occur between Jews and others, and since the Christians had no traditional protection or legal status as a group, the outcomes of such disputes would be experienced as "persecution."

Finally, it should be noted that the narrative insertion texts show a relatively high christology, a belief in the divine status of Jesus. This can be associated with the time after the schism, insofar as the Christians were no longer in the synagogue and no longer faced the charge that any such christology is blasphemous. Moreover, the Christians had reached the ethnic boundary and faced the gentile world, though they may not have fully crossed over into that world. The object of cultus was in part Jesus, because of whom they had been expelled from the synagogue, but they were not ready to set Jesus up as a human-made god comparable to local pagan divinities. Jesus was a figure who came out of a Jewish religious world with its monotheist theology, but he had to transcend the limits of an ethnic social presence. The ritual commemoration of Jesus was these people's substitute for the recently-destroyed Temple, the former center of the Jewish religious world. The high christology that was already to be found in Christianity would now be highlighted so that there would be a functioning continuity, a continuation of a sacred transcendence, amidst the changes implicit in a community's being put at the margins of Judaism. The same historical events that would conspire to deprive these people of their visible reference to a transcendent God - the Roman disestablishment of Temple Judaism and the synagogue's banishing them from the locus of Torah legitimacy - forced them to make the Transcendent manifest again. Hence these Christians would emphasize the high christological facet of the Jesus tradition.

Ambivalence in the late sayings and discourses

The portions of the Gospel of John that lend themselves to interpretation with the concept **ambivalence** are found in the latest of the three layers of literary material, the layer that is made up of sayings and discourse texts that had been inserted into a gospel that had already been composed out of at least two sets of narrative material. This latest layer is the one that has a number of verbal parallels with the First Letter of John. It probably reflects the Johannine Christians in about the years 95-112.[2] These materials include some passages that are most recognizable to modern Christians, focusing as they do on the theme of divine love and Christian unity. They can obviously be interpreted with concepts other than ambivalence; so what follows is proposed merely as **an** interpretation.

Ambivalence differs in notable respects from the social forum, jurisdictional dispute, and schism; ambivalence manifests itself as an attitude or feeling that is experienced by the individual while the other three refer to situations in one's environment or situational processes that involve a number of people. This is not to suggest that ambivalence does not have a social dimension to it or that the others do not have their personal or individual experiential aspects. The ambivalence that is of concern to us here is occasioned by non-neutral orientations toward other people, groups, and collective cultural expressions; such an other-directed orientation or attention is itself more than individual. And the social forum, jurisdictional dispute, and schism all could not occur without individuals participating in them in a wide-awake fashion. But ambivalence is manifest in the first instance in the experience of the individual while the others come to notice **as** situations or processes that lie beyond the individual. One can think of oneself having had an experience of ambivalence, but only of a number of people, possibly including oneself, having been involved in any of the other three. Ambivalence is a social psychological object while the others are sociological ones.

Second, ambivalence is less objectively evident than are the other three phenomena. In the terms used back in Chapter One, borrowed from the writings of Georges Gurvitch, this is a question of "levels in depth." A social forum is more likely to be identified as a social forum by means of unsubtle observation than ambivalence is likely to be identified as ambivalence by such means. The social forum is analogous to objects that are closer to the surface of a pond than some other objects and hence more readily detected and recognized. Gurvitch proposed a full spectrum of levels of objective availability in the social world, running from the ecological and morphological surface, encompassing such social facts as population density and spatial arrangement, to mental states and psychic acts in which a number of people share.[3] Ambivalence would appear to be at the latter end of the spectrum; it would appear to be a shared mental state. The sociologically interesting phenomenon is not the mere existence of ambivalence among a number of people but the association between ambivalence and social phenomena that appear at other levels in depth. It would be a gross exaggeration to speak of a schism, for example, "causing" ambivalence or of ambivalence "causing" a schism; "causation" implies a lack of any spontaneous response on the part of the individuals who are involved in a schism and who may feel ambivalence. Nevertheless, one who beholds a schism as a participant, who sees value in a social group as it once existed as a united entity and yet who sees value in a stance that helped precipitate the schism, can be reasonably expected to experience ambivalence as a spontaneous response to the situation; the ambivalence would make sense **as a spontaneous response** (and, by the way, not as an effect occurring independently of the person's act of beholding it or independently of a personal openness to spontaneous responses).

When ambivalence is used as an interpretive concept, it is applied to a number of instances. The implicit suggestion is that, for example, a person can behold a schism on more than one occasion, and respond each time in a similar way, thereby making it meaningful to say that the person remained ambivalent over the schism. Again, two different people can behold the same schism and each experience ambivalence. The repeated feeling by one person is not the same feeling in the sense of it being the identical experience, and the experiences by different people are not the same experience in the sense of their making a singular response to the schism. There is no question of a unitary, identical state of mind but of a similarity, an analogy between experiences, a homology of some sort. This in turn reflects a situation in which one can regard one's own personal response from a similar vantage to that in which one regards a response taken by another, and thereby "know" of a similarity between the two responses. One knows of the other's response first, and then associates one's own response with it, regarding one's own response from the vantage of the other.[4] Ambivalence in the sense intended here is not an inarticulate state of being ill at ease but a reasonable sort of judgment to which any number of people can arrive.

In the sayings and discourse material of the third Johannine textual layer, there are a number of junctures at which ambivalent responses to social circumstances would be reasonable and meaningful. In one of them, reference is made to what I have termed the missed opportunity, as the Johannine Christians would have seen it, for the non-christian Jews to recognize and accept their Messiah. There is not only mention of non-belief on the part of Jews but also, in the Prologue to the gospel, of creation in general failing to grasp the Creator. It is noteworthy that this particular kind of ambivalence - an ambivalence in the face of missed opportunity - is thus mentioned not only in the context of the non-believing Jews but as part of a cosmological statement. The Johannine Christians became sensitized to this kind of ambivalence, presumably from having experienced it in the social forum situation, and then in the jurisdictional dispute and schism processes. By the time of the inserted discourse and sayings material, they were predisposed to see ambivalence as a meaningful response to the inherent limitedness of the physical and everyday worlds. This particular kind of ambivalence consists of a context in which one finds oneself (the Johannine Christians in a Jewish context and the human in the context of creation) with a generalized inability to be open to a detectable value that transcends that context.

Another object that occasions ambivalence is what in a later parlance would be called "revelation"; the revelation in question is a divine communication through Moses. In this case, the same object (Torah) does not suggest so much a missed opportunity as a movement toward what were from the perspective of the Johannine Christians both good and bad outcomes. One the one hand the Law led to Jesus, spoke about Jesus (according to the Christians); it hence led to Christianity itself. On the other hand the Law led to a Judaism in the local community and elsewhere that was not only non-christian but anti-christian; it was also the law of the authorities who insisted, according to the narrative texts, upon the execution of Jesus. The "flavor" of this ambivalence does not have the character of the limitedness of one's own environment but of the common ground one shares with a bitter opponent.

A slightly different ambivalence occurs when the topic of revelation through Jesus comes up. There is no question yet, of course, of this revelation producing something Christian and something non- or even anti-christian at the same time; that would not happen until some Christian entity had become sufficiently established to consider itself orthodox and some other Christian entity heterodox. Nevertheless, the Johannine Christians could not avoid the fact that Jesus' revelatory teachings proved ineffective for purposes of persuading most of the Jews in Palestine, and that the revelatory tradition (as it would be regarded from the Christians' perspective) was failing to persuade many Jews in the Johannines' local community. What the Johannine Christians would regard highly was ineffectual in a highly visible way.

Another experience of ambivalence is occasioned by appreciating the richness of the Hebrew Bible. It is not a matter in this case of approaching the scriptures as revelation but as an impressive tradition to which someone like Flavius Josephus can point as a body of legitimatory antiquities. The Christians certainly retained a claim on these scriptures, and we have noted Johannine allusions to them. In Chapter Six of this study a concern with the richness of the Law was noted in the sayings and discourses inserted into the fourth gospel. The traditions unique to Christianity, in contrast, were not nearly as impressive; Christian writings as such were only in the process of being written and circulated. The Hebrew Bible made the Jesus tradition, which the Christians regarded favorably and associated with themselves, look paltry. The Hebrew Bible occasioned this experience of ambivalence, but it was neither the scriptures nor the Christians that were its object; the Jesus tradition, an object of commitment and identity on the one hand and a mere religious novelty on the other, was the object of this particular ambivalence; and the perception of it in such a light was occasioned by the Hebrew Bible.

It is interesting to note that the very literary form assumed by major sections of the third Johannine textual stratum - the disputation - lends itself to being interpreted in terms of ambivalence. In the disputation it is not simply the fact of a disagreement that is represented, but arguments designed to persuade are put into the mouth of Jesus. These arguments are not particularly persuasive, since in most cases they presuppose a Christian perspective and theology rather than prove a Christian doctrine to be true; hence it is not because of their inherent force that they were preserved but because of some other reason; it is the **attempt** to persuade that is highlighted in such passages. The opponents - usually depicted as Jewish critics of Jesus - are deemed worthy of persuasive effort and are not simply ignored or dismissed; yet it is clear that from the perspective of the Johannine Christians the opponents lack insight or any grasp of the truth. Such critics are functioning intellectuals who speak on behalf of a community, and as such they are not unlike the intellectual who is responsible for the insertion of these sayings and discourse materials into the gospel. The very form of a dispute honors the opposition as an equal to oneself, while at the same time articulating a claim that the opponent is unequal to the task of arriving at a truth without help from oneself. The ambivalence associated with this is one in which another person is accepted as a social equal but is taken to be vincibly wrong-headed and hence responsible for perpetrating error; this latter consideration suggests that the other is in one respect at least a moral unequal to a reader who is sympathetic to the Christian disputant's position.

Judaism in general enjoyed a higher status in the world of the Roman Empire than did earliest Christianity. It was officially recognized in a number of cities and can therefore be credited with the political clout to obtain that recognition. Its intellectuals had a place in the hellenistic world of letters, and there were fortunes in Jewish hands. A schism that separated Christians from Jewish organized life would inevitably involve ambivalence over being separated from the high status associated with ancient Judaism. This appears in the literary material under consideration as a sensitivity to the fact that the opponents of Jesus rejected him as uneducated and as not really being Jewish. This was neutralized in the texts on the one hand with an individualism of sorts, wherein the authenticity of an individual religious experience would be deemed more important than one's position with respect to Jewish organized life, and on the other hand with an appeal to a religious universalism, a theme already present in Jewish tradition, wherein a divine salvific plan would encompass all people. However, these two responses are themselves opposed to each other; the religious person focuses on an individual religiosity on the one hand and a collective, even universal, apparatus on the other. This creates an inherent ambivalence to Christian religiosity in which one's effort is always less than adequate, lacking either in personal depth or in cosmic reach; so long as both of these are valued the slighting of either of them in the course of enhancing the other is experienced with ambivalence.

A similar ambivalence arises when the everyday world is relativized by an orientation toward a cosmic religion. The "things of this world" are seen as trivial compared to the things of God; in the third Johannine literary layer this is expressed as a death joined to a union with God. But such a relativizing is itself an ironic focus on that which is relativized; carried to an extreme it would entail an obsession with this-worldly avoidances and non-involvements. Hence, the things of the world would still occasion experiences of value, but the valuations would be imported from the perspective of a cosmos rather than of immediate ends. The resultant ambivalence is one in which the activities of everyday life are labelled both with value and without value at the same time.

Finally, it is worth noting that a separation from the Jewish world both accommodates and is accommodated by a favorable appreciation of the wider, non-jewish world. A positive orientation toward the whole of humanity has already been mentioned above. Nevertheless, the early Christians had to face the stubborn fact that most of the known whole of humanity was not accepting Christianity. This occasions ambivalence over the non-jewish world, an ambivalence to be experienced in tandem with that occasioned by the Jewish world.

Overcoming ambivalence in the late sayings and discourse material

One of the most notable features of the later texts of the fourth gospel is their high christology; Jesus is not only taken to be a messiah but one enjoying a divine status. It is interesting to see how this belief can affect the Johannine Christians amidst their experiences of ambivalence. It would not be the case of their ambivalence causing or creating their high christology; the latter can be found as a received tradition among the Christians (e.g., in Paul's writings) prior to any schism, and it is the schism that appears to have occasioned most of the ambivalence. It would be a case, on the contrary, of a pre-existing belief coming to be emphasized because it helps address felt ambivalence, and a case of its becoming more widespread among the early Christians.

In the context of an ambivalence over the missed opportunity, a high christology increases the value of the opportunity that is perceived to be missed, in the sense that the non-christian Jews would not only be failing to recognize their messiah but their God as well. This would help resolve the ambivalence by leading the subject to decide all the more affirmatively about that which had been missed, and be drawn **relatively** less toward the Jewish community. The psychological dynamic would be away from indecision and toward defining oneself as a Christian. By the same token those among the synagogue Jews in the Johannines' local community who had not rejected the Jesus tradition but who had not accepted a high christology could see the non-acceptance of Jesus by their fellow Jews as a missed opportunity and still decide not to join the Christians at the time of schism out of loyalty to the synagogue community. The psychological dynamic for these people would also be away from indecision, but toward identifying themselves as Jews all the more definitively; their favorable orientation toward Jesus would weaken over time.

A high christology would have the effect of relativizing the revelational aspect of the Hebrew Bible. Jesus himself would be the new center of any revelational history. Hence the fact that the Hebrew scriptures led to a non-christian Judaism for some as well as to Christianity for others, would become less of a problem. These traditional writings would be used for purposes other than that of finding out truths about the normative will of God; they would be used by the Christians as prayer texts, statements of moral principle, sources of practical wisdom, and the like. It is notable that the precise way rabbinical Judaism would later use the Hebrew scriptures - as containing a Law that reveals God's will apart from and additional to natural moral principles - is a way the early Christians did not use them.

Ambivalence occasioned by the embarrassing fact that Jesus himself had been unable to persuade the Palestinian Jews would be resolved by placing some negative valuation on the latter. This dynamic may have been responsible for the negative aspect of the references to "the Jews" in the later layer of literary material in the Gospel of John. Modern Christians, of course, are embarrassed not by the unpersuasiveness of Jesus, since they approach the Jesus traditions from a world in which Christianity is a widely-accepted religion and source of legitimacy, but they are embarrassed by the negativeness of some of these passages. A reasonably sophisticated reader in the modern world can see these passages in the light of something like their originary context, but those who refuse to do so because they resist reasonable sophistication either experience an ambivalence of their own or adopt an anti-semitic stance. One should point out, however, that those Christians who resist a sophisticated hermeneutic are precisely those who see themselves as a cognitive minority and face the embarrassing fact that people around them are often not persuaded by their erstwhile efforts at evangelization. Their own temptation to vilify the modern age is analogous to the dynamics that seem to lie behind some of the Johannine material. In general these texts can be seen to be more revelatory about the humanness of the Johannine Christians than about the character of "the Jews."

A high christology rather straight forwardly addresses the ambivalence occasioned by a comparison of the rich Hebrew literary tradition to the upstart Christian traditions. The ambivalence disappears when the value of Christianity is enhanced by the divine status that is accorded its central figure Jesus, who comes to be seen as the incarnate Word. This is a benign resolution to the experience of ambivalence insofar as the Hebrew tradition does not suffer in anyone's estimation in the process. The balance is created in the subject by compensating a literary lack of prestige with a prestige-endowing doctrinal claim.

The high christological position of the later Johannine sayings and discourse material is not the only stratagem to be found in that textual layer to address ambivalence. There is also a stratagem of religious populism, a belief that the ordinary person's religiosity is as adequate as and even better than the religiosity of the specialists and virtuosi. This shows up when the critics of Jesus are depicted as dismissing Jesus as an uneducated person; the dismissal itself confirms what ordinary people "know" about educated religious specialists. But a far more striking stratagem is that which turns to the internal side of the emerging Christian community; in this stratagem there is a concern with highlighting a Christian identity and a "love ethic" among the Christians themselves. In this light the disputation texts can be seen as strengthening the Christian identity by counterposing a Christian position and a Jewish one. A heightened Christian identity reinforces a collective Christian apparatus, over against claims of individual religious experience as well as over against any Jewish particularism. Any serious divisions within Christianity would complicate if not undermine the Christian identity; hence, the unifying love ethic ("that they all may be one") can be seen as a concomitant disposition.

NOTES

1. See Pierre Bourdieu, "The uses of the 'people.'" In Pierre Bourdieu, In Other Words. Essays Towards a Reflexive Sociology (Stanford, California: Stanford University Press, 1990), pp. 150-155, especially the opening paragraphs.

2. See Chapter Two of this study.

3. Georges Gurvitch, "Sociologie en profondeur," in Georges Gurvitch (ed.), Traité de Sociologie (Paris: Presses Universitaires de France, 1962), pp. 157-171.

4. This is, of course, the "taking the role of the other" activity spoken of repeatedly in George H. Mead, Mind, Self, and Society (Chicago: University of Chicago Press, 1934).

Ch. 8 The Social Construction of Johannine Ultimacy[1]

The Johannine Christians, as the expression is used in the present discussion, were the people to whom the biblical Gospel of John and its predecessor texts were addressed, and by whom these texts were initially used. The gospel, according to my source critical analysis (see Appendix), was composed in three principal stages. The first stage, written in the mid 60's of the first century C.E. by a Palestinian Jew who had been close to the Christians of Jerusalem and who would migrate or had migrated to another community, took the form of an anonymous (later, "Beloved") disciple narrative. Some twenty years later further narrative fragments were written or collected at a time soon after Christians had begun to be excluded from synagogues and soon after the Johannine Christians had ceased identifying themselves with a local Jewish community. These narrative fragments were edited into the basic Beloved Disciple text, perhaps as marginalia adjacent to specific parts of that narrative that they paralleled. This enlarged version of the Johannine gospel evidently had an impact on the author of the Gospel of Luke. Meanwhile, the Johannine Christians themselves experienced a parting of ways from the followers of John the Baptist. A third stage of composition resulted in discourses, often on the themes of love and unity, being edited into the text of the gospel sometime between 95 and 112 C.E.; this produced substantially the Fourth Gospel as it appears in modern Greek New Testaments. This three-stage process enables us to speak of three cohorts of Johannine Christians.

The fact that different parts of the Gospel of John were written at different times for a community has enabled us to make reasonable inferences about that community that pertain to the different stages of its development.[2] In the present case our interest is in the later two layers of the fourth gospel; the texts of these later layers are marked by a "high christology," a view of the messiah that sees him as the Son of God. Here, this belief will not be isolated and explored as a symbol or doctrine, but considered in the context in which it became a central tenet of the Johannine Christians. That context was one that represents a specific conjuncture in religious history at which the local Christian and non-christian Jews had experienced a schism, and in which the Christians had interpreted the related conflict as a persecution.

The Johannine Christians saw themselves in a continuity with the Jewish religious tradition, even while making invidious comparisons between themselves and "the Jews"; the opening passages of the gospel in particular make a number of allusions to the Hebrew Bible.[3] They therefore symbolized the ultimate with references to God, the Jewish monotheist deity. The actual wording that is used, however, is not "Lord" (*ho kyrios*) but usually "Father." There is a seeming insistence on referring to God from the perspective of Jesus, who speaks, in the text, of God as his Father. The few departures from this practice theologize about Jesus' sonship by speaking of a Word spoken by God to God, using allusions to the first creation account in Genesis, or they speak of a Holy Spirit.

The expression, "ultimacy," refers to a form of knowledge, broadly defined. It does not refer to a kind of mere consciousness since it does not describe one's awareness per se but suggests implications about that of which one is aware. Those implications are not comparable to objective statements of the kind that we usually associate with knowledge, because in speaking of the ultimate we are speaking of it in terms of its relevance for various aspects of our environment rather than in terms of its observed qualities. Thus I may say of a house that it is beige in color, and my statement may be called "knowledge"; I know that the house is beige. I may also say that I know of such a house, and that statement would pertain to my consciousness rather than to the house itself. If I say it is the most important house in town, I am not speaking of something I know about it in the same sense as my knowing that it is beige, and yet I am not explicitating my consciousness of that house. Ultimacy refers to "knowledge" in the sense of not being about one's own consciousness per se, but not in the sense of associating qualities to some object.

Knowledge in the broad sense, according to which "ultimacy" refers to a kind of knowledge, is an object of sociology. The discipline includes a sociology of knowledge, which focuses on the cognitive priorities that structure people's consciousness of the world about them. Ultimacy is such a priority. The sociology of knowledge searches for elective affinities between knowledge systems and typical social experiences. It cannot affirm that a given social system and its attendant typical experiences cause a particular kind of knowledge, nor can it either affirm or call into doubt the valid or true nature of the knowledge system that is under consideration. Rather, the sociology of knowledge focuses on the prevalence of a particular kind of knowledge in a particular social world, a prevalence that reflects a pattern of priority that is rendered more reasonable than otherwise by the experiences that are typical in a given part of the social world. A mathematicalized physics is neither more valid or less so because commercial relations in the market economy render quantitative assessments of objects more reasonable than would otherwise be the case; nevertheless, a world structured to a great extent by a market economy, a world in which every physical object has a quantitative price, can be said with good reason to give priority to quantitative interpretations of the objects and processes that physics studies.

In studying Johannine ultimacy from a sociology of knowledge approach, I am suggesting first that ultimacy is a category that seems relevant to what the texts of the Fourth Gospel seek to communicate and that there were typical social aspects of life in the Johannine world that had an elective affinity for approaching the environment in a way that gave priority to ultimate matters. By "ultimate matters" I am referring to that to which the human mind refers when it puts everything else into perspective and that for which humans tend to sacrifice everything and which they would not lose for anything.

My examination of the textual layers of the Gospel of John revealed both structural and cultural processes. The earliest layer suggested a social form that I have termed the "social forum," a continuing social interaction that draws individuals into lines of activity that they would not pursue alone, that occasions spontaneous responses that constitute departures from received tradition and normalcy, that receives a coherence out of a shared faith or ideal, and in which the participants position themselves with respect to some matter. The participants in the social forum were drawn into group religious expressions to which they responded in ways that departed from Jewish tradition but were nevertheless in many respects coherent from the perspective of Jewish religion; they positioned themselves for or against giving prominence to the late Jesus of Nazareth as messiah. The second textual layer of the Fourth Gospel suggested a social form that I have termed the "jurisdictional dispute." There seems to have been a dispute among different religious movements over the exercise of religious influence. The third textual layer of the gospel suggested that a schism had taken place, a separation that was regretted. The structural process that we can see as we move from considering the earliest to considering the second and then the third layer is a process in which a jurisdictional dispute emerges in a social forum and evolves into a schism.

In addition to this structural process

there is a cultural one, a process in which there was a change in symbolic material in the Jewish world of the Johannines' community. In order to place the Johannine high christology, the cultural material in question, into its social context, it is necessary first to consider ultimacy in general as a sociological problem. Ultimate questions from a social scientific standpoint are theses, systems of belief and relevance that obtain for social actors. They are cases in point of what Alfred Schutz called "provinces of meaning" (**Sinngebieten**).[4] The logic and coherence of one province of meaning, according to Schutz, cannot be simply transferred to another; the attitude of everyday life, for example, cannot be transferred to science, and vice-versa. The coherence of a science cannot be applied to a fantasy. Schutz also identified religion as such a province. All such provinces are social constructs not only in the simple sense of being "learned," imparted to one person by another, but also in the sense that the imagination required to entertain them must be one that knows interaction.

Let me explain. An imagination that does not know interaction, for example that of a dog that runs in its sleep, is imprisoned in a world of stimuli and responses. The dog that is running in its sleep is merely re-experiencing stimuli that had been retained in memory and that had been associated with running responses; the phenomenon is not entirely unlike playing a tape recording and seeing the sound track lights or meters respond. An imagination that knows interaction, however, can have an entirely different experience. One endowed with such an imagination can first entertain the thesis of an object that is other, that is independent of one's own stimuli. Such a one can also make one's own self an object of contemplation from the vantage point of the other. Such a one can distinguish between a sensation that is peculiar to one's own body and a response that an other would have to one's own planned gesture or statement, and moreover one can distinguish the other's anticipated response to one's own statement from the other's anticipation of a response on one's own part to the other's statement. One can surprise the other by not responding as the other expected, and one can anticipate responding to that surprise. The imagination that knows interaction knows of play and interplay, tease and conversation, sequences and juxtapositions - in short, relevance structures that form meaning provinces.[5]

Ultimate reality (a variety of "other") and ultimate meaning (self contemplated from the vantage of the ultimate reality) are aspects of a particular polythetic social mind. By "social mind" I mean simply a person whose imagination knows interaction in the sense described above, and can therefore entertain forms of awareness that presuppose the self-other dialectic. By polythetic I mean that some relevance systems are nested within other ones. For example, I may ask a student why she has done an assignment; she may say in astonishment, "Because you told me to do it!" Then I may ask why she does what I tell her to do. She may respond that she wants to learn sociology or to earn a degree. If I keep asking why she wants to do such things, I can usually lead the student back to a basic wish to do something worthwhile in life or to do worthwhile things in general, to be a contributing citizen of the world. The actions needed in the doing of the assignment are nested within the desire to complete the work, and that in turn is nested within a broader plan, and the broader plan is nested within an even more general approach to life. When speaking of ultimacy, the suggestion is that a given person or group of people has an ultimate action-impulse within which all other activities are potentially nested. They have a prehension of an ultimate reality and of implied responses by the self or selves to that ultimate reality.

Now in a sociology of the Johannine Christians' ultimacy, the focus is on the social interactions that helped form the imagination that supports such a nesting of everyday actions and broader plans within such an ultimate action-impulse. I will use a portion of the latest, discourse layer of the gospel for illustrative purposes; these are the opening words of the Prologue:

> [1]There was a speech in Genesis, and the speech was to God, and the speech was divinity. [2]In Genesis this was to God. [3]All things came to be through this one, and apart from him nothing came to be that had come to be. [4]In him was life, and the life was the light of humans. [5]And the light shines in the darkness, and the darkness has not caught it.

The translation speaks of "Genesis" in order to preserve the Greek allusion to the Book of Genesis, which in most English translations is reproduced by the use of identical words: "In the beginning God made..." (Gen. 1.1); "In the beginning was the word..." (John 1.1). Similarly, there is a reference to light in both texts: "And God said, 'let light become'" (Gen. 1.3); "And the light shines in the darkness..." (John 1.5). The audience of the gospel was expected to think of the biblical creation poem upon hearing the opening three syllables (*'EN 'APXH*), and again when hearing the reference to light. This was evidently familiar phraseology, in the same manner that an English-speaking Christian who had been raised in a religiously literate environment would recognize the expression, "In the beginning...." The text presupposed a Greek-speaking Jewish background.

The first image that the text brings to the imagination is that of speech, specifically speech to God. By this speech all things were made, so that all things, according to the author, comprise a speech to God. Life itself is included in this speech to God, and whoever would see this would be enlightened; however, light eludes the darkness so that the divine speech is not caught. "Light" brings to the imagination a second image, and it stands in contrast to darkness. This metaphorical language suggests two social situations from which the author proceeds to articulate the Johannine theology: creative discourse and non-comprehended discourse. Creative discourse is a conversational process in which one knows what the other will understand from one's own statement but after speakinq finds that the other is placing one's own thought into a different life-perspective and thereby leads one to elaborate one's own thought in a wholly unanticipated way. Good conversations do that; they lead down paths that were unknown before hand and will never be traveled with precisely the same strides again. Good exchanges of letters and good meetings are like that, as are good seminars; all of the participants discover something that they had not thought of before. Moreover, it is even the case that no two persons had come to the exact same thought, since the perspective from which each receives the discourse cannot be exchanged for the perspective of the other. This is the creative process, so relished in the intellectual and political worlds and indeed in everyday life itself that people play and tease with it for the simple delight of doing so. This is the essential form of the creative imagination that enables humans to go well beyond stimuli and responses.

Non-comprehended discourse is minimally discourse insofar as one correctly anticipates what the other will understand from one's own statement and therefore utters it in order to occasion the desired meaning in the other's mind, but the other places it in no creative perspective, much less the other's own perspective. One's thought is not given back to oneself with new implications that lead one to think something new. The addressee understands in a lexical sense but does not know why one has said what had been said; pertinent words have been pronounced but the point not taken, much less dwelt upon and revised. The problem is not a lack of intelligence but a lack of a genuine participation in the same good conversation. We might think of someone who had been hired to work with an already established, creative group of people for whom the task at hand is not a mere job but a project to which they are committed; the hireling is not meeting the activities at hand with the same broader purpose.

The Johannine text speaks of the ultimate in such terms. There is the creative speech by which all things are made and by which life is given, and there is the non-comprehension of this, like a darkness that does not catch light. We need to reiterate in this context that the Johannine Christians had parted ways with the rest of the local Jewish community, whom they associated with the wider non-comprehending "world." This was a very serious matter to the Johannine Christians; their gospel discusses it repeatedly. "The Jews," as the gospel's later layers call them, fully understood the Johannines' words; had they read a text such as the gospel verses given above they would have caught the allusions to Genesis and would have taken the expression, *theos*, in the same monotheist way as did the Johannines. The Jews who rejected the Johannine Christians as fellows were nesting their everyday activities within broader plans and purposes ever as much as were the Johannines, and their broad plans and purposes were no doubt also a speech to God. But they were not making the point with the same statements as those of the Johannine Christians, and they were not, evidently, in a comprehending conversation with the Johannines. And similarly the Johannine Christians were not in a comprehending conversation with the local non-christian Jews. A schism is a regretted parting of ways, a break that the participants wish were not occurring. The counter tendency toward reunion, even while failing to prevent the schism from occurring, is based upon the common heritage of symbolic and community life that leaves the opposed parties surprised at each other's non-comprehension.[6]

But there is more than this to the ultimacy that was constituted in the Johannine discourse. In this discourse, the Johannines not only nest their activities in a separate, distinct "speech to God," but they seek the sacred or ultimate in the unacknowledged. Once more taking up the passage quoted above:

> 9The true light which
> enlightens every human was coming
> into the world. 10He was in the
> world, and the world came to be
> through him, and the world did not
> know him. 11He came to his own, and
> his own did not accept him.

First the world does not know to seek for its own creative principle, and the portion of the world called "home" by that principle does not accept the Homecomer. The Johannines cultivated an irony that they expressed in this text, the world's ultimate denial of selfhood. How could they have come to appreciate such an irony and find it in the center of their theology?

The situation of irony is one in which the person or people who should be aware of something, who are most intimately associated with it, are not so, and those who are relative outsiders to a situation or are distant from a matter prove to be keenly aware of it. The former take some matter of great seriousness for granted while the latter appreciate its precarity.[7] Is it not the wealthy, for example, who can spend with abandon, and those of modest means who economize? In the instance of Johannine Christians, it is "the world" that knows life and creativity in a taken-for-granted manner and, according to the author, lack an appreciation of the generation of life and creativity. It is the "home" of the "true light," Judaism, that would not treasure light. The perspective of the author presupposes a lack of cultural products as products, both products of the world in general and of Jewish tradition; the

Johannines lacked such cultural products but were sensitive to the generation of them. This can only describe a situation of some disappointment.

In disappointment over cultural matters the individual seeks to be addressed by texts that are engaging; such texts may have been "tasted" in the sense that some of them have raised questions that could be answered in the course of a further dialogue with them and perhaps with other texts, but further access thereto has been denied. Such a denial may take the form of a denial of access to documents and discourses - as might occur in an exclusion from a synagogue - or, perhaps more to the point, a denial of the very validity of one's quest for cultivation, the broader project into which one's questions and searches for answers are nested. The very relegation of Johannine Christians' interest to the status of subaltern culture, perhaps "cult" in a negative sense, by those who take the ways of the world and the riches of an ancient wisdom for granted, engenders a preparedness for cultural and religious pursuits among the very people whose interests had been so relegated. Disappointment in that kind of circumstance is propaedeutic to an openness to values that could be cultivated by means of the discourse-related and text-related activities that are denied to cognitive minorities in general.

Implicit in this ironical situation of disappointment is an experience of genuine quests in "good conversations" among the members of an out group, albeit in an absence of the sophistication that a heritage of cultivation can supply; and also implicit is a knowledge about cultural riches in the hands of some others, riches that are thought to be lying fallow in some way. This kind of irony of the disappointed may arise in the typical biography of a stratum of people who tended to become Johannine Christians, but another circumstance may be equally relevant; the destruction of the Temple in Jerusalem had once again made the whole of Judaism precarious. The cultural space-and-time co-ordinates of the Jewish world had been undermined, and the Law that had once functioned in concert with the Temple rituals and in the Temple life-world began to serve a new purpose in a new life. The Law would begin to dominate Jewish life at precisely the time Christians, including the Johannines, sought their quests in another aspect of Judaism. The turn Jewish tradition was taking could only be disappointing to the Johannines, and in the end exclusive of them. In addition the Johannine community, having been excluded from the synagogue in the course of a schism in its local Jewish community, lost the status of being legitimately Jewish at all, and from that time onward they would be disappointed outsiders to a community life that they valued.

What would the disappointed seek and where would they seek it? Having known a tradition that would speak of a monotheist Ultimate, they would of course seek that same God; but having been brushed aside in the name of cultural truth, they cannot be expected to set about replicating that which excluded them. Johannine Christianity would not be an Islam, setting up a rival monotheist legal order in place of the nascent post-Temple Jewish one. The sense of irony would lead to finding the traces of Ultimacy in the persecuted, in the teacher who had been turned over to the powers of the world for crucifixion. Jesus had already been identified as the messiah by the Johannines at an earlier point in time, but in the years following the schism they would dwell upon the **persecuted** Jesus, the one whom the authorities in the old Jerusalem had sought to kill. If Paul had thought of the messiah as the new Adam, the Johannines had in mind something of a new Isaac bound and waiting on the wood for sacrifice under the knife of a new Abraham.

> For God loved the world so that he
> gave the only son, so that everyone

> who believes in him may not die but have eternal life. (3.16)
>
> No one has greater love than this, that someone lay down his life for his friends. (15.13)

For those with a sense of irony it would come as no surprise that both the world and the cultural home of the principle of life would seek to impose death on that principle.

What emerges from this is a theodicy of the culturally disinherited. Precisely people who know value but not approval would be disposed to depict ultimacy with the imagery of irony. And even upon discovering the experiential foundation of such religious imagery, they would not be "cured" of it, led to abandon it upon gaining self-insight, since it has the intrinsic intellectual merit of not claiming to have captured the Ultimate within the limits of human conceptual constructs. By its very nature irony appreciates without comprehending, senses that the process of inference and stances of reasonability cannot cope with reality as the latter mockingly runs riot. The ironical imagination knows the ridiculous and the tragic and hence seems to speak of reality to people who also know such. Such an irony prepares people to glory in conditions that would otherwise be seen as deprivation. They sense that such is the condition for coming to their particular ironic appreciation of the cosmos and of their place in the cosmos.

> Amen amen I say to you, unless a grain of wheat die falling into the ground, it remains alone; but if it die, it bears much fruit. He loving his life loses it, and hating his life in this world will keep it forever. (12.24-25)

If the ultimate is that for which people would sacrifice everything, the Johannine followers of Jesus took their particular religious pursuit as their ultimate.

NOTES

1. Revised paper presented at the 1993 Workshop in the Sociology of Early Christianity in Durham, England, and at the 1993 meeting of the Association for the Sociology of Religion in Miami Beach, Florida. I am indebted to Peter Staples and the late Joseph Fitzpatrick for helpful comments, suggestions, and encouragement.

2. For methodological principles pertaining to the phenomenon of "layers of tradition" in gospel texts, see Anthony J. Blasi, Early Christianity as a Social Movement (Bern and New York: Peter Lang, 1988), pp. 199-217.

3. Irving M. Zeitlin, Jesus and the Judaism of His Time (Cambridge: Polity Press, 1988), points out that the intentions of Jesus himself need to be situated inside the Jewish

setting; I am suggesting that the trajectory of Johannine Christianity must similarly begin there.

4. See, e.g., Alfred Schutz and Thomas Luckmann, Strukturen der Lebenswelt, Band I (Frankfurt am Main: Suhrkamp, 1979), p. 49; The Structures of the Life-World, translated by Richard M. Zaner and H. Tristram Engelhardt, Jr. (Evanston: Northwestern University Press, 1973), pp. 23-24.

5. See George H. Mead, Mind, Self, and Society (Chicago: University of Chicago Press, 1934).

6. Norman R. Petersen, The Gospel of John and the Sociology of Light. Language and Characterization in the Fourth Gospel (Valley Forge, Pennsylvania: Trinity Press International, 1993) does not appreciate the shared nature of the symbolic universe of the Christians and Jews of the Johannine world. In the gospel, the Jews' non-comprehension and non-acceptance of the word is a problem that is addressed with literary irony. The "special language," as Petersen terms it, of the Fourth Gospel is full of allusions to the Hebrew Bible. Its "special" character derives from the function it serves of linguistically marking the sacred/profane divide. What divides the Johannine Christians and the Jews from whom they have become separated is not the language in which their theologies are clothed but the Christians' theology itself. It simply does not follow, as Petersen seems to assume, that separate or opposed groups need have separate or divergent languages. I must also take exception to Petersen's use of the term "anti-society" when referring to the Johannine community; when sociologists of religion speak of a group defining itself as other than or apart from a dominant society, they call it a "sect." Johannine Christians

may well have been sect-like in this sense. The term "anti" suggests the usage of Victor Turner, who spoke of "anti-structure," a transitory reversal of normal social barriers and constraints by the very people who usually observe them - e.g., people on a pilgrimage. Such would not apply to the Johannine Christians. See Victor Turner, Dramas, Fields, and Metaphors. Symbolic Action in Human Society (Ithaca: Cornell University Press, 1974).

7. Paul D. Duke, Irony in the Fourth Gospel (Atlanta: John Knox Press, 1985), focuses largely on irony as a literary phenomenon in the Gospel of John, rather than on what I have called the "situation of irony"; yet there are resemblances and relationships between the two objects of investigation. Following D.C. Muecke, Duke speaks of three essential elements of literary irony: 1) a double-layered or two-storied phenomenon, 2) some kind of opposition between the two levels, and 3) an element of "innocence" or unawareness (p. 13). Notably, as "a remarkably indirect mode of communication" (p. 147), irony presupposes a relationship of shared knowledge, values, and expression between a writer and a reader. "Indeed the power of irony, as is the case with symbolism, imagery, and metaphor, lies in the eloquent implicitness of its silence." (p. 30) Yet irony is not mockery; author and reader can still identify with the victim of the irony. (p. 32) Duke sees the ironic passages of the gospel as later additions to the earlier source material (p. 150).

Ch. 9. New Community Discourse

The separation of the Johannine Christians from the community of the local synagogue of their community left them with the three alternatives of either breaking up, assimilating themselves into other local communities, or forming a new, Johannine Christian identity. Some from among their number may have chosen the first of these alternatives, but we have no evidence of that having happened. We do have the third layer of Johannine texts (Column B in the Appendix) as evidence that at least a critical mass of them had formed a new identity, and over time they evidently did assimilate into other Christian communities. Their immediate situation as identifiable Johannines was complicated, however, by the fact that there were already other Christians. As a result of their earlier history, the Johannine Christians, whose separation from the synagogue came about three decades after the time of Paul, had to clarify their identity vis-a-vis other Christians as well as other Jews.

Affirmation of identity: election

Judging from a number of texts, the Johannine Christians appear to have affirmed their identity in terms of election. The Prologue, for example, contains two typical election texts:

> ...Whoever received him, he gave to them power to become children of God.... (1.12)
>
> ...From his fullness we have all received grace upon grace.... (1.16)

The notion of Christians being "children of God" did not begin with this third literary layer of the Fourth Gospel; one can find it in Paul's Letter to the Galatians (e.g., Gal. 4.4-6). Yet the Johannines took this imagery and made it their own. As they understood matters, they had received, or accepted, Jesus, and thereby received power to become children of God. The Father chose them, as many were chosen, but they accepted the Son and therefore received a "fullness," a "grace upon grace." Given the lessened social status they apparently received as a consequence of becoming Christians, they could evidently use the language of election by way of compensation rather than self-congratulation. The compensation took the form of an enhanced afterlife that depended upon the action of the risen Jesus:

> The Father loves the son and has

> given all in his hands. (3.35)
>
> You did not choose me, but I chose you.... (15.16)

The imagery of election through being children of God, likened long beforehand by Paul to adoption, is not articulated in such legal terms in the Fourth Gospel. Nevertheless, the image is very significant one, bearing much freight. To be the children of someone is to participate in an identity and in a particular nexus of the parents' several social networks. Just as one acquires "family friends," relatives, a level of respect, neighbors, and a name from one's parents, the Johannines acquired these by virtue of being Christians. Similarly, they acquired the strained relations and the social distance from certain others that was analogous to what one had by virtue of family identity. An identity of this nature is not a mere particularity, analogous to a philosophical unit or to an atom, but a recognizable social complex of on-going relationships and repute.

This kind of imagery also conveys the impression that one did not become a Johannine Christian out of a mere velleity, any more than one becomes a child of a parent - be it adoptive or natural - by virtue of merely willing so. The vast majority of people are simply not passionately philosophical; they do not make life decisions on the basis of purely intellectual convictions. And one would not expect the Johannine Christians to opt for Christianity in a vacuum out of a rationalist conviction in some doctrine such as the Incarnation. They would not have been converting first, in most cases, and enduring the social consequences second. Rather it would often be the case that they had been marginalized from the synagogue community first, perhaps even being labeled "Christians" as well as some other negative epithets, and then from a position of relative social weakness found the Johannines to be a congenial community. The experience would be that of being converted by external situations rather than by some autonomously working faith-development process. Christianity - both as an identity and a symbol system - would make sense as much because of the situation one found oneself in as because of one's personal theology. In this kind of a situation, one would feel elect rather than electing. One would receive graces, or perhaps somewhat more actively, accept them.

While no identity is a matter of pure choice and while the Johannines' identity as Christians would be no exception, it would be mistaken to take this to an extreme and to see their identity as a passive conferral. People in marginal situations, people who do not find total acceptance in some one uncomplicated social status, try out several identities before settling upon one that they will keep for a while. Twentieth century young adults do this, especially with styles of dress and appearance, until their very visual experimentation comes to mark their social transitoriness and marginal place in society. Religious "seekers" do much the same, trying out different "conversions" until one particular conversion seems more or less plausible and satisfactory.[1] This may be the kind of reason why the Johannine texts speak not only of being elect but also of receiving and accepting, or more specifically, of believing. Thus, they are likely to have been in a religious or philosophical quest, perhaps a quest engendered in part by their discomfort or experience of less than total acceptance within the local synagogue community.

Quests

The spiritual quest typically takes the form of a search for dimensions of life and meaning that are more profound and more subtle than the superficial codes of social approval and disapproval. The Johannine texts seem to liken such superficialities to material rewards, though the references to material goods are clearly symbolic:

> Work not for the food that perishes but for the food that lasts into eternal life, which the son of humanity will give you.... (6.27)

The perspective that goes beyond social approval and disapproval is even more explicit in a prayer that the text has Jesus directing toward the Father:

> I have given them your word, and the world hates them because they are not of the world, just as I am not of the world. I do not pray that you take them from the world but that you keep them from evil. (17.14)

Such texts seem to suggest solace or security as this might be occasioned by a quest for deeper dimensions of life. This solace or security seems to take the form of an acceptance by God.

> Amen amen I say to you, he who receives anyone I send receives me, and he receiving me receives him who sent me. (13.20)

This saying was undoubtedly derived from earlier versions of it, present in the wider Christian tradition (see Mk. 9.37, Mt. 10.40, Lk. 10.16, 1 Thess. 4.8), but what is interesting in the present context is the fact that the Johannines found it important and appropriated it in their own words.

In order to understand the spiritual quest, it should be held in contrast to popular religious appeal. In the first century popular religion was therapeutic in nature, and sometimes, judging from the occasional disclaimers that appear in the gospels, a matter of wonder working. The latest layer of the fourth gospel laments, "Unless you see signs and wonders, you will not believe" (4.48b). The Johannines seem to have distinguished themselves from many of their contemporaries, at least in their own minds, by pursuing a quest for the more meaningful and profound rather than in some cultivation of spectacle.

A separate identity from that of the Jewish community

By the time of the third textual layer of the Gospel of John, the local synagogue Jews and Johannine Christians appear to have been in agreement that they were separate communities. For the Johannines, this was a matter of the Jewish community not accepting their religious affirmations; in this respect they placed the local synagogue Jews in the cognitive category of the "world," along with others who did not accept the Christians' testimony and the quest associated with it. Statements about belief and disbelief thereby operated as markers of others' identities versus the Johannines' own.

> Amen amen I say to you that what we know we pronounce, and to what we see we testify, and our testimony is not accepted. (3.11)

The texts go beyond the making of social distinctions; they bring tension, even hostility, into evidence. These social divides are made to seem momentous by the use of the religious language itself.

> If they persecuted me, they will persecute you also; if they kept my word, they will keep yours also. (15.20)

The religious beliefs and the social divides corresponding to them did indeed have important consequences for the individuals involved, so that giving them cosmic significance seemed perfectly plausible.

> They will excommunicate you from the synagogue. Indeed an hour is coming when everyone who has killed you will think that he is carrying out a worship service to God. (16.2)

Inevitably a universe of discourse that does not tie in to one's quest for ultimate meaning will seem disconnected from ultimate meaning itself. It will be thought never to go beyond superficialities. Logically, of course, this does not follow at all, but what is reflected in these texts is the social distance separating Jewish and Johannine universes of discourse, not any logical analysis of the possibilities available under pluralist conditions. These statements appear in contexts that pertain to the Jewish community in the gospel narrative:

> How can you believe, when you accept glory from each other and not seek the glory that is from the only God? (5.44)
>
> He coming from above is over all; he being of the earth is of the earth and converses of the earth. (3.31)
>
> For God did not send the son into the world to condemn the world but so that the world may be saved through him. He who believes in him is not condemned, but he not believing has been condemned already, since he has not believed in the name of the only son of God. (3.17-18)

And the texts attribute a lack of understanding to the Jewish community as well:

> Amen amen I say to you, it was not Moses who has given you bread from heaven, but my Father gives you the true bread from heaven. (6.32)

And they go on to describe Jews as being most incredulous about the very people with whom the Johannine Christians had begun to identify themselves:

> So the Jews said to themselves, "Where is he (Jesus) about to go that we will not find him? Is he about to go to the diaspora of the Greeks and teach the Greeks?" (7.35)

Such textual material is best understood as an embodiment of the social negotiation of identity. By becoming non-Jewish, the Johannines were becoming "Christian," in the sense of almost Gentile Christian - not only in the opinion of their former associates in the synagogue, but also in their own view.

Johannines and other Christians as a new community

The passage in the Fourth Gospel that is popularly known as the "Parable of the Good Shepherd" is actually an allegory that is composed of two juxtaposed images (see 10.1-15). One image likens Jesus to a gate through which a shepherd enters and leads the sheep out. It is thieves who climb over at some other place in order to seize the sheep. This image seems designed to maintain a separateness between the following of Jesus and other religions, including synagogal Judaism. The second image makes Jesus the shepherd rather than the gate. The use of two images for Jesus is consistent with another passage in the third literary layer of the gospel, the Prologue, where Jesus is introduced as both speech to the divine and divinity itself ("There was a speech in genesis, and the speech was to God, and the speech was divinity" 1.1). After the double image is presented in the allegory, a very interesting statement follows:

> And I have other sheep that are not from this yard; it is necessary for me to bring them, and for them to listen to my call, and become one flock, one shepherd. (10.16)

The passage appears to recognize other Christian groups and to call for a formation of a single identity for all of them. This implies first that the Christian group in the image - presumably the Johannines - was not or had not been in any unity with one or more other Christian groups but was in the process of merging or at least contemplating a merger with the other groups.

Once the Johannine Christians had articulated the symbols with which to express their identity, it became possible for them to focus on themselves as a community. There are passages that focus on the quality of the community life of the group:

> I am giving you a new command, that you love one another; as I loved you, you should also love one another. By this all will know that you are my disciples, if you have love for one another. (13.34-35; see also 15.12)

This is the kind of discourse in the gospel that has parallels with the First Letter of John. The Johannine Christians would have recognized it as typical of the discourse of an author known to them, perhaps one of their own - the author of The First Letter of John. This would be the case even if in the gospel this textual material is placed in the mouth of Jesus, and even if the author of the gospel's third layer of textual material had not been the author of the letter but imitating that author.[2] They would have known very well that this kind of discourse had been written with their community in mind rather than coming out of earlier Christian tradition.

This community seems to have been formed around a liturgy that bears some resemblance to that of the wider Christian community. One of its texts that refers to the ritual consumption of the communion bread and wine does so with rather outrageous phraseology that seems calculated to "turn off" non-Christians:

> He who munches on my flesh and drinks my blood has eternal life, and I will raise him on the last day. (6.54)

This is followed by a curious statement that steps back from the superficially cannibalistic understanding of the sentence; it speaks of a "true food" and "true drink" (*alethes brosis, alethes posis*), and I translated it with the word "real" to express the text's suggestion that there are other foods and drinks that would not be the genuine articles: "For my flesh is real food, and my blood is real drink" (6.55). The focus of the discourse shifts from the show of cannibalistic discourse, which is perhaps a feint, to questions of true or genuine food and drink. Few readers, of course, would be so literalist as to miss there being some spiritual rather than narrative intent in the quasi cannibalistic part of the text, but the intent is to separate the conversationalists (author and reader) from those who mock the quasi cannibalistic sounding language from outside the conversation, and to imply that there is something less than genuine in what those people have to say, and even imply that there is something less than genuine in what they have to offer; in contrast, it suggests that there was something quite genuine in what there was to be had within the community. From the Johannine perspective this genuineness is a matter of being in communion with Jesus and divinity:

> He who munches on my flesh and drinks my blood remains in me and I in him. As the living Father sent me and I live through the Father, so that person who munches on me will live through me. (6.56-57)

The gospel's many references to living in another and vice versa cannot be understood in a denotative sense because it would be contradictory to say that A is in B while B is in A. Rather, the gospel likens Jesus to a vine that is made up of branches that remain in him and he in them, all under the care of the Father (see chapter 15 of the gospel). If we were to spell this out in modern parlance, we would say that the community had a collective identity that the text also identifies with Jesus; the burden of the text is to merge the two identities. In the way that the textual material of the third layer dwells on a dual aspect of Jesus (speech to God, and divinity), it also dwells on a dual aspect of the community that it identifies with Jesus. It is a community brought together, according to the texts, through divine intervention (God dwelling in it) and addressing God in union with the "Speech to God."

> Holy Father, keep them in your name, which you have given me, so that they may be one, as we. (17.11)

The text, ostensibly presenting a prayer spoken by Jesus in the presence of his disciples, explicitly brings later Christians such as the Johannines into the picture:

> Not only for these (the disciples) do I pray, but also for those who believe in me because of their word, so that all may be one.... (17.20-21a)

Where an earlier layer of the gospel tradition may speak only of the relationship between Jesus and the Father ("...I am in the Father and the Father in me..." 14.11), the third layer speaks also of the new Christian community and its blind contemporaries:

> A little while yet and the world will see me no more, but you will see me because I live and you will

> live. On that day you will know that I am in my Father and you in me and I in you. (14.19-20)

The text sees not only eucharistic imagery, such as food and drink/body and blood, in this light, but also baptismal imagery:

> Amen amen I say to you, unless someone is born of water and spirit, one cannot enter into the kingdom of God. (3.5b)

In theological language, the concerns of the Johannine community had turned to an ecclesiological consciousness.[3]

NOTES

1. For a presentation of the convert as an active agent, see James T. Richardson, "The active vs. passive convert: Paradigm conflict in conversion/recruitment research." Journal for the Scientific Study of Religion 24: 2: 163-179. For an application to the young adults of the 1960's and 70's, see Wade Clark Roof, A Generation of Seekers. The Spiritual Journeys of the Baby Boom Generation (San Francisco: Harper, 1993). For a general discussion of conversion as a quest for greater significance in everyday life, see Anthony J. Blasi, A Phenomenological Transformation of the Social Scientific Study of Religion (Bern and New York: Peter Lang, 1985), pp. 91ff.

2. I am introducing these qualifiers simply because I am neither defending nor rejecting the thesis that the author of First John was responsible for the third layer of the gospel material.

3. In my _Making Charisma. The Social Construction of Paul's Public Image_ (New Brunswick, New Jersey: Transaction Publishing, 1991) I noticed the Pauline tradition, well after Paul's lifetime, taking something of an inward turn, focusing increasingly on the Christian community. This may well be a generational effect; i.e., later generations of Christians may have been facing matters of intra-communal life rather than of conversion, eschatology, and relations with non-Christian Jews.

Ch. 10 The Un-syncretizing of Johannine Christianity[1]

As was the case with all early Christian texts, the Gospel of John came to be written in a complex context. It had an acknowledged backdrop of Hebrew/Jewish tradition, but that tradition itself represented a synthesis of differing historical influences. First century C.E. Judaism was the Judaism of the Septuagint, a Greek-language compendium of writings that encompassed pre-mosaic legends, several editions of the exilic minority's legal code (together with its theologized monarchical history), prophetic protest literature, etc. There had not been a widespread consensus yet over a Hebrew text (though that was soon to come), much less over how the books that were to be included in such a canon were to be understood in the contemporary Hellenistic world. Indeed, it would be later in counterposition to Christianity in the fourth century that Judaism would define itself in terms of an oral Torah commentary on the written Torah.[2] Moreover, first century Judaism outside Palestine was a Hellenized species, and one can argue that even in Jerusalem the diaspora flavor greatly affected what there was to be found during the time of Jesus.

Hellenism affected the early Christians, of course, directly as well as by virtue of a Jewish mediation. Hellenism was a culturalism if not a coherent culture, an approach to the world that gave various schools and traditions each a fair hearing, and confronted each with the demand that it make a good case for itself. One finds in Hellenism an appreciation for argument, a weakness perhaps for facile retort, but a capacity for further reflection and rationality as well. There was a cosmopolitanism about it all that called for principles - divine or otherwise - that could conceivably hold true for all peoples for all times. In short, Hellenism was quite different from any kind of traditionalism, and by virtue of that pluralizing difference could transform any given tradition. Thus we see people such as Flavius Josephus and Paul/Saul of Tarsus trying out one tradition at an early point in life and adopting another in adulthood.

One cannot forget the reality of the Roman Empire, which collected representations of the gods and goddesses in its Pantheon. The Empire consisted of a world-class administrative apparatus that was informed by a too parochial originary civic culture. Its cultural life resembled in some respects what we find today in the modern university and in the multinational corporation - very often interesting and productive at the level of line personnel, where external influences can have relatively free play, but rather afflicted by puerile ambitions at the top. In such contexts martyrs gain respect if not public endorsement, and people in general distinguish between their civic and their individual lives. The civic life is one of giving the powers of the day their due as necessity requires, and the individual life seeks an existence in some realm that has its own legitimacy.[3] In this regard we need to set aside the old saw that the ancient world knew only collective, not individual, identities. The reality of empires rendered it impossible for most people to identify with the political powers, and therefore most people had selves that were detached from the large-scale political units. Hence personal responsibility emerged in Hebrew literature in the prophetic era, once the domestic monarchs had become puppets of foreign imperial powers, well before the Roman era. The Romans did nothing to bring imperial power any closer to the will of the smaller communities, nor to prevent individuals from being caught between cross pressures that originated in the several, juxtaposed communities.

Syncretism

In complex societies, differing and even

opposing religions or systems of ultimate concern routinely come into contact with each other. Farmers who would sell a surplus or cash crop, craftspeople who would market their wares, and merchants who would follow their trade routes through their known worlds must all come to understandings amidst conditions of cultural pluralism. Mores of public conduct come to be established independently of any one tradition, or for that matter an expedient practice that may have originated in any one culture may become a common property of many peoples. Moreover, domestic occurrences as intermarriage and the employment of "outsiders" as teachers or as overseers over children bring about cultural borrowing within the intimacy of the household. This should be understood as the normal state of affairs in complex societies such as the Roman Empire. Roger Bastide used to refer to the processes that occur within this kind of context as the "interpenetration of civilizations."[4]

Amidst such a pluralism of ultimacies, it will occur that people of vastly differing cultural origins may recognize in one another a genuine spiritual quest. They may respect each other's parallel consciousnesses of the ultimate, but not know in the least how they may themselves learn anything from each other. This would not quite be syncretism, however spiritually liberating an experience it might be. A second kind of occurrence that can be found in the complex society is one in which a sense of the ultimate that had been cradled in one's tradition of birth assumes an expression, after a conversion, in a second culture; this too is not quite syncretism, though it may lead toward it. A third kind of occurrence is the accounting for some other person's or group's quest for the ultimate in terms of one's own tradition's theology; this too is not quite syncretism. Similarly, theologizing from one tradition about the religious symbols of another (somewhat in the manner of the "science of religious studies" is not syncretism. In syncretism there is a dialogue of symbols that themselves have differing origins, differing cultural genealogies.

In syncretism, origins can be set aside as having little importance. This would not be entirely unlike the practice of empires insofar as an acceptance if not loyalty to a present reality takes primacy over "antiquities." One's sense of the ultimate may arise, cradled in the symbol system of one's birth, and then express itself pluralistically in a symbolic mixture; or one may develop a spiritual quest from the outset with materials of varying ancestry. Similarly one may theologize, i.e. apply the system and depth of ratiocination and insight, with either unicultural or pluralistic symbols. Or again, one may be religiously unmusical but conform to practices that are syncretistic. I mention all this only to point out that "syncretism" is a word that has a neutral meaning; it speaks of a pluralism of religious wording and action that can serve the purposes of both profound and superficial religiosities.

Syncretism in pre-schism Johannine experience

What we have of the literary materials proper to the Johannine Christians prior to their break with the local synagogue comes to us by virtue of their having been edited into the post-schism Gospel of John. It may be that there had been other materials that had been edited out, just as the early extant materials had been edited in. Thus, it may be necessary for us to depend on a rather limited body of literary evidence, in contrast to what the case would have been had we some independent, pre-schism document. The early layer of material (Column A in the Appendix) nevertheless provides some clues.

First, there is quite a bit in the material about John the Baptizer. The Baptizer's tradition, of course, did not make it into subsequent non-christian Jewish scripture, but in his time he was clearly a

Palestinian Jewish personage. The awkward presence of the Baptist material along with narratives about Jesus seems to have led to repeated mentions in the gospel, of John having a secondary role. Thus John came from divinity (Jn. 1.6), but as a witness to the light (1.7), not as the light itself. He confesses that he is not the messiah (1.20) and that he only baptizes with water (1.26). John even speaks in such a way that two of his disciples follow Jesus (1.37). The early layer materials even explain that Jesus and John pursued their ministries in the same Judean vicinity (3.22-23), and that when the Pharisees realized that Jesus was drawing more disciples than John, Jesus withdrew to Galilee (4.1-3). The text goes out of its way to quote "many," saying, "John worked no sign, but all that John said about this man was true." (10.41)

Baptism itself was a Jewish practice that the Christians retained. The text in fact explains that it was not Jesus himself who introduced the practice but that his disciples had been responsible for it: "...Jesus himself did not baptize, but his disciples did...." (4.2) This and Jesus' stated observance of the Jewish feasts suggest that at the earliest layer of the Johannine literary tradition there is an explicit openness to the Jewish symbol system.

There are occasional references to light and darkness in this first literary layer. John the Baptizer is said to have come as a witness about the light. (1.7) Jesus is presented as disappointed that Nicodemus comes to see him in the dark of night: "The light has come into the world, and humans prefer the darkness...." (3.19b) The theme turns up in Jesus' teaching: "I am the light of the world. He who follows me will not walk in darkness but have the light of life." (8.12) The reference to light as an image for divinity and the work of divinity was certainly not peculiar to early Johannine Christianity; it is found in Egyptian symbolism from centuries before, in the Dead Sea scroll material, and in Roman symbolism. The contrast of light and darkness is also reminiscent of Persian imagery of a great heavenly conflict.[5]

The early material also cites the Hebrew scriptures and personages - Isaiah (Jn. 1.23; 12.38-41), Elias (1.25), Moses (1.45, 7.19), Jacob and Joseph (4.5), Psalms (Jn. 12.13; 19.24), and Zechariah (Jn. 12.14). This, of course, would also be true of later Christian writings, if for no other reason than early texts such as these Johannine passages cite the Hebrew Bible. But it is also the case that the early Johannine layer tellingly accepts a popular, non-canonical, Jewish legend, that of the water stirring up to cure the lame in the Bethzatha Pool in Jerusalem (5.7); this even seems to be used to prefigure the stirring of the Sea of Galilee when Jesus approaches walking on it (6.18-19).

The narrative of Jesus' stay among the Samaritans illustrates the Johannine early openness to non-Christian influences even while asserting both a Jewish and a Christian identity. Jesus enters a Samaritan town, Suchar, and sits on a well. Despite a taboo against Jewish men talking with Samaritan women, he asks a Samaritan woman for water. (4.5-8) When she sees that Jesus is a prophet, she raises the question about on which mountain, the Samaritan or the Judean one, God should be worshipped.

> Madam believe me, an hour is coming when you people will worship the Father neither on this mountain nor in Jerusalem. You worship what you do not know; we worship what we know, since salvation is from the Jews. God is spirit, and for those who worship him it is necessary to worship in spirit and truth. (4.21-22)

Christianity seems to introduce, at this juncture, a belief that particularistic differences may have once had a point ("since salvation is from the Jews") but that it did not matter any more because an hour was coming in anticipation for which "spirit and truth," not religious real estate, would be important. "Spirit and truth," of course, seems to be a Hellenistic principle.

Finally, a point should be made about Jesus' Galilean origin. It seemed important from at least one Jewish perspective that the Messiah come from King David's tribal town, Bethlehem (see Jn. 7.41-42). Rather than offer a genealogy, infancy narrative, or childhood account to explain away Jesus' Galilean origin, the early Johannine layer offers no response on the subject of Jesus' earthly ancestry. The issue does not seem at all troubling; Jesus worked signs and no one should worry about ancestry. This seems to reflect an openness to "outside" influences and "mixed" origins that would be congruent with if not an aspect of a spirit of syncretism.

The limits of syncretism in a crisis situation

As suggested above, syncretism involves a juxtaposition of symbolic materials that come from different traditions. It does not imply a unity, such as an integration of separate theological systems into a new synthesis could achieve. It does not imply an awakening of a home tradition of religiosity cradled anew in a foreign religious expression, or an appreciation of a foreign religiosity through a translation into one's own familiar symbols; both of these processes would tend to prevent any schism. Rather, syncretism reflects a default situation, in which unlike religious expressions appear together in a forum, without any great issue being made of any incongruities that may by occasioned. It has also been suggested, in a previous chapter, that there seems to have been an inequality of access to cultural goods in the local Jewish community. Those who had more purely Jewish education seemed satisfied with the community's religious conventions, while the cultural have-nots seemed to be pursuing a religious quest that led them into a Christianity that had a "high christology."

We have also suggested in a previous chapter that the community in which the schism was about to take place, had assumed the social form of a forum; i.e., there were frequent, probably regular, interactions that were characterized by a face-to-face give-and-take, from which new cultural materials and new positions could emerge. It is in this kind of circumstance that an internal cultural inequality can lead to crises of unity, in which groupings can come to take stands on an issue and create argumentative expressions that more sharply divide the community. This seems to be what happened in the Johannines' local community; the cultural "haves" purified their Judaism and the cultural "have nots," marginalized from local Jewish life, outlined their Christianity with increasingly sharply-drawn lines.

Desyncretization

The process of desyncretization involves an identity group in designating some symbolic materials as proper to its religious system and designating other symbolic materials as foreign. When this occurs amidst a schism, two desyncretization processes would be occurring simultaneously. In the case of the synagogue where the Johannines had at least for a time found a religious home, it appears to be the non-christian Jews who initiated a desyncretization process; at least a Johannine line from one of the later narrative levels of literary tradition speaks of being excluded from the synagogue (Jn. 9.22). It will be recalled that much of the disputation material found in this later literary stratum involves claims by Jesus' critics that they stand firm with Moses and the Torah; this seems to imply, as suggested, that the Christians' critics had greater access than did the Christians to the Jewish cultural materials. Otherwise, why would a later layer of the Johannine material dwell so much on Jesus scoring debating points with such critics?

For the Christians, it would hardly seem

satisfactory to be identified merely as people who had become marginally Jewish by being excluded from the synagogue. Their identity came to form around a high christology, as a doctrinal content, and a comforting Spirit, as a principle of the new group's life (Jn. 14.15-18). Part of the formation of a Johannine Christian identity was a rejection of any compromise with those within the local Jewish community who were not hostile to the Jesus tradition but who did not accept a high christology. In the later discourse material, the Johannine text depicts such Jews as uncomprehendingly staying in a sinful slavery:

> Then Jesus said to the Jews who had believed him, "If you keep my word you are truly my disciples, and you will learn the truth, and the truth will free you." They answered him, "We are the seed of Abraham, and we have never been enslaved to anyone. Why are you saying, 'You will become free?'" Jesus answered them, "Amen amen I say to you, everyone who commits a sin is a slave of the sin. The slave does not stay in the household forever, the son does. So if the son frees you, you will really be free. I know that you are the seed of Abraham. (Jn. 8.31-37a)

They can escape if they are freed by Jesus - i.e., join the Christians. This appears to call upon Jews who are friendly to the Jesus tradition to decide against Jewish identity and for a Christian one.

The fact that the Johannine Christians and the synagogue had parted ways left the Johannines in a situation that was not entirely unlike that of the Gentile Christians. It will be recalled that Paul had organized Gentile Christian churches in Ephesus in Asia Minor and Greece. References in the "Good Shepherd" section of the fourth gospel suggest a willingness on the part of the Johannines to identify with these Gentile Christians. Then other later discourse passages speak of all being one. This would inevitably lead to a certain amount of pluralism **within** the Christian world, insofar as Johannine and non-johannine Christians would be merging their respective traditions; but insofar as all these traditions would be identifiably Christian the result of all this would not be primarily a new syncretism.

Discussion

There has been something of a fad in the late twentieth century to treat the canon of the New Testament as something of a political accomplishment. In the same way as "history" may be defined as the victors' versions of disputed narratives, it is suggested that victors in post-constantinian Christianity edited out of their list or *kanon* books that did not serve their purposes or served the purposes of factions that they deemed heretical. Thus, various gospels, acts, and letters that have for centuries now been dismissed as apocryphal, are read as serious early Christian literature, and they are given as much weight as the traditional canon of books. Whatever books one wishes to accept for religious purposes is not a scientific but a theological matter; and while there is a valid point to interpreting the process of labeling factions "heretical" as an aspect of post-constantinian power structures, the evidence from my source critical study of the Gospel of John suggests a caution against sweepingly equating canon with power or associating it with victors.

First, the Christian identity crystallized well before the time of Constantine. We in fact have seen it crystallizing between the compositions of the earliest and later major literary layers of the Gospel of John - some time about the year 75 C.E.

Second, the Johannine Christians who formed this identity and included some symbolic materials and excluded others, were the losers in an intra-communal conflict; they had been excluded from a synagogue. In terms of access to cultural materials, they appear to have been the weaker party in the conflict all along.

Third, while post-constantinian Christianity, often allied as it was with political and economic elites, would not always elicit or deserve our sympathies, it was unable to excise from tradition the texts that made it uncomfortable. The bad light the fourth gospel casts upon religious authorities, for example, could not be deleted, without jeopardizing the Christian identity of the ecclesiastical apparatus. The love ethic found in the gospel, so foreign to the ways of political structures in general, could not be banished from the tradition without changing it into a different tradition altogether. The individualism that is resident in the gospel texts, stressing as they do the belief and insight rather than convention and inheritance, cannot be suppressed in favor of group conformity and nationalism, without jeopardizing the claims of a post-constantinian group to be Christian at all. It is in the nature of tradition texts to attract and even, as in the case of the Gospel of John, incorporate commentary and adumbration, but not to delete anything essential to the original material; specifically, the early narrative materials seem to comprise a whole story.

Fourth, the desyncretizing process that appears to have been in progress as the Gospel of John was taking shape, cannot be isolated historically from an accompanying process of identifying with non-johannine Christian churches and thereby preparing the way for an intra-Christian pluralism. There seems to be a difference between desyncretization on the one hand, with its avoidance of certain identity-threatening materials, and sect formation on the other, with its avoidance of pluralism of any kind.

I would hope these observations leave syncretism and desyncretization as neutral, descriptive terms rather than as judgmental labels.

NOTES

1. This chapter was originally written for the 1994 meeting of the Society for the Scientific Study of Religion in Albuquerque, New Mexico, at the suggestion of Otto Maduro.

2. Jacob Neusner, From Testament to Torah. An Introduction to Judaism in Its Formative Age (Englewood Cliffs, New Jersey: Prentice-hall, 1988), pp. 115ff.; this oral Torah was oral in the sense that Moses was said to have spoken rather than to have written it, but of course by the time it came to be accepted it was in written form.

3. Twentieth century sociologists of religion would refer to this as "privatization"; see Thomas Luckmann, The Invisible Religion (New York: Macmillan, 1967).

4. Roger Bastide, *Les Religions Afro-Brésiliennes: Contribution à une Sociologie des Interpénétrations des Civilisations* (Paris: Presses Universitaires de France, 1960).

5. For observations on the Gospel of John and dualism in the Qumran and Persian writings, see Raymond E. Brown, *The Gospel According to John (i-xii)* (New York: Doubleday, 1966), pp. LXII-LXIII.

Ch. 11. The Similitude of Modernity in the Gospel of John

The fourth gospel is not a modern work; it does not reflect a world in which power, class, and law need be self-limiting and need work by indirection through high culture, education, religion, and other "soft," non-*Realpolitik* aspects of life.[1] Nevertheless, it does not reflect a world that lacks individualism or a world in which people's cultural decisions are made for them ascriptively by virtue of their ethnic origins or family memberships. Over and over again the Gospel of John seeks to confirm faith and reinforce belief; its author(s) earnestly desire the readership/audience to turn away from "the world" and to believe in the messiahship of Jesus. It is in this sense that this gospel bears a "similitude of modernity."

As has been suggested with different phraseology in Chapter 10, this similitude-of-modernity character of the gospel reflects, at least in part, an imperial social condition. Prior to being included in an empire, a small nationality may evolve its culture in a relative vacuum, more or less in isolation from alternative symbol systems. This pre-imperial situation allows for a unity of the nationality's religion with its political order. Or more precisely, the effective social world, the agents and institutions that make a difference in everyday life and have empirical consequences for people, serves as a "plausibility structure"[2] for the symbol system with which the people refer to ultimate reality and meaning. Everyday political and social life reinforces rather than threatens the religious system.

Empires and inter-nationality commerce destroy the cozy relationship between total societies on the one hand and systems of religion and ultimate reality and meaning on the other. The rulers and merchants whose whims, estimations, and practices have practical consequences for one cannot be expected to play by the same rules as one would have, left to oneself; they cannot be expected to have the same values as one's own values, or to engage in the same customary practices as one would on one's own. Moreover, when one needs deal with these others, one may not even be able to follow one's own preferred rules, uphold one's own values, or follow one's own customs. By the very fact that the imperial condition of pluralism presents alternatives, one finds oneself **choosing** one's rules, one's values, and one's customary practices. One's actions no longer follow as a matter of course but become a matter of faith and commitment. It is in such circumstances that schisms over matters of faith become conceivable.

The imperial condition, as well as its attendant similitude of modernity, was not new in the first century C.E. Much of the Hebrew Bible seems to have been edited from a perspective in which imperial pluralism was being resisted. Moreover, first century Judaism itself knew a plurality of factions - a circumstance which the Qumran documents have made clear. The Roman world inherited a pluralistic environment from its Hellenistic predecessors, and this pluralistic character had pervaded Judaism. Pharisaic Judaism confronted this situation by resisting any comfortable accommodation with it, as did Christianity; the two would do so in different ways, however, developing their two separate subsocieties, their two separate plausibility structures.

In the pre-imperial circumstance birth can define one's self-concept and conceivable life trajectory; one receives a social "place" in the world and lives in it to the fullest if one can. In the imperial circumstance, however, one needs define oneself in parallel systems of life. It is indicative, for example, that many of the people named in the New Testament had two names - Saul/Paul, John/Mark, etc. One may have a political or civic self (citizen, affiliate of a citizen, etc.), a commercial self, and a religious self. One may also describe one's life trajectory from the perspective of these several parallel systems of life. All this is quite significant for the Gospel of John because it means that a decision within one system - e.g., to be a Christian rather than a Jew, once the schism between the two had taken place - may or may not have consequences within another system. This is a matter of the relative privatization of religion: When someone made an issue of Christianity in the political framework, a private realm of life would thereby be made less private, and no little bitterness would result. This kind of process is what has come down to us through historical sources as "persecution" and reactions to persecution.

The cure of the man born blind

A good example of the Fourth Gospel's similitude of modernity is evident in the narrative of the cure of the man born blind (Jn. 9.1-41). As it is found in the earliest textual layer of the gospel (Column A in the Appendix), the narrative begins with Jesus rejecting the suggestion that a blind man's condition is either an indication of his moral status or that of his parents. As the narrative develops it both affirms that one's moral status depends upon an individual act of will rather than birth, and rejects one kind of magical or "enchanted" interpretation of medical conditions, substituting a more cosmological one.

The introductory discourse "frames" the narrative to follow, providing it an editorial context in which the reader is to interpret events:

> And while walking along he saw someone blind from birth. And his disciples asked him, "Rabbi, who sinned, this man or his parents, for him to be born blind?"
>
> Jesus answered, Neither he nor his parents sinned, but it was that the works of God be shown in him."

Jesus cures the man's blindness, and the locals take the cured man to the Pharisees, who cannot see the cure in a benign light because the cure had been accomplished on the Sabbath. After the cured man is thrown out of the gathering of Pharisees, Jesus seeks him out and elicits an affirmation of belief from him. Then the narrative has Jesus speaking the editorial judgment upon the whole proceeding: "I came into this world in judgment, so that those not seeing may see and the seeing become blind."

The stance presented by the narrative cannot be missed. The man's blindness is a metaphor for spiritual blindness, for a lack of individual faith. Such a spiritual blindness, no more than the man's physical blindness, does not come from being born to a sinful nation; in this respect an "anti-semitic" stance cannot be attributed to the Gospel of John. Rather those choosing not to see the miraculous evidence, i.e. those endeavoring to interpret it in some evil light, are not suffering from an inherited sin or even from some prior one. Rather, the strenuous effort to become blind is itself that upon which the writer would have judgment cast. The man who gained sight, however, did so in order that the workings of God could become evident both to himself and to others. All this speaks of a basic moral individualism.

The secularization of thinking

The term, "secularization," has taken on a variety of meanings in both popular parlance and in sociology, including the separation of religion from other institutions, the decline of religion, and the rise of non-religious concepts to construe religion itself. It is the last of these meanings that can be applied to the Gospel of John. One can well argue that the gospel presupposes the first two kinds of secularization, wherein at least Christian religiosity had been separated from state cult, from nationality, and perhaps even from family, and the Roman destruction of Jerusalem had represented a fall of an established religion. But less arguably and more surely it is a fact that the gospel uses such metaphors as word, light, and sign to describe what the Christian religion is about. The authorial account of it does not limit itself to the narrative and myth behind the Christians' ritual but essays some philosophical explication. This is to say that the gospel theologizes.

Theologizing is an activity that occurs when there is a difference between the cognitive categories with which a faithful population understands and the categories that are internal to its religious tradition. The faithful inhabit a world that may or may not separate religion from other institutions but that certainly separates the religious culture from some other cultural aspect of everyday life. The theologizing activity bridges the two (or more) cultures, interpreting the religion in non-religious terms, and applying religious imperatives to otherwise non-religious activity. This latter process creates or expands a religious system of ethics. To the extent that such "bridging" is necessary, theological activity in this sense is an aspect of secularization. It is notable that as a "new" religion, upon its separation from synagogue Judaism, Christianity had to assume a secularized form from the time of its very beginning.

One aspect of this secularizing process evident in the fourth gospel is that gospel's "realized eschatology." As is well known, the early Christians appear in many instances to have had an expectation that the world as it was known would come to an end; the Christ would appear in glory at the end of time. Some passages in the fourth gospel, however, refer to the earthly life of Jesus of Nazareth as the definitive coming of the Christ or Messiah. This has the effect of naturalizing the temporal dimensions of Christian life; it places the life of the church in the everyday calendar rather than marginalizing the secular calendar by means of a psychology of impatient expectation. This, of course, bears a similitude to modernity.

In much the same way, the Gospel of John presents a psychological rather than a cosmological dualism to the reader. In a psychological dualism, the individual chooses good over evil, faith over hard heartedness, acceptance of God's overtures over the world's enticements. In a cosmological dualism there are two sovereign principles in the universe, a good god and an evil one, or alternatively, two powerful entities mediating between a monotheist God and the world. James H.

Charlesworth has compared the Gospel of John to the Qumran Rule in order to illustrate the contrast between these two kinds of dualism.[3] The effect of focusing on a psychological dualism rather than a cosmological one is to bring the experience of good and evil into the parameters of everyday life, to naturalize it, rather than leave it in a realm of religious doctrine. This is another case of a "bridging" activity. It too bears a similitude to modernity.

According relative autonomy to religion

The process of naturalizing various dimensions of life illustrates only one side of secularization, for when a separation between religion and non-religion is taken for granted in such naturalization processes, it is not non-religion alone that can stand out alone. Religion too can stand out apart from the non-religious; it can be accorded a semi-autonomy as a province in its own right.[4] Carried to an extreme, as it has been in our times, this process results in a "privatized" religion, a matter of consumer preference. In the fourth gospel such an extreme has not been reached; those who do not prefer "the light" are condemned, according to the Gospel. Those who do not respond to Jesus with faith are thought to be morally deficient in some way.

Nevertheless, religion has its own province in life, according to the Gospel; Jesus is presented as having a kingdom that is not of the world, but a kingdom just the same. The trial before Pilate makes it obvious that the world's government cannot cope with matters that come from the religious realm.

Social dialectic

One way of thinking about the similitude of modernity in the Gospel of John is to conceive of social experience becoming dialectical in a two-fold way. All social experience is dialectical in the sense of reflecting a merging of the perspectives of self and other, but there is a two-fold or doubled dialectic in which one knows oneself as not only "not another" but also "not my usual not-other." In the simple dialectic there is one's community - or more precisely, "the" community - and there is oneself in it. In the more complex, as-if modern dialectic, there is one's community that includes oneself but is not oneself, there is oneself in it, and additionally there is a wider world that is also not oneself but that is not one's usual community. That wider world has sufficient importance in one's life for it to be involved in the self-definition, but one's community, which is also involved in one's self-definition, lays claims on one in a way that the wider world does not. One is <u>in</u> the wider world, as one is in an empire, but one is "one with" one's community in a way that one cannot be "one with" a wider world or empire. It is the particular dialectical condition of not being the same thing as the community while being "one with" it, and of being aware of this because of its not being the same kind of experience as being in a wider world, that I wish to bring into consideration.

If one's community is the only social presence one knows, if one lives for all practical purposes in isolation from any wider world, that community need not be sentimental about its meaningfulness for the individual; it can be taken for granted. Such a community is one's own by default; it needs no ideology proclaiming that it is a particularly good community. But if there are alternatives, the community may well have an ideology that makes invidious comparisons, to the disadvantage of the wider world and that world's alternative communities. Then there needs be an ideology that identifies the individual with the community, though the individual experiences the community's presence precisely as "not self," other. It is in the experience of this more complex social dialectic that belongingness and identity become issues of everyday life.

The forum is a social form that presupposes such a more complex kind of social dialectic. The forum is occasional; a collectivity of people are not gathered much of the time, but come together often enough to engage in forum-like activity. Issues of community identity are conceivable in the forum, and schisms can issue from it. Once there occurs a multiplicity of groupings of people who had formerly been members of the same community, the unity of each such grouping similarly becomes important.

The experience of this kind of complex social dialectic, with its similitude of modernity, did not begin for the first time in the Hebrew/Jewish/Christian tradition with the Johannine faction. There had long been factions in the Hebrew world, and the first century Jewish world appears to have had many factions. Among the latter were the Christians, who do not appear to have been unified themselves from their origin. The Johannines, of course, had become identifiably Christian (versus Jewish) during the time of the composition of the Gospel of John. The conflict experienced by the Johannines, not surprisingly, involved the negotiation of their non-Jewish identity and establishing their community in communion with other emerging Christian groupings. Such a negotiating and establishing line of activity is only conceivable in a world that bears at least a similitude to modernity. In such a social context, one can well understand the presence of the controversy passages, where Jesus and "the Jews" argue with each other; and one can understand the appeal of the fourth gospel's references to "being one with" and "remaining in" or "abiding in," when speaking of the Christian identity-group. The Jesus of the Gospel of John is a paragon of "being in union with" - with his disciples, his people, and with his Father. The Johannine Jesus is depicted as a savior for a collectivity that has been made well aware of its identity.

NOTES

1. For an account of modern (including postmodern) culture that is articulated in such terms, see Anthony J. Blasi, "Power, class, law: The complementarity of *Realpolitik* and soft sociologies." Sociologia Internationalis 32:1 (1994): 47-54.

2. Peter L. Berger, The Sacred Canopy. Elements of a Sociological Theory of Religion (Garden City, New York: Doubleday, 1967), p. 48, distinguishes "between situations in which an entire society serves as the plausibility structure for a religious world and situations in which only a subsociety serves as such."

3. James H. Charlesworth, "A critical comparison of the dualism in 1QS 3:13-4:26 and the 'dualism' contained in the Gospel of

John." In James H. Charlesworth (ed.), John and the Dead Sea Scrolls (New York: Crossroad, 1991), pp. 76-106.

4. Phenomenological sociologists speak of "provinces of meaning" when different aspects of life are cognized in different ways, in different cognitive languages as it were. Amidst secularization, religion is experienced as such a province. On provinces of meaning, see Alfred Schutz and Thomas Luckmann, The Structures of the Life-World, translated by Richard M. Zaner and H. Tristram Engelhardt, Jr. (Evanston, Illinois: Northwestern University Press, 1973), esp. pp. 24-25.

APPENDIX: TEXT OF JOHN SEPARATED INTO SOURCES

SOME NOTES ON THE TEXT

The translation of my source criticism of the Greek text of the Gospel of John is intended to present which passages were considered to be those of the "Beloved Disciple" layer of tradition, which those of other narrative passages that were inserted into it, and which late discourse materials that were inserted into the merged narrative formed out of the first two layers. A few notes are added in order to explain some of the source critical decisions I have made. For reasons of space, no attempt is made here to argue for the individual decisions. In general, the interest here is in the social worlds of the *origins* of the texts; so indications of "seams" are allowed to prevail over indications of literary forms, which are taken to be redactive and hence reflective of only the final edition of the gospel. It is in part because of the interest in originary texts that the results of the source criticism differ from reconstructions that have been made by others, who have been more interested in what the final redactor had in hand when forming the present gospel.

Column A contains a primitive narrative that appears to have provided the basic chronology of events as presented in the gospel. A_1 at the end seems to be an early appendix. Column B contains discourse material, often characterized by parallels with The First Letter of John, and frequently introduced with "Amen amen I say to you." Column C contains other materials. Because these sometimes originated from different sources, subscripts are used to distinguish among them.

Underlined texts indicate close Greek parallels, suggesting either that variants of the same account or saying have been included in the gospel, or that a key word in the primitive narrative cues in an addition from elsewhere. Parentheses with chapter and verse citations in columns B and C refer to the location of the close parallels of a preceding underlined text; the parallels are usually in column A. Superscript capital letters note redactive material from the final edition of the gospel.

Chapter and verse sidenotes introduce translation notes, observations, and close parallels from elsewhere in the New Testament.

A

1

6There came to be a
human, sent from
divinity, named
John. 7This man
came as a witness to
testify about the
light, to make all
believe through him.
8He was not the
light, but would
testify about the
light.

B

1There was a
speech in genesis,
and the speech was
to God, and the
speech was divinity.
2In genesis this was
to God. 3All things
came to be(1.6)
through this one,
and apart from him
nothing came to be
that had come to be.
4In him was life,
and the life was the
light of humans.
5And the light
shines in the
darkness, and the
darkness has not
caught it. 9The
true light(1.8) that
enlightens every
human was coming
into the world.
10He was in the
world, and the world
came to be through
him, and the world
did not know him.
11He came to his
own, and his own did
not accept him.
12But whoever
received him, he
gave to them power
to become children
of God - to those
who believed in his
name; 13they
were born not from
blood or from the
will of flesh or

C_1

NOTES

[1.1]See 1 Jn. 1.1

[1.7]See Acts 19.4

[1.10]See 1 Jn. 3.1

[1.12]See 1 Jn. 3.1

15John(1.6) testified about him and called out, "This was he of whom I spoke, 'He who is coming after me is created prior to me because he has priority over me.'"(1.30)

19And this is John's testimony(1.7) when the Jews sent priests and Levites from Jerusalem to him to ask him, "Who are you?"

A

[20b]...and he
confessed, "I am not
the Christ." [21]And
they asked him, "Who
then? Are you
Elias?" And he
said, "Not I." "Are
you the prophet?"
And he answered,
"No." [22]Then they
said to him, "Who
are you? That we
may give an answer
to those who sent
us: What do you say
about yourself?"
[23]He said: "I - a
voice of one crying
out in the
wilderness,
'Straighten the way
of a lord,'" as
Isaiah the prophet
said. [24]And there
were those sent from
the Pharisees, [25]and
they asked him,
"Then why do you
baptize if you are
not the Christ or
Elias or the
prophet?" [26]John
answered them, "I
am baptizing with
water. Among you
stands someone whom
you do not know,
[27]who is coming
after me, the thong
of whose sandal I am
not worthy to
loose."

B

from the will of a
man but from
divinity. [14]And the
word became flesh
and pitched tent
among us, and we
have beheld his
glory, glory as of
an only son from a
father, full of
grace and truth -
[16]because from his
fullness we have all
received grace upon
grace; [17]for the Law
was given through
Moses, grace and
truth came to be
through Jesus
Christ. [18]No one
has ever seen
divinity; the only
son of divinity, who
is near the bosom of
the Father - it was
he who drew
revelation forth.

C_1

[20]And he confessed[(1.20b)] and did not deny...

NOTES

[1.18]See 1 Jn. 4.12

[1.20]Repeating "and he confessed" suggests some editing had been done here. See Lk. 3.15 and Acts 13.25 for parallels.

A

28 These events
occurred in Bethany
beyond the Jordan,
where John was
baptizing.
35 The next day[A]
John was standing as
well as two of his
disciples, 36 and
looking at Jesus
walking by he said,
"Look! The lamb of
God." 37 And the two
disciples listened
to him talking and
followed Jesus.
38 Jesus turning and
seeing them follow
said to them, "What
do you want?" They
said to him,
"Rabbi," which
translates as
"teacher," "where
are you staying?"
39 He said to them,
"Come and see."
They went then and
saw where he was
staying and stayed
that day with him.
It was about four
o'clock.
40 Andrew the
brother of Simon
Peter was one of the
two listening near
John and following.
41 He first found his
own brother, Simon,
and said to him,

C_1

29 The next day[(1.35)] he
saw Jesus coming to
him and said, "Look!
The lamb of God[(1.36)]
who is taking away
the sin of the
world. 30 This is
the one I talked
about: a man is
coming after me[(1.27)]
who is created prior
to me because he has
priority over
me.[(1.15)] 31 And I did
not know him, but so
that this may be
revealed to Israel I
have come baptizing
with water."[(1.26)]
34 And I have seen
and testified that
this is the son of
God."

C_2

NOTES

[A]again

[1.30]Inconsistent
w2ith 1.27

[32]And John
testified, "I have
seen the spirit
descend from heaven
as a dove and remain
over him. [33]And I
did not know
him,[(1.31)] but he who
had sent me to
baptize with water -
it was he who said
to me, 'Over
whomever you see the
spirit descend and
remain, it is he who
baptizes with a holy
spirit.'"

A

"We have found the
Messiah," which
translates as
"Christ." 42He
brought him to
Jesus. Looking at
him Jesus said, "You
are Simon Johnson;
you will be called
'Kephas,'" which
translates as
"Peter."
43The next day he
wanted to leave for
Galilee, and he
found Philip. And
Jesus said to him,
"Follow me."
44Philip was from
Bethsaida, out of
the town of Andrew
and Peter.
45Philip found
Nathaniel and said
to him, "We have
found him about whom
Moses wrote in the
Law and whom the
prophets were
about - Jesus
Josephson who is
from Nazareth.
46And Nathaniel said
to him, "Can
anything good be
from Nazareth?"
Philip said to him,
"Come and see."
47Jesus saw
Nathanael coming to
him and said about
him, "Look! Truly

NOTES

1.43"He" refers to the active agent in the preceding material, i.e., Andrew. If this were an insertion a redactor would have attempted to clarify the subject by replacing the pronoun with its antecedent.

A

an Israelite in whom
there is no deceit."
[48]Nathanael said to
him, "How do you
know me?" Jesus
answered, "Before
Philip called you,
when you were under
the fig tree, I saw
you." [49]Nathanael
answered him,
"Rabbi, you are the
son of God, you are
king of Israel."
[50]Jesus answered
him, "Because I told
you that I saw you
down below the fig
tree you believe?
You will <u>see</u> more of
these."

B_1

[51]And he said to
him, "Amen amen I
say to you, you will
<u>see</u>[(1.50)] heaven
opened and the
angels of God
ascending and
descending over the
son of humanity."

NOTES

[1.47b-48]The absence of a major role for Nathaniel in the Fourth Gospel argues for this being primitive material.

[1.51]The addressee, "you," suddenly shifts to the plural in the Greek, suggesting this is an insertion.

2 C_1

[12]After this he went
down into
Capharnaum; he, his
<u>mother</u>, his
brothers, and his
disciples stayed
there not many days.
[13]And the Passover
of the Jews was
near, and Jesus went
up to Jerusalem.
[14]And in the Temple
he found those who
were selling oxen,
sheep, and pigeons,
and the coin
changers seated.
[15]And making a whip
from cords he drove
all out of the
Temple - the sheep
and oxen - and he
poured out the coins
of the money
changers and
overturned the
tables, [16]and to
those selling the
pigeons he said,
"Take those out of
here. Do not make
my Father's house a
house of commerce."[B]
18Then the Jews
answered him, "What
signs do you show us
for you to do such
things?" [19]Jesus
answered, "Destroy
this shrine and I
will raise it in

NOTES

[B17]His disciples remembered that it is written, "The zeal for your house consumes me."

[2.19]See Mk. 14.58; v. 19 presupposes knowledge of events of 70 C.E.

three days." [20]Then
C_1
the Jews said,
"Forty-six years
this shrine was
built, and you raise
it in three days?"
[21]But he was talking
about the shrine of
his body.[C] [23]While he
was in Jerusalem
during the
Passover,[D] many
believed in his name
when they saw what
signs he worked.
[24]But Jesus himself
did not entrust
himself to them
because he knew all
[25]and had no need
for anyone to
testify about
people, for he knew
what was in
humanity.

NOTES

[C][22]Then when he was raised from the dead, his disciples remembered that he said this, and they believed in the scripture and in the word that Jesus spoke.

[D]during the feast

C_3

1And one Tuesday
there was a wed-ding
in Cana of Galilee,
and the mother(2.12)
of Jesus was there.
2Jesus was invited
to the wedding, as
well as his
disciples. 3And
with the wine being
short Jesus' mother
said to him, "They
have no wine." 4And
Jesus said to her,
"Mother, what is
this to me and you?
My hour has not come
yet." 5His mother
said to the
servants, "Do
whatever he tells
you." 6There were
six stone water jugs
sitting there for
the purification of
the Jews, holding up
to fifteen or
twenty-five gallons.
7Jesus told them,
"Fill the jugs with
water." And they
filled them to the
top. 8And he said
to them, "Now draw
some and carry it to
the head-waiter."
They did so. 9When
the headwaiter
tasted the water-
become-wine and did
not know where it

C_3

came from (but the
servants who had
drawn the water
knew) the head-
waiter called the
bridegroom 10and
said to him,
"Everyone places the
good wine out first
and when they are
high the lesser
wine. You have
saved the good wine
until now." 11Jesus
worked this first of
his signs in Cana of
Galilee and showed
his glory, and his
disciples believed
in him.

NOTES

2.11 See Lk. 9.32.

3 C_4

[3b]"Amen amen I say
to you unless
someone is born
anew, one cannot see
the kingdom of God."
[4]Nicodemos[(3.1)] said
to him, "How can an
adult human be born?
He cannot enter his
mother's womb a
second time and be
born, can he?"
[5a]Jesus answered,
[6]"What is born from
the flesh is flesh,
and what is born
from the spirit is
spirit. [7]Do not
wonder that I told
you, that it is
necessary for you to
be born anew. [8]The
spirit blows where
it wills and you
hear its sound, but
you do not know from
where it comes and
where it goes; so is
everyone born of the
spirit." [9]Nicodemos
answered, "How can
such happen?"
[10]Jesus answered,
"You are a teacher
of Israel and you do
not know such
things?"

NOTES

[3.5b]See 1 Jn. 4.7b.

[3.7]"You to be born" is plural; elsewhere it is singular. The statement must be a citation from an earlier part of C_4 that has been replaced by A and B material.

[E]a leader of the Jews

A

[1]There was a man of the Pharisees named Nicodemos.[E] [2]He came to him at night and said to him, "Rabbi, we know that you are a teacher come from divinity, for no one can perform these signs that you do unless God is with him. [3a]Jesus answered, [19b]"The light has come into the world, and humans prefer the darkness over the light, since their works were evil. [20]For everyone who practices evil hates the light and does not come to the light, lest his works be in evidence."

[22]Afterwards Jesus and his disciples went into Judean territory, and he stayed there with them, and they baptized. [23]John also was baptizing, in Ainon, near Saleim, since there were many waters there, and many arrived and were baptized. [24]For John was not thrown

B_1

[5b]Amen amen I say to you, unless someone is born[(3.3)] of water and spirit, one cannot enter into the kingdom of God.

[11]Amen amen I say to you that what we know we pronounce, and to what we see we testify, and our testimony is not accepted. [12]If I speak of earthly things to you and you do not believe, how will you believe if I speak to you of heavenly things? [13]And no one has ascended into heaven except he who had descended from heaven - the son of humanity. [14]And as Moses lifted up the serpent in the wilderness, so it is necessary for the son of humanity to be lifted up, [15]so that everyone who believes in him may have eternal life. [16]For God loved the world so that he gave the only son, so that everyone who believes in him may not die but have eternal life. [17]For

B_1

God did not send the son into the world to condemn the world but so that the world may be saved through him. 18 He who believes in him is not condemned, but he not believing has been condemned already, since he has not believed in the name of the only son of God.[F]

21 But he who acts in truth comes to the light[3.20] so that his works may be revealed to have been wrought in divinity.

31 He coming from above is over all; he being of the earth is of the earth and converses of the earth. He coming from heaven is over all; 32 what he has seen and heard - to that he testifies, and no one accepts his testimony. 33 He who accepts his testimony has certified that God is genuine. 34 For he whom God has sent speaks God's words,

C_1

25 Then there was a dispute over purification between some of John's[3.23] disciples and a Jew. 26 And they came to John and said to him, "Rabbi, the man who was with you beyond the Jordan about whom you have testified, see, he is baptizing and all are going to him. 27 John answered, "No person can receive even one thing unless it is given[3.35] him from heaven. 28 You yourselves bear me witness that I said, 'I am not the Christ,' but that I am sent before him. 29 He who has the bride is the bridegroom, but the friend of the bridegroom, who stands and hears him, rejoices greatly at the bridegroom's voice. Then this joy of mine has been completed. 30 He must grow, and I diminish."

A

into prison yet.

4

[1]Then when Jesus
realized that the
Pharisees had heard,
"Jesus was making
more disciples and
baptizing more than
John," [2](though
Jesus himself did
not baptize, but his
disciples did)
[3]he left Judea and
went to Galilee
again. [4]It was
necessary to go
through Samaria.
[5]Then he went into a
Samaritan town
called Suchar near
the field that Jacob
gave to his son
Joseph. [6]Jacob's
Well was there. So
Jesus, tired from
the trip, sat right
down at the well at
about noon time. [7]A
Samaritan woman came
to draw water.
Jesus said to her,
"Give me some to
drink." [8]For his
disciples had gone
on into the town to
buy food. [9]So the
Samaritan woman said
to him, "How is it
that you, a Jew, ask
for a drink from me,
a Samaritan woman?

NOTES

[3.16]See 1 Jn. 4.9

[F19a]and this is the judgment:

[3.21]See 1 Jn. 1.7

[3.31a]See 1 Jn. 4.4b

[3.31b]See 1 Jn. 4.5

B_1

for he gives the
spirit limitlessly.
[35]The Father loves
the son and has
given[(3.27)] all in his
hands. [36]He who
believes in the son
has eternal life,
but he who
disbelieves the son
will not see life,
but the wrath of God
stays on him.

C_1

[10]Jesus answered her, "If you knew the gift of God and who it is saying to you, '<u>Give me some to drink</u>,'(4.7) you would have asked of him and he would have given you living water."
[11]The woman said to him, "Sir, you have no bucket and the shaft is deep; where then do you have the running water?
[12]Surely you are not greater, are you, than our father Jacob who provided us with this shaft and himself drank from it, and his sons and cattle?"
[13]Jesus answered her, "Everyone who drinks from this water will thirst again. [14]But whoever would drink from the water that I will give will never thirst, but the water that I will give will well up within with water leaping up to eternal life."
[15]The woman said to him, "Sir, give me this water, so that I would neither

NOTES

4.2 is inconsistent with 3.22 and 4.1.

4.10"Living" also means "running" water, as in a stream.

4.11"Shaft": Unlike 4.6, the term here can mean either "well" or "shaft." This is an ap-parent allusion to the LXX version of Gen. 21.19 <u>phrear hudatos zontos</u> - "well of living water" from which Hagar drew water for her child.

A

For Jews do not
associate with
Samaritanesses."
16 He said to her,
"Go, call your
husband and return."
17 The woman answered
him, "I have no
husband." Jesus
said to her, "You
have spoken well, 'I
have no husband,'
for you have had
five husbands and
now you have one who
is not your husband.
You have spoken the
truth." 19 The woman
said to him, "Sir, I
see that you are a
prophet. 20 Our
fathers worshiped on
this mountain, and
you people say the
place where it is
necessary to worship
is in Jerusalem."
21 Jesus said to her,
"Madam believe me,
an hour is coming
when you people will
worship the Father
neither on this
mountain nor in
Jerusalem. 22 You
worship what you do
not know; we worship
what we know, since
salvation is from
the Jews. 24 God is
spirit, and for
those who worship

B

23 But an hour is
coming(4.21) and is
now, when the true
worshipers will
worship the
Father(4.21) in spirit
and truth. For the
Father also seeks
such worshiping him.

C_1

thirst nor come here to draw."

NOTES

[4.16ff.] Jesus responds to the difficulty raised by the woman in 4.9. As is evident from the fact that the disciples went into the town to buy food, Jewish men associated with Samaritan men. The fact that Jesus even spoke with the woman elicits surprise in 4.27. The Jewish-Samaritan problem is the theme in the primitive pericope from beginning to end.

him it is necessary
to worship in spirit
and truth." 25The
woman said to him,
"I know that a
Messiah[G] is coming;
when he comes, he
will announce
everything to us."
26Jesus said to her,
"I am he speaking to
you." 27And just
then his disciples
came and were
surprised that he
was conversing with
a woman, though
nobody said, "What
do you want?" or"Why
are you talking with
her?" 28Then the
woman left her water
jug and went into
the town and said to
the people, 29"Come
see a man who told
me everything I have
done. Isn't he the
Christ?" 30They
came out from the
town and went to
him.

31In the meantime
the disciples were
urging him, "Rabbi,
eat." 32But he said
to them, "I have
food to eat about
which you don't
know." 33So the
disciples were
saying to each

other, "Did anyone
bring him something
to eat?" 34Jesus
said to them, "My
food is doing the
will of him who sent
me and finishing his
work. 35Do you not
say, 'Four months
yet and the harvest
comes'? Look, I
tell you, 'Lift your
eyes and see the
fields,' for they
are already white
for the harvest."
39Many of the
Samaritans from that
town believed in him
on the basis of the
word of the woman
testifying "He told
me everything I have
done." 40When the
Samaritans came to
him, they urged him
to stay with them,
and he stayed there
two days. 41And
many more believed
on the basis of his
word, 42and they
were saying to the
woman, "We no longer
believe on the basis
of your talk, since
we have heard for
ourselves and we
know that this is
truly the savior of
the world." 43After
the two days he left

B_1

36He who <u>harvests</u>[4.35]
is receiving pay and
is taking in the
crops for eternal
life, so that he who
plants and he who
harvests may
likewise rejoice.
37For here the
saying is true: "One
person plants and
another harvests."
38I sent you to
harvest what you
have not labored
over. Others have
labored, and you
came upon their
crops.

NOTES

4.36In context this presupposes an existent Samaritan mission; the Samaritan religion planted and the Jewish Christians reaped.

A

from there for
Galilee. 46 Then he
went again to Cana
of Galilee, where he
had made the water
wine.

And there was a
royal officer whose
son was ill in
Capharnaum. 47 When
he heard that Jesus
arrived in Galilee
from Judea, he went
to him and asked
that he come down
and heal his son,
since he was about
to die. 50 Jesus
said to him, "Go,
your son will live."
The man believed
what Jesus told him
and went. 51 While
he was still on his
way down his
servants met him
saying that his boy
was living. 52 Then
he inquired about
the hour in which he
had recovery. They
told him at one in
the afternoon the
fever left him.
53 Then the father
knew that at that
hour Jesus told him,
"Your son will
live," and he
believed him, and
his whole household
as well.[J]

B

44 For Jesus himself
testified that a
prophet has no
respect in his own
country[H(4.43)]

48b Unless you see
signs and wonders,
you will not be-

NOTES

[J54]This was the second sign Jesus performed, again having come from Judea into Galilee. [1]Afterwards there was a feast of the Jews, and Jesus went up to Jerusalem.

NOTES

4.44 is inconsistent with 4.45b; it parallels Mt. 13.57, Mk. 6.4, and most closely Lk. 4.26.

[H45]So when he went to Galilee, the Galileans welcomed him, having seen all that he had done in Jerusalem at the feast, since they too went to the feast.

[4.46b]This differs enough from the Q parallels (Mt. 8.3-13; Lk. 7.1-10) to be independent. John's "son" closer to Matthew's "boy" than to Luke's "slave."

[4.48b]"You" shifts to the plural.

[I48a]Then Jesus said to him...[49]The royal official said to him, "Sir, come down before my boy dies!" 4.49 seems to be a redactive a resumptive repetition to accommodate 4.48.

A

5

2There is by the
Sheep Gate in
Jerusalem a pool
that is named
Bethzatha in Hebrew,
having five
colonnades.
3A multitude of the
disabled, blind,
lame, and paralyzed
lay in these.[K]
5There was a man
there, disabled for
thirty-eight years.
6Seeing him lying,
and knowing that it
had been for a long
time, Jesus said to
him, "Do you want to
become healthy?"
7The disabled man
answered him, "Sir,
I have no one to
place me in the pool
when the water stirs
up. I come to it,
another goes down
before me." 8Jesus
said to him, "Get
up, pick up your
bedding, and walk."
9And immediately the
man became healthy
and picked up his
bedding and walked.
But it was the
Sabbath that day.
13The healed man did
not know who it was,
since Jesus

C_1

10So the Jews were
saying to the cured
man, "It is the
Sabbath, and
you are not
permitted to pick up
your bedding." 11He
answered them, "He
who made me healthy,
it was he who told
me, 'Pick up your
bedding and walk.'"
12They asked him,
"Who is the man who
told you, 'Pick up
and walk'?" 15The
man went and
announced to the
Jews that it was
Jesus who had made
him healthy.(5.6)
16And on this basis
the Jews persecuted
Jesus, because he
did such things on
the Sabbath.(5.9)

NOTES

5.2"Jerusalem" with definite article, unlike 5.1.

K5.4, found in modern NTs, is post-Johannine.

A

withdrew, a crowd
being in the place.
[14]Afterwards Jesus
found him in the
Temple and said to
him, "See, you have
become healthy; sin
no more, lest worse
happen to you."

B_1

[19]So Jesus answered
them, "Amen amen I
say to you, the son
cannot do anything
of his own, but only
what he would see
the Father(5.18)
doing. For whatever
things He would do,
those the son does
likewise. [20]For the
Father loves the son
and shows him all
that He is doing,
and He will show him
greater works, so
that you may marvel.
[21]For just as the
Father raises the
dead and makes them
live, so also the
son makes those whom
he wishes live.
[22]For the Father
does not judge
anyone, but He has
given over all
judgment to the
son,(5.27) so that all
would honor the son
as they honor the
Father. He not
honoring the son
does not honor the
Father who sent him.
[24]Amen amen I say to
you, he who hears my
word and believes
Him who sent me, has
eternal life and
comes not to
judgment;(5.29) but he

C_1

[10]So the Jews were
saying to the cured
man, "It is the
Sabbath, and you are
not permitted to
pick up your
bedding." [11]He
answered them, "He
who made me healthy,
it was he who told
me, 'Pick up your
bedding and walk.'"
[12]They asked him,
"Who is the man who
told you, 'Pick up
and walk'?" [15]The
man went and
announced to the
Jews that it was
Jesus who had made
him healthy.(5.6)
[16]And on this basis
the Jews persecuted
Jesus, because he
did such things on
the Sabbath.(5.9)
[17]Jesus answered
them, "My Father(5.19)
is still working
now, and I am
working." [18]Because
of this, the Jews
then wanted even
more to kill,
because he not only
broke the Sabbath,
but he was also
calling God his own
father, making
himself equal to
divinity.

NOTES

5.15ff. These verses refer to the Jerusalem authorities as "the Jews," and 5.16 explains what would be subsequent to the narrated event.

5.24 See 1 Jn. 3.14

B_1

has crossed over
from death to life.
25 Amen amen I say to
you, a time comes
and is here, when
the dead will hear
the voice of the son
of God, and those
who heard will live.
31 If I were to
give testimony about
myself, my testimony
would not be true.
32 He giving
testimony about me
is another, and I
know that the
testimony that He
gives about me is
true. 33 You have
sent to John, and he
has given testimony
to the truth. 34 But
I do not accept
testimony from
humanity; however I
say these words so
that you may be
saved. 35 He was the
lamp, lit and
shining; but you
wished to rejoice in
its light for a
time. 36 But I have
a greater testimony
than John's; for the
works that the
Father has handed
over to me for me to
complete, the very
works that I
perform, testify

B_2

26 For just as the
Father has life in
Himself, so also he
has handed over life
to the son to have
in himself. 27 And
He has handed over
to him authority to
pass judgment, (5.22)
because he is a son
of humanity. 28 Do
not marvel over this
- that a time comes
in which all who are
in the graves will
hear his voice 29 and
those who have done
good deeds will come
out to a
resurrection of
life. But those who
have practiced evil,
to a resurrection of
judgment. (5.24) 30 I
cannot do anything
by myself; as I hear
I judge, and my
judgment is just,
because I do not
seek my will but the
will of Him who sent
me.

B_1

about me that the
Father has sent me.
[37]And the Father Who
sent me, He has
testified about me.
You have never heard
His voice or seen
His form, [38]and you
do not have His word
staying among you,
because you do not
believe in the one
whom He sent. [39]You
search the
scriptures because
you suppose you have
eternal life in
them; and they are
what testify about
me. [40]And you do
not wish to come to
me to have life.

[41]I do not accept
glory from humans,
[42]but I have come to
know you people,
that you do not have
among yourselves the
love of God. [43]I
have come in my
Father's name, and
you do not accept
me. If another were
to come in his own
name, him you would
accept. [44]How can
you believe, when
you accept glory
from each other and
not seek the glory
that is from the
only God?

B_1

[45]Do not suppose
that I will accuse
you before the
Father. He accusing
you is Moses - he in
whom you have hoped.
[46]For if you
believed Moses, you
believed me also,
for he wrote about
me. [47]But if you do
not believe his
writings, how do you
believe my
utterances?

A

6 1 Afterwards
Jesus went to the
far shore of the Sea
of Galilee.[M] 2 A big
crowd followed him,
because they saw the
signs that he worked
for the disabled.
3 Jesus went up the
mountain and sat
there with his
disciples.[N]
5 Then lifting the
eyes and seeing that
a big crowd was
coming to him, Jesus
said to Philip,
"Where would we buy
bread so they would
eat?" 6 He was
saying this in
bantering with him,
since he knew what
he was about to do.
7 Philip answered
him, "Two hundred
days' wages is not
enough for them to
each receive a
little." 8 One of
his disciples, An-
drew the brother of
Simon Peter, said to
him, 9 "Here is a
youngster who has
five barley loaves
and two fish. But
what is this for so
many? 10 Jesus said,
"Have the people
recline." There was

NOTES

[M](the Sea) of Tiberias.

[N]4 It was near the Passover, the feast of the Jews.

A
much grass in the
place. So the five
thousand or so men
reclined. [11]Then
Jesus took the
loaves and, having
given thanks, handed
them out to those
lying down; likewise
also the fish, as
much as they wanted.
[12]And when they were
satisfied, he said
to his disciples,
"Gather up the
leftover pieces,
lest any be lost."
[13]So they gathered
them up and filled
twelve baskets of
fragments from the
five barley loaves
that were left over
when they had eaten.
[14]Then, seeing what
sign he had worked,
the people were
saying, "Truly this
is the prophet who
is coming into the
world." [15]Then
Jesus, knowing that
they were about to
come and seize him
to make a kingdom,
withdrew again by
himself to the
mountain.

[16]As evening came
his disciples went
down to the sea
[17]and getting into a

A

boat were going
across the sea to
Capharnaum. And it
had already become
dark and Jesus had
not yet come to
them. 18And the sea
was stirred up with
a great wind
blowing. 19Then
when they had rowed
three or four miles,
they saw Jesus
walking on the sea
and approaching the
boat, and they were
frightened. 20But
he said to them, "It
is I, do not be
frightened." 21So
they wanted to take
him into the boat,
and immediately the
boat landed at the
place where they
were heading. 22The
next day the crowd,
which had stood on
the far shore of the
sea, had seen that
there was no other
boat there but the
one and that Jesus
had not set out with
his disciples in the
boat but that only
his disciples had
left. 23But boats
from Tiberias came
near to the place
where they ate

B_1

26Jesus answered
them, "Amen amen I
say to you, you do
not <u>look for</u>(6.24) me
because you saw
signs, but because
you ate from the
bread and were
filled. 27Work not
for the food that
perishes but for the
food that lasts into
eternal life, which
the son of humanity
will give you. For
the Father set his
seal on him - God
has." 28Then they
said to him, "What
should we do to work
the works of God?"
29Jesus answered
them, "This is the
work of God, that
you believe in him
whom He sent."
30Then they said to
him, "Then what sign
do you perform, that
we may see and
believe you? What
do you work? 31Our
fathers ate manna in
the wilderness. As
it is written,' He
has given them bread
from heaven to
eat.'" 32Then Jesus
said to them, "Amen
amen I say to you,
it was not Moses who
has given you

B_2

[36]But I told you
that you have both
seen me and not
believed.
[37]Everyone whom my
Father is giving me
will come to me, and
I will not cast out
him coming to me,
[38]because I have
come down from
heaven not so that I
would do my will but
the will of Him who
sent me.(6.44) [39]This
is the will of Him
who sent me, that I
not lose any from
His whom he has
given me, but raise
every one of them up
on the last day.(6.44)

NOTES

[6.26]This is inconsistent with 6.14-15

[6.36]This verse refers to a previous section of this discourse, which the redactor has not used.

A

bread.[0] [24]When the crowd saw that Jesus was not there, or his disciples, they entered the boats and went to Capharnaum looking for Jesus. [25]And finding him across the sea they said to him, "Rabbi, when did you come here?" [43a]Jesus answered them,... [44]"No one can come to me unless the Father who sent me drew him, and I will raise him on the last day. [45]It is written in the prophets, 'And all shall be taught by God.' Everyone who has heard and learned from the Father comes to me. [46]Not that anyone has seen the Father except he who is from God; he has seen the Father." [59]He said these things when teaching in the synagogue in Capharnaum.

[60]Then many of his disciples, after hearing this, said, "This saying is hard. Who can listen to it?" [61]But

B_1

bread from heaven, but my Father gives you the true bread from heaven. [33]For the bread of God is what is coming down from heaven and giving the world life." [34]Then they said to him, "Sir, give us this bread always." [35]Jesus said to them, "I am the bread of life. He who comes to me will not hunger, and he who believes in me will never thirst."

[40]For this is the will of my Father, that everyone who sees the son and believes in him should have eternal life; and I will raise him up on the last day.[(6.44)] [41]Then the Jews grumbled[(6.61)] about him because he said, "I am the bread coming down from heaven," [42]and they were saying, "Isn't this Jesus, Joseph's son, whose father and mother we know? Now how does he say, 'I have come down from heaven?' [43]Jesus answered

B_2

51 I am the living
bread(6.48) that has
come down from
heaven. Whoever
should eat of this
bread will live
forever, and
moreover the bread
that I will give for
the life of the
world is my flesh.
52 Then the Jews
argued with each
other, "How can this
man give his flesh
for eating?" 53 So
Jesus said to them,
"Amen amen I say to
you, unless you eat
the flesh(6.63) of the
son of humanity and
drink his blood, you
do not have life in
yourselves. 54 He
who munches on my
flesh and drinks my
blood has eternal
life, and I will
raise him on the
last day. 55 For my
flesh is real food,
and my blood is real
drink. 56 He who
munches on my flesh
and drinks my blood
remains in me and I
in him. 57 As the
living Father sent
me and I live
through the Father,
so that person who
munches on me will

NOTES

°the Lord having given thanks

6.51ff. A second eucharistic discourse.

A

Jesus, knowing in
himself that his
disciples were
grumbling about
this, said to them,
"Does this
scandalize you?
62Then what if you
were to see the son
of humanity ascend
to where he was
beforehand? 63It is
the spirit that
makes live; the
flesh accomplishes
nothing. The speech
that I have spoken
to you is spirit and
is life. 64But some
of you disbelieve."
For Jesus knew from
the outset who
disbelieved and who
was the one who
would betray him.
65And he said, "This
is why I have told
you that no one can
come to me unless it
is granted him from
the Father."
66Because of this
many of his
disciples went away
from among the
following and no
longer accompanied
him. 67So Jesus
said to the twelve,
"Do you also wish to
leave?" 68Simon
Peter answered him,

B_1

that you gave me,
that they may be one
as we are one: (17.2 B_1
them "Do not grumble
among one another.
47Amen amen I say to
you, he who believes
has eternal life.
48I am the bread of
life. (6.51) 49Your
fathers ate the
manna in the
wilderness and
died. (6.58) 50This is
the bread that is
coming down from
heaven, so that
anyone who would eat
of it would also not
die.

B_2
live through me.
58This is the bread
that has come down
from heaven, such as
the fathers did not
eat and died.(6.49)
He who munches on
this bread will live
forever.

NOTES

6.49The verse
suggests some social
distance from Jews.

A

7
1 And afterwards
Jesus moved about in
Galilee. For he did
not wish to move
about in Judea
because the Judeans
sought to kill him.
10 But when his
brothers went up to
the feast, then he
also went up, not
openly but as in
secret.
14 But at the

B_1

6b "My time is not
here yet,[(7.8)] but
your time is always
right. 7 The world
cannot hate you, but
it hates me because
I testify about it,
that its works are
evil."

C_1

2It was close to
the Jews' feast of
Tabernacles. 3So
his brothers said to
him, "Depart from
here and head for
Judea, so that your
disciples may see
you do your works.
4For no one works in
secret when he wants
himself to be before
the public. If you
do such things, show
yourself to the
world." 5For his
brothers did not
believe in him.
6aSo Jesus said to
them, 8"You go up to
the feast. I am not
going up to that
feast because
my time has not yet
been completed."
9Having said this he
stayed in Galilee.
11Then the Jews
sought for him at
the feast(7.10) and
were saying, "Where
is he?" 12And there
was much whispering
about him in the
crowds. While some
were saying, "He is
good," others were
saying, "No, on the
contrary he misleads
the crowd."
13However, no one
was conversing

C_1

openly about him for
fear of the Jews.

A

middle of the feast
Jesus went up to the
Temple and taught:
19 "Didn't Moses give
you the Law? Yet
none of you follows
the Law - why do you
seek to kill me?"
20 The crowd
answered, "You have
a demon. Who is
seeking to kill
you?"
25Q Some of the
Jerusalemites were
saying, "Isn't this
the man they are
trying to kill?
26 And look, he is
talking openly and
they are saying
nothing to him. Do
the rulers know,
perhaps, that this
man is actually the
Christ?" 31 Many in
the crowd believed
in him and were
saying, "When the
Christ comes, will
he perform more
signs than this man
was doing?" 32 The
Pharisees heard the
crowd whispering
these things about
him, and the high
priests and
Pharisees sent
officers to arrest
him. 40 Those from
the crowd who

B$_1$

15 Then the Jews
wondered, "How does
this uneducated man
know letters?
16 Then Jesus
answered them, "My
teaching(7.14) is not
my own but that of
Him who sent me.
17 If anyone should
wish to do His will,
he will know about
the teaching,
whether it is from
God or whether I
talk from myself.
18 One who talks from
himself seeks his
own glory. But one
seeking the glory of
someone who sent him
is genuine, and
there is no deceit
in him."
27 "But we know
where this man is
from. When he
comes, no one knows
where the Christ(7.26)
is from." 28 Then
Jesus called out,
teaching in the
Temple, "You know
me, and you know
where I am from, and
I have not come from
myself, but it is
the true One who
sent me whom you do
not know. 29 I know
Him, since I am from
Him; He sent me."

C_1

21 Jesus answered
them, "I did one
work and all are
surprised 22 because
of it. Moses gave
you[(7.19)] circumcision
- not that it is
from Moses but from
the fathers - and
you circumcise a man
on the Sabbath.
23 If a man receives
circumcision on the
Sabbath lest the Law
of Moses be broken,
are you angry with
me because I made a
whole man healthy on
the Sabbath?
24 Don't judge by
appearance, but
judge with right
judgment."

30 So they tried to
arrest[(7.12)] him, and
no one laid a hand
on him[(7.44)] because
his hour had not yet
come.

NOTES

[Q]Then

[7.15]This seems continuous with 5.47.

[7.21ff.]This appears to continue the dispute begun in 5.17.

[7.33ff.]This passage seems to be occasioned by the un-successful efforts to arrest Jesus (7.30 and 7.32).

[7.34]Parallels Thomas 38.2.

A

listened to him[R]
were saying, "This
is truly the
prophet." [41]Others,
"This is the
Christ," but "Is the
Christ coming from
Galilee? [42]Did the
scripture not say
that the Christ is
coming from the seed
of David and out of
Bethlehem, where
David was from?"
[43]There was
disagreement in the
crowd over him.
[44]Some of them
wanted to arrest
him, but no one laid
a hand on him.
[45]So the officers
went to the high
priests and
Pharisees, who asked
them, "Why didn't
you arrest him?"
[46]The officers
answered him, "Never
has anyone spoken
like this." [47]So
the Pharisees
answered them, "Have
you been misled?
[48]Have any of the
rulers believed in
him, or any of the
Pharisees? But this
crowd, which is
ignorant of the Law,
is accursed." [50]One
of them, Nicodemos,

B_1

[33]Then Jesus said,
"I am with you a
little time yet, and
I am heading to him
who sent me. [34]You
will seek me and not
find me, and where I
am you cannot come."
[35]So the Jews said
to themselves,
"Where is he about
to go that we will
not find him? Is he
about to go to the
diaspora of the
Greeks and teach the
Greeks? [36]What is
this saying, 'You
will seek me and not
find me, and where I
am you cannot
come'?"[(7.37)]

C_1

[37]On the last day,
the great one of the
feast, Jesus stood
up and called out,
"If anyone thirsts
[38a]who believes in
me, [37]let him
<u>come</u>[(7.36)] to me and
drink. [38b]As the
scripture said,
rivers of living
water flow from
within him."[V]

NOTES

[7.37]Having the last day of the feast precede the return of the guards to the high priests and Pharisees (7.45) breaks the chronology of the narrative. This is evidently an insertion.

[R]these sayings

[V39]He said this about the spirit, which those who believed in him are about to receive. For there was no spirit yet since Jesus was not yet glorified.

[7.53-8.11]This passage, generally regarded as non-Johannine, is omitted.

8

A

[12]Another time
Jesus was talking to
them, saying, "I am
the light of the
world. He who
follows me will not
walk in darkness but
have the light of
life." [13]Then the
Pharisees said to
him, "You are
testifying about
yourself; your
testimony is not
true."
[14]Jesus answered
them, "Even if I
testify about
myself, my testimony
is true because I
know where I came
from and where I am
going. But you do
not know where I
come from or where I
am going. [15]You
judge according to
the flesh; I am
judging no one.
[16]But if I judge, my
judgment is true
because I am not
alone; I am with the
Father who sent me."
[19]Then they said
to him, "Where is
your father?"
Jesus answered,
"You know neither me
nor my Father. If
you knew me, you

B

[17]"And it is also
written in your Law
that the testimony
of two people is
true.[(8.16)]
[18]I am one
testifying about
myself and the
Father who sent me
testifies about me."

C_1

21 Another time he
said to them, "I am
heading out and you
will look for me,
and you will die in
your sin. <u>Where</u>[8.14]
I am heading you
cannot come."
22 Then the Jews were
saying, "Since he
says, 'Where I am
heading you cannot
come,' is he killing
himself?" 23 And he
said to them, "You
are from below, I am
from above. You are
of this world, I am
not of this world.
24 So I said to you,
'You will die in
your sins.' For if
you do not believe
that I AM, you will
die in your sins."
25 So they were
saying to him, "Who
are you?" Jesus
said to them, "I
have been telling
you that from the
beginning. 26 I have
much to say and
<u>judge</u>[8.16] about you,
but He who sent me
is <u>truth</u>,[8.31] and
what things I heard
from Him I am
proclaiming to the
world.[S] 28b When you
lift up the son of
humanity, then you

NOTES

S27 They did not
realize that he
spoke to them about
the Father. 28a Then
Jesus said to them,

8.20 A break here,
shifting to a higher

A

would also know my
Father." [20]He was
making these
statements while he
was teaching at the
treasury in the
Temple, yet nobody
arrested him be-
cause his hour had
not come yet.
[30]When he was
proclaiming these
things, many
believed in him.

B_1

[31]Then Jesus said to
the Jews who had
believed[(8.30)] him,
"If you keep my word
you are truly my
disciples, [32]and you
will learn the
truth,[(8.26)] and the
truth will free
you." [33]They
answered him, "We
are the seed of
Abraham, and we have
never been enslaved
to anyone. Why are
you saying, 'You
will become free'?"
[34]Jesus answered
them, "Amen amen I
say to you, everyone
who commits a sin is
a slave of the sin.
[35]The slave does not
stay in the
household forever,
the son does. [36]So
if the son frees
you, you will really
be free. [37a]I know
that you are the
seed of Abraham."

C_1

37b"But you want
to kill me because
my word finds no
place in you. 38I
proclaim what I have
seen from the
Father, and you,
then, should do what
you have heard from
the Father." 39They
answered him, "Our
father is
Abraham."(8.33) Jesus
answered them, "If
you are the children
of Abraham, do the
works of Abraham.
40Now you want to
kill someone who has
spoken to you the
truth(8.32) I heard
from God. Abraham
didn't do that."
41"We do the works
of our father," they
said to him. "We
have not been born
in illegitimacy. We
have one Father,
God." 42Jesus said
to them, "If God
were your Father,
you would love me,
for I set out from
God and have
appeared. For I did
not come on my own,
but He sent me.
43Why don't you
understand my
discourse? Is it
because you cannot

B_1

[54b]If I glorify
myself, my glory is
nothing. The one
who glorifies me is
my Father, whom you
say is our divinity.
[55]And you do not
know him, but I know
him. And were I to
say I don't know
him, I would be a
liar[(8.44)] like you.
But I know him and
keep his word.

[47]He who is of God hears the statements of God. Therefore you do not hear, since you are not of God.

NOTES

[8.47]See 1 Jn. 4.6. This seems to be cued in by 8.46b.

[8.54b-55]This seems to break the flow of thought. I take it as an insertion occasioned by 8.44.

C_1

listen to my speech?
[44]You are of the
father, the devil,
and you wish to do
your father's
desires. He was
from the beginning
the downfall of
humanity, and he
does not stand in
the truth because
there is no truth in
him. When a lie
talks, it talks from
its own, since its
father is also <u>a
liar</u>.(8.55) [45]But
because I speak the
truth you do not
believe me. [46]Which
one of you accuses
me of sin? If I
speak truth, why do
you not believe me?
[48]The Jews answered
him, "Do we speak
evilly, 'You are a
Samaritan' and 'You
have lost your
mind'?" [49]Jesus
answered, "I have
not lost my mind,
but I honor my
Father and you
dishonor me. [50]But
I do not seek my
glory. There is one
seeking and judging.
[51]Amen amen I say to
you, if anyone keep
my word, he will not
see death in

C_1

eternity." [52]Then
the Jews said to
him, "Now we know
you have lost <u>your
mind</u>.(10.20) Abraham
died, and so did the
prophets, and you
say, 'If anyone keep
my word, he will not
taste death
forever.' [53]Are you
greater than our
father Abraham, who
died? And the
prophets died. What
are you making
yourself?" [54a]Jesus
answered, [56]"Your
father Abraham
rejoiced that he
might see my day.
He both sees and
rejoices." [57]Then
the Jews said to
him, "You aren't
even fifty years
old, and you have
seen Abraham?"
[58]Jesus said to
them, "Amen amen I

NOTES

8.48"lost your mind" -lit., "have a devil"

8.52"forever" - lit., "into the ages," the same expression as "in eternity" in 8.51.

A

9 [1]And while
walking along he saw
someone blind from
birth. [2]And his
disciples asked him,
"Rabbi, who sinned,
this man or his
parents, for him to
be born blind?"
[3]Jesus answered,
"Neither he nor his
parents sinned, but
it was that the
works of God be
shown in him."
[6]Having said these
words, he spat on
the ground and made
clay out of the
saliva and smeared
his clay above the
eyes. [7]And he said
to him, "Get up to
wash in the pool of
Siloam."[T] So he
went and washed, and
came seeing. [8]Then
the neighbors and
those who had seen
him before - because
he had been a beggar
- were saying,
"Isn't this the man
who sits and begs?"
[9]Some were saying,
"This is he," others
"No, but he looks
like him." The man
himself said, "I am
he." [10]So they were
saying to him, "Then

B_1

[4]It is necessary
that we work the
works[(9.3)] of him who
sent me during the
day; night is
coming, when no one
can work. [5]When I
am in the world, I
am the light of the
world.

C_1

say to you, before Abraham came to be, I AM." [59]They picked up stones to throw at him, but Jesus hid and left the Temple.

NOTES

[9.1]This makes an abrupt break from 8.59, suggesting it came from a different source.

[9.4]The abrupt change in the chain of thought suggests that this is an insertion.

[T]which translates as "sent."

A
how were your eyes
opened?" [11]He
answered, "The man
called Jesus made
clay and smeared my
eyes and said to me,
'Get up, to Siloam,
and wash.' Then
after going and
washing, I began to
see." [12]And they
said to him, "Where
is he?" He said, "I
don't know."
[13]They took him
who was once blind
to the Pharisees.
[14]But it was a
Sabbath on the day
Jesus made clay and
opened his eyes.
[15]Then again the
Pharisees too asked
him how he began to
see. He said to
them, "He smeared
clay on my eyes, and
I washed, and I see.
[16]Then some of the
Pharisees were
saying, "This man is
not from God, since
he does not keep the
Sabbath." But
others were saying,
"How can a sinful
man work such
signs?" And there
was a division among
them. [17]Then they
spoke to the blind
man again: "What do

C_1

[18]Then the Jews did not believe it about him, that he was blind and began to see, until they called the parents of him who had begun to see. [19]And they asked them, "Is this your son, whom you say was born blind? Then how does he see now?" [20]Then his parents answered, "We know this is our son and that he was born blind. [21]But we do not know how he sees now, or who opened his eyes we do not know. Ask him. He is an adult; he speaks for him-self." [22]His parents said these words because they feared the Jews. For the Jews had already decided that if anyone confessed him to be the Christ that person would be put out of the synagogue. [23]That is why his parents said, "He is an adult. Ask him." [24]Then[U] they called the man who was blind and said to him, "Give glory to God: We know that

NOTES

[9.24]Parallels 9.17, and comes from the doublet of 9.1-17.

[U]for the second time

A

you say about him,
since he opened your
eyes?" He said, "He
is the Prophet."
34They answered him,
"You were born with
sins through and
through, and you are
teaching us?" And
they threw him out.
35Jesus heard that
they threw him out,
and finding him he
said, "Do you
believe in the son
of humanity?" 36He
answered, "And who
is he, sir, that I
may believe in him?"
37Jesus said to him,
"You have seen him
and he who is
talking with you,
that is he." 38He
said, "Sir, I
believe." And he
worshiped him.
39And Jesus said, "I
came into this world
in judgment, so that
those not seeing may
see and the seeing
become blind."
40Pharisees heard
these words, since
they were with him,
and they said to
him, "Are we also
blind?" 41Jesus
said to them, "If
you were blind, you
have no sin at all.

A

But now that you
say, 'We see,' your
sin remains."

C_1

this man is a
sinner." [25]He
answered, "Whether
he is a sinner I do
not know. I know
one thing, that I
was blind and now I
see." [26]Then they
said to him, "What
did he do to you?
How did he open your
eyes?" [27]He
answered, "I told
you already and you
didn't listen. Why
do you want to hear
again? Do you want
to become his
disciples?" [28]And
they reviled him and
said, "You are a
disciple of that
one, but we are
disciples of Moses.
[29]We know that God
had spoken to Moses,
but we do not know
where this one is
from. [30]The man
answered them, "Now
this is amazing; you
do not know where he
is from, and he
opened my eyes."
[31]"We know God does
not listen to
sinners, but if
someone is a
worshiper and does
his will, he listens
to this one."
[32]"Never has it been

C_1

heard that someone
opened the eyes of
someone who had been
born blind. [33]He
could not have done
anything if he were
not from divinity."

NOTES

[9.22]A possible reference to the Jamnia exclusion.

[9.24]Parallels 9.17; comes from a doublet.

A

10 [V20]Many of them
were saying, "He has
lost his mind[(8.52)]
and raves. Why
listen to him?"
[21]Others were
saying, "Such words
are not crazed. Can
insanity open the
eyes of blind
people?"
[X22b]It was winter,
[23]and Jesus walked
about in the
courtyard of Solomon
in the Temple.
[39]They tried to
arrest him again,
and he escaped from
their grasp. [40]And
he went away beyond
the Jordan again, to
the place where John
was baptizing the
first time; and he
stayed there. [41]And
many came to him and
were saying, "John
worked no sign, but
all that John said
about this man was
true." [42]And many
believed in him
there.

B_1

[1]Amen amen I say to
you, that person who
does not enter the
sheep yard by the
gate but climbs over
another place, is a
thief and guerilla.
[2]But he who enters
through the gate is
a shepherd of the
sheep. [3]The gate
keeper opens for
him, the sheep
listen to his
call,[(10.27)] he calls
his own sheep by
name, and he leads
them out. [4]When he
has taken all his
own out, he goes
before them and the
sheep follow him,
because they know
his voice. [5]They do
not follow some
other but flee from
him, because they do
not know the call of
others.[W] [7b]Amen amen
I say to you, I am
the gate of the
sheep. [8]All who
came before me were
thieves and
guerrillas, but the
sheep did not listen
to them. [9]I am the
gate; if anyone
enters by me he will
be saved, and he
will go in and go
out and find

C_1

because you are not
from my sheep.
[27]The sheep that are
mine listen to my
call,[(10.3)] and I
recognize them and
they follow me,
[28]and I give them
eternal life. [29]My
Father, who has
given them to me, is
greater than all,
and no one can
steal[(10.10)] from the
Father's grasp. [30]I
and the Father are
one." [31]Again the
Jews picked up
stones in order to
stone him. [32]Jesus
answered them, "I
showed you many good
works from the
Father. For which
of them do you stone
me?" [33]The Jews
answered him, "We do
not stone you
because of a good
work but because of
a blasphemy, and
because you, a
human, make yourself
a god." [34]Jesus
answered them, "Is
it not written in
your Law, 'I said,
you are gods'? [35]If
it called those to
whom the word of God
came *gods* (and the
scripture cannot be

NOTES

[10.1ff.]The prior refusal of the blind man to follow the Pharisees seems to occasion this allegory.

[V19]Again a division broke out among the Jews because of these sayings.

[W6]Jesus told them this figure of speech, but they did not understand what he was talking about. [7a]Jesus said again to them

[10.21]"insanity" - lit., "a demon."

[X22]Then came the Rededication Feast in Jerusalem.

[10.24b]See Lk. 22.67a

[10.25a]See Lk. 22.67b

B_1

pasture. [10]The
thief does not come
but to steal, kill,
and destroy; I came
that they may have
life and have it
abundantly. [11]I am
the good shepherd;
the good shepherd
lays down his life
for the sheep.
[12]The hireling is
not a shepherd; the
sheep are not his
own. He sees the
wolf coming, leaves
the sheep and
flees,[Y] [13]because he
is a hireling and is
not concerned about
the sheep. [14]I am
the good shepherd,
and I recognize mine
and mine recognize
me, [15]as the Father
recognizes me and I
recognize the
Father, and I lay
down my life for the
sheep. [16]And I have
other sheep that are
not from this yard;
it is necessary for
me to bring them,
and for them to
listen to my call,
and become one
flock, one shepherd.
[17]It is for this
reason that the
Father loves me: I
lay down my life so

B_1

that I may take it
up again. [18]Nobody
takes it away from
me, but I lay it
down myself. I have
power to lay it
down, and I have
power to take it up
again. I received
this charge from my
Father.

NOTES

[Y12b]And the wolf
seizes and scatters
them.

A

11 [1]There was a
man who was ill,
Lazarus of Bethany,
the town of Mary and
her sister Martha.[z]
[3]So the sisters sent
a message to him,
saying, "Sir, he
whom you make your
friend is ill."
[6]When he heard that
he was ill, he still
stayed two days in
the place where he
was. [7]Then after
this he said to the
disciples,
[11b]"Lazarus, our
friend, has fallen
asleep, but I will
go to wake him up."
[12]Then the disciples
said to him, "Sir,
if he has fallen
asleep he will
recover." [13]Jesus
had spoken of his
death, but they
supposed that he was
speaking about
resting in sleep.
[14]So Jesus told them
plainly, "Lazarus
died, [15]and I am
glad for you that I
was not there, so
that you may
believe. But let us
go to him. [16]Then
Thomas, who is
called Twin, said to

A

his fellow
disciples, "Let us
also go that we may
die with him."
[17]Then having
gone, Jesus found
that he had already
been in the tomb
four days. [20]Then
when Martha heard
that Jesus was
coming, she met him.
But Mary sat inside
the house. [21]Martha
said to Jesus, "Sir,
if you would have
been here my brother
would not have died.
[22]But I also know
now that whatever
you ask God, God
will grant you."
[23]Jesus said to her,
"Your brother will
arise."

NOTES

[z2]It was the Mary
who anointed the
Lord with perfume
and wiped his feet
with her hair, whose
brother was ill.

[11.7]Repeating "said"
suggests a break.

A

24 Martha said to
him, "I know, he
will rise in the
resurrection on the
last day." 25a Jesus
said to her, 26b "Do
you believe this?"
27 She said to him,
"Yes sir, I have
believed that you
are the Christ, the
son of God, who is
coming into the
world." 28 After
saying this she left
and called her
sister Mary, saying
privately, "The
teacher has arrived
and is calling you."
29 But when she heard
she started up and
went to him.
30 Jesus had not come
into the village
yet, but was still
in the place where
Martha had met him.
32 So Mary, as she
came to where Jesus
was, saw him, fell
at his feet, and
said to him, "Sir,
if you had been here
my brother would not
have died." 34 And
he said, "Where have
you placed him?"
They said to him,
"Sir, come and see."
35 Jesus cried.
38 Then Jesus,

B_1

[A]25b I am the
resurrection(11.24)
and the life. He
who believes in me,
though he die, will
live, 26a and everyone
who lives and
believes in me will
never die.

NOTES

[A]again

C_1

[31]Then the Jews who
were with her in the
house and consoling
her, seeing Mary
start up and leave,
followed her,
thinking she was
going to the tomb to
weep there. [33]Then
Jesus, when he saw
her weeping and the
Jews who came with
her weeping, was
stirred in spirit
and was himself
upset. [36]The Jews
were saying, "See
how close a friend
he was to him."
[37]But some of them
said, "Couldn't he
who opened the blind
man's eyes make it
so that this man
wouldn't die?"
[41]Then they
removed the stone.
Jesus raised his
eyes upward and
said, "Father, I
thank you because
you hear me. [42]I
know you always hear
me, but I spoke for
the benefit of the
crowd standing
about, so that they
may believe that you
sent me."
[44b]...Jesus said
to them, "Untie him
and let him go."

C_1

[45]Then many of the
Jews who had come to
Mary and had seen
what he had done,
believed in him.[B]

NOTES

[11.44b]"them" - this term is in the masculine, but no crowd, or even disciples, was mentioned in the material in column A.

[B46]Some of them went to the Pharisees and told them what Jesus had done.

A

stirred within
himself,[E] went to
the tomb. It was a
cave, and a stone
lay over it.
39Jesus said,
"Remove the stone."
Martha, the sister
of the deceased,
said to him, "Sir,
it smells now, for
it is the fourth
day." 40Jesus said
to her, "Didn't I
tell you that if you
believe you will see
the glory of God?"
43And having said
these words, he
called out in a loud
voice, "Lazarus,
come out." 44aThe
dead man came out,
bound hand and foot
with burial cloth
and his face wrapped
in a face cloth.
47Then the high
priests and
Pharisees convened
the Sanhedrin and
were saying, "What
do we do since this
man is working many
signs? 48If we let
him continue, all
will believe in
him," and, "The
Romans will come and
take away our place
and nation." 49One
of them, Caiaphas,

A

who was high priest
at that time, said
to them, "You know
nothing at all,"
50and "You do not
understand that it
is useful to you for
one man to die for
the people lest the
whole nation
perish." 51He did
not say this on his
own, but since he
was high priest at
that time he
prophesied that
Jesus was about to
die for the nation.[C]
53So from that day
they were resolved
to kill him. 54So
Jesus no longer
moved about openly
among the Judeans
but went from there
to the region near
the wilderness, to a
town called Ephraim,
and he stayed there
with the disciples.
57The high priests
and Pharisees had
given orders that
anyone who knew
where he was should
report it so that
they could arrest
him.

C

[55]It was close to
the <u>feast</u>(10.54)[D]
and many went up
from the region to
Jerusalem before the
feast to purify
themselves. [56]They
were looking for
Jesus and saying to
each other while
standing in the
Temple, "What do you
think? He won't
come to the feast,
will he?"

NOTES

[C52]and not for the nation only but so that the children of God who were scattered may gather as one.

[11.54]"Judeans" - same word that usually means "Jews," understood in a geographical sense here.

[D55]of the Jews

A

12 1Then Jesus
went to Bethany six
days before the
feast; Lazarus, whom
Jesus raised from
the dead, was there.
2They made a banquet
for him there, and
Martha was serving,
but Lazarus was
among those
reclining with him.
3Then Mary took a
pound of costly
pistik nard perfume
and anointed the
feet of Jesus; she
wiped the feet with
her hair. The house
was filled with the
aroma of the
perfume. 4Judas the
Iscariot, one of his
disciples, who was
about to betray him,
said, 5"Why wasn't
this perfume sold
for three hundred
denarii and given to
the poor?" 6He said
this not because he
cared for the poor
but because he was a
thief and pilfered
the money box of its
contents. 7Jesus
said, "Leave her,
that she may keep it
for the day of my
burial. 8For you
will always have the

A

poor among you, but
me you do not always
have." 12The next
day the great crowd
that was coming to
the feast - the
people having heard
that Jesus was
coming to Jerusalem,
13were taking the
palm fronds, going
out to meet him, and
crying out,
"Hosanna! Blessed
he who is coming in
the Lord's name!"
and,"The king of
Israel!" 14But
Jesus, finding a
little donkey, sat
on it. As it is
written, "Fear not,
daughter of Sion.
Behold your king is
coming, seated on
the colt of a
donkey."[E]

C_1

[9]Then a great crowd[(12.12)] of Jews learned that he was there, and they came out not only because of Jesus but also to see Lazarus[(12.17)] whom he raised from the dead. [10]But the high priests had resolved to kill Lazarus [11]since many of the Jews were heading off because of him and believing in Jesus.

NOTES

[12.3]"pistik" - most translations use a later meaning, "genuine."

[12.12]translated here as "the people" to show a shift to the plural.

[E16]At first his disciples did not know of these words, but when Jesus was glorified they remembered that these had been written about him and that he did these things.

A

17Then the crowd
that was with him
testified about the
time he called
Lazarus from the
grave and raised him
from the dead.
18Therefore the
crowd met him also,
since they heard
that he had worked
this sign. 19Then
the Pharisees said
to themselves, "See,
you can do nothing
about it. Look, the
world has gone after
him."
20There were
Greeks who were
among those going up
to worship at the
feast. 21These
approached Philip,
who was from
Bethsaida of
Galilee, and asked
him, "Sir, we wish
to see Jesus."
22Philip went and
told Andrew; Andrew
and Philip went and
told Jesus. 23But
Jesus answered them,
"The hour has come
for the son of
humanity to be
glorified."
27"Now my soul is
troubled, and what
should I say,
'Father, save me

B_1

24Amen amen I say to
you, unless a grain
of wheat die falling
into the ground, it
remains alone; but
if it die, it bears
much fruit. 25He
loving his life[12.27]
loses it, and he
hating his life in
this world will keep
it forever. 26If
anyone serve me, let
him follow me. And
where I am, there
will my server also
be. If anyone serve
me, the Father will
honor him.

C_1

[34b]"We heard from the Law that the Christ will remain forever," and "How do you say that it is necessary for the son of humanity to be lifted up?[(12.31)] Who is this son of humanity?" [35]Then Jesus said to them, "For a little time yet the light is among you. Walk while you have the light,[(12.46)] lest the dark catch you," and "He who walks in the dark does not know where he is going. [36a]While you have the light, believe in the light, so that you become children of the light.

NOTES

[12.25]"life" - *psuche*, the same word as "soul" in 12.27, which cues in this sayings passage.

[12.34ff.]The contrast in tone with the crowd in 12.12ff. suggests that this passage is from a different narrative.

A

from this hour'?
But I came to this
hour for this.
28Father, glorify
your name." Then
came a voice from
heaven: "I both
glorified it and
will again glorify
it." 29Then the
crowd that stood and
had heard said it
was thunder; others
said, "An angel had
spoken to him."
30Jesus answered,
"This voice did not
sound for me but for
you." 31Now is the
judgment of this
world. Now will the
ruler of this world
be cast out. And if
I am lifted up from
the earth, I will
draw all to
myself."[F] 36bJesus
proclaimed these
things, and leaving,
hid from them. 37He
had worked many such
signs before them,
but they did not
believe in him, 38so
that the saying of
Isaiah the prophet
would be fulfilled.
It said, "Lord, who
believed our report?
And to whom was the
arm of the Lord been
revealed?"

B_1

44But Jesus called
out, "It is not me
in whom he who
believes in me
believes,(12.37) but
He who sent me,
45and he who sees me
sees Him who sent
me. 46I have come
into the world as
light,(12.35) so that
everyone who
believes in me would
not stay in the
dark. 47And if
anyone should hear
my words and not
keep them, it is not
I who judges him,
for I did not come
to judge the
world,(12.31) but to
save the world.
48He who refuses me
and does not accept
my words has his
judgment. The word
that I have spoken -
it judges him on the
last day, 49because
I did not speak on
my own, but the
Father who sent me
had given me the
command what to say
and what to
proclaim. 50And I
know that his
command is eternal
life. So the things
I proclaim, I
proclaim as the

C_1

[42]Still many of the rulers also believed in him, but they did not confess it lest they be put out of the synagogue.
[43]For they loved the glory of humans more than the glory of God.

NOTES

[F33]He said this signifying by what death he was about to die. [34]Then the crowd answered him

[12.36a]See Lk. 16.8b.

[12.42]This appear to be an insertion qualifying 12.37, if not completely contradicting it.

A

39 Therefore they
could not believe,
because Isaiah said
again: 40 "He has
blinded their eyes,
and hardened their
heart, lest they see
with their eyes,
comprehend with the
heart, turn, and I
heal them."
41 Isaiah said these
things because he
saw his glory, and
he talked about him.

13

1 Now before the
Passover Feast,
knowing that the
hour had come for
him to leave this
world for the
Father, and having
loved his own who
were in the world,
Jesus loved them to
the end. 2 And as a
dinner began, when
the devil had
already put it into
the heart of Judas
Simon Iscariot to
betray him, 3 Jesus,
knowing that the
Father had given all
over to his hands
and that he came
from divinity and
was going to God,
4 got up from the
dinner and took off

B_1

Father has asked me.

A

his robe and, taking
a towel, girded
himself. [5]Then he
poured water into a
basin and began to
wash the feet of the
disciples and wipe
them with the towel
with which he was
girded. [6]Then he
came to Simon Peter,
who said to him,
"Sir, are you to
wash my feet?"
[7]Jesus answered,
"You do not know now
what I am doing, but
you should know
after these things."
[8]Peter said to him,
"You should never
wash my feet."
Jesus answered him,
"If I don't wash
you, you will have
nothing more to do
with me." [9]Simon
Peter said to him,
"Sir, not only my
feet but also hands
and head." [10]Jesus
said to him, "He who
has bathed has no
need to wash, except
for the feet, but is
clean all over. And
you are clean, but
not all," for he
knew who was to
betray him. That is
why he said not all
were clean.

A

[12]Then when he
had washed their
feet and put his
robe on and reclined
again, he said to
them, "Do you know
what I have done to
you?

NOTES

[13.10]Plural second person, refers to the disciples present.

A

13You call me
'Teacher' and 'Sir,'
and that is correct,
for I am. 14If then
I, 'Sir' and
'Teacher,' washed
your feet, so should
you wash one
another's feet.
15For I have given
you an example so
that as I did to
you, you also should
do. 17If you know
these things, happy
are you if you act
on them."
21Having said
these things, Jesus
was troubled in
spirit, and he
testified, "Amen
amen I say to you,
one of you will
betray me." 22The
disciples looked at
one another, at a
loss over whom he
was talking about.
23One of the
disciples was
reclined close
beside Jesus, the
one whom Jesus
loved. 24So Simon
Peter nodded to him
to find out whoever
he was talking
about. 25So leaning
thus near Jesus'
chest he said to
him, "Sir, who is

B_1

16Amen amen I say to
you, a servant is
not greater than his
master or a
messenger greater
than he who sent
him.

18"I do not speak
about all of you. I
know whom I have
chosen. But so that
the scripture may be
fulfilled, 'He who
ate my bread lifted
his heel against
me.' 19I say this
to you now before it
happens, so that you
may believe when it
happens that I AM.
20Amen amen I say to
you, he who receives
anyone I send
receives me, and he
receiving me
receives him who
sent me."

A

it?" [26]Jesus
answered, "That is
he, to whom I will
give this piece of
bread when I dunk
it." Then having
dunked the bread
he took it and gave
it to Judas Simon
Iscariot. [27]And
then after the piece
of bread, Satan
entered into that
person. So Jesus
said to him, "Do
quickly what you are
doing." [28]But no
one reclining knew
to what end he said
this to him. [29]For
some thought, since
Judas held the money
box, Jesus was
telling him to buy
something we needed
for the feast, or to
give something to
the poor. [30]Having
taken the piece of
bread, he left
immediately. It was
night.
[31]When Judas had
left, Jesus said,
"Now the son of
humanity is
glorified, and God
is glorified in him.
[32]If God is
glorified in him,
God will also
glorify him in him,

NOTES

[13.16]Cued in by 13.13-14; it would be redundant if in the original material.

[13.18]Inserted to solve the problem of Jesus blessing Judas in.

[13.20]A saying cued in by interpreting foot washing as a welcoming.

A

and glorify him
immediately. [33b]I
am with you for a
little while, and
you will seek me."
[36]Simon Peter
said to him, "Sir,
where are you
going?" Jesus
answered him, "Where
I am going you
cannot follow me
now, but you will
follow later."
[37]Peter said to him,
"Sir, why can I not
follow you now? I
will lay down my
life for you."
[38]Jesus answered,
"You lay down your
life for me? Amen
amen I say to you,
the cock will not
crow until you deny
me three times."
14 [1]"Do not let
your heart be
troubled. Believe
in God and believe
in me. [2]There are
many rooms in my
Father's home. If
not, would I have
said to you that I
was leaving to
prepare a place for
you? [3]And though I
go and prepare a
place for you, I am
coming again and I

B_1

[33a]Children,

[G33c]"Where I am going
you cannot
come,[(13.36)] and I say
this to you now.
[34]I am giving you a
new command, that
you love one
another; as I loved
you, you should also
love one another.
[35]By this all will
know that you are my
disciples, if you
have love for one
another."

NOTES

[G33b]And as I said to
the Jews,

[13.34]See 1 Jn. 3.11
and 3.23

A

will take you to
myself so that where
I am you will also
be. 4And where I go
you know the way."
5Thomas said to
him, "Sir, we don't
know where you are
going. How can we
know the way?"
6aJesus said to him,
6c"No one comes to
the Father but
through me."
8Philip said to
him, "Sir, show us
the Father and it
will be enough for
us." 9Jesus said to
him, "So long I am
with you and you do
not know me, Philip?
He who has seen me
has seen the Father.
Why do you say,
'Show us the
Father'? 10Do you
not believe that I
am in the Father and
the Father is in me?
The words that I
speak to you I do
not proclaim on my
own, but the Father
does his work in me.
11Believe me, I am
in the Father and
the Father in me;
but if not me,
believe the words on
account of the
works.

B_1

6b"I am the way,[(14.5)]
the truth, and the
life."

7"If you know
me,[(14.9)] you know my
Father also. And
from now you know
him and have seen
him."

12"Amen amen I say
to you, he who
believes in me will
do the works[(14.11)]
that I do, and he
will do greater than
these because I am
going to the Father.

A

14 Whatever you ask in my name, I will do." 21 He who has my commands and keeps them - it is he who loves me. He who loves me will be loved by my Father, and I will love him and show myself to him."

22 Judas (not Iscariot) said to him, "Sir, what happened that you are about to show yourself to us and not to the world?" 23 Jesus answered, 28 "You heard me say to you, 'I leave and I come to you.' If you love me, you would rejoice when I go to the Father because the Father is greater than I. 29 And now I have told you before it happens, so that when it happens you may believe. 30 I will no longer talk about many things with you, for the ruler of the world is coming, and he has nothing over me, 31 but that the world may know that I love the Father, I do as my Father commanded.

B_1

13 And whatever you ask in my name, I will do (14.14) it, so that the Father will be glorified in the son.

15 "If you love me, keep my commands. (14.21a) 16 And I will ask the Father and he will give you another advocate to be with you forever, 17 the spirit of truth that the world cannot accept, because it does not see or know it. You know it because it stays with you and you in it. 18 I will not leave you orphaned; I am coming to you. 19 A little while yet and the world will see me no more, but you will see me (16.18; 16.16) because I live and you will live. 20 On that day you will know that I am in my Father (14.11) and you in me and I in you."

B_2

NOTES

[14.13]1 Jn. 3.22.

[14.14]Virtually identical to 14.13a

[14.15]1 Jn. 5.3

[14.18b]This would not appear to have originated in a narrative in which Jesus had not left yet.

[23b]"If anyone love
me he will keep my
word, and my Father
will love him and we
will come to him and
make a home with
him. [24]He who does
not love me does not
keep my words, and
the word that you
hear is not mine but
the Father's, who
sent me.

25 I have said these
things to you while
remaining with you.
26 But the advocate,
the holy spirit,
which the Father
will send in my
name, will teach you
all and recall for
you all that I said
to you. 27 Peace I
leave you, my peace
I give you. Not as
the world gives do I
give to you. Let
your heart not be
troubled or timid."
15 1 "I am the true
vine, and my Father
is the gardener.
2 He removes every
branch on me that
does not bear fruit,
and clears each that
does bear fruit, so
that it would bear
much fruit. 3 You
are already cleared
by the word that I
have spoken to you.
4 You remain on me
and I in you. As a
branch cannot bear
fruit from itself
unless it remain on
the vine, so you
cannot unless you
remain on me. 5 I am
the vine, you the
branches. He who
remains on me and I

with him - he it is
who bears much
fruit, because apart
from me you can make
none.
6 If anyone not
remain on me, he is
thrown out as a
branch and withers,
and they gather them
up and throw them
into the fire, and
it burns. 7 If you
remain on me and my
words remain in you,
ask whatever you
wish and it will
happen for you. 8 My
Father is glorified
in this, that you
bear much fruit and
become my disciples.
9 As the Father
loved me and I loved
you, stay in my
love, as I kept the
commands of my
Father and remain in
His love. 11 I have
spoken these things
to you so that my
joy will be in you
and your joy be
completed. 12 This
is my command, that
you love one another
as I loved you.
13 No one has greater
love than this, that
someone lay down his
life for his
friends. 14 You are

B_1

my friends if you do
what I command you.
15 No more do I call
you slaves, because
the slave does not
know what his master
is doing. But I
have called you
friends because I
have made known to
you all that I heard
from my Father.
18 If the world
hates you, know it
has hated me, the
first of you. 19 If
you are of the
world, the world
would befriend its
own; but because you
are not of the
world, but <u>I chose
you</u>[(15.16)] out of the
world, the world
therefore hates you.
20 Recall the saying
that I told you, "No
servant is greater
than his master."
If they persecuted
me, they will
persecute you also;
if they kept my
word, they will keep
yours also. 21 But
they will do both of
these things to you
because of my name.
Since they did not
know Him who sent me
22 if I did not come
and talk to them,

B_2

16 You did not choose
me, but <u>I chose
you</u>[(15.19)] and
destined you to go
and bear fruit and
for your fruit to
remain, so that
whatever you ask of
the Father in my
name He would grant
to you. 17 I command
you these things so
that you love one
another.

NOTES

[15.12] See 1 Jn. 3.11 and 3.23.

[15.16] This breaks the train of thought. Bearing fruit recalls 15.1ff.; asking in Jesus' name 14.13-14.

[15.20] "Servant" is the same term as "slave" in 15.15, which cites 13.16. 15.15 is continuous with 15.20.

[15.20b-21] Most read 15.21b with the preceding, creating logical problems in the passage.

B_1

they had no sin.
But now they have no
excuse for their
sins. [23]He who
hates me also hates
my Father. [24]If I
had not done the
works among them
that no one else
did, they had no
sin. But now they
have seen and have
hated both me and my
Father. [25]But it is
to fulfill the
saying that is
written in their
Law: "They hated me
gratuitously."
[26]When the advocate
comes, whom I will
send you from the
Father, the spirit
of truth who goes
forth from the
Father, he will
testify about me.
[27]You also will
testify because you
are with me from the
beginning.
16 [1]"I have spoken
these things to you
that you not be
scandalized. [2]They
will excommunicate
you from the
synagogue. Indeed
an hour is coming
when everyone who
has killed you

B_2

[4]"However, I have
spoken these things
to you[16.1] that when
their hour[16.2] comes
you would remember
what I said to you.
I did not say these
things to you from
the beginning
because I was with
you. [5]But now I am
heading toward him
who sent me, and
none of you asks me,
"Where are you
going?" [6]But
because I have said
these things to you
sorrow has filled
your heart. [7]But I
am telling you the
truth; it is to your
benefit that I
leave. For if I do
not leave, the
advocate will not
come to you. But if
I go, I will send
him to you. [8]And
when he comes he
will prove the world
wrong about sin,
righteousness, and
judgment. [9]About
sin, because they do
not believe in me.
[10]About
righteousness,
because I am heading
to the Father and
you will no longer
seeme. [11]About

B_1

will think that he
is carrying out a
worship service to
God. [3]And they will
do these things
because they know
neither the Father
nor me."

NOTES

[16.2]"Indeed" - the term is usually "but"; however, here it seems to have an additive rather than adversative sense.

A

18 Then they were
saying, "What is he
saying, this 'little
while'? We do not
know what he is
talking about."
19 Knowing that they
wanted to question
him, Jesus also
spoke, "Is it about
this that you are
seeking among
yourselves, that I
said a little while
ago both, 'You will
not see me,' and a
little while later,
'You will also see
me'? 25 I have told
you these things in
figures. An hour is
coming when I will
no longer speak in
figures but announce
to you openly about
the Father. 26 On
that day you will
make requests in my
name, and I will not
say to you that I
will ask the Father
for you. 27 For the
Father Himself is
your friend, because
you have befriended
me and have believed
that I came from
God. 28 I came from
the Father and
entered the world.
Again I am leaving
the world and going

B_1

20 Amen amen I say to
you, you will weep
and mourn, but the
world will rejoice.
You will grieve, but
your grief will
become joy. 21 The
woman has grief when
with child because
her hour comes. But
when she gives birth
to the child she no
longer re-members
the distress[16.33]
because of the joy
that a human has
come into the world.
22 You also have
grief now, but I
will see you again
and gladden your
heart, and no one
will take your joy
away from you.
23 And on that day
you will not make
requests[16.26] of me
for anything.

Amen amen I say
to you whatever you
ask of the
Father[16.26] in my
name he will give
you. 24 Until now
you did not ask for
anything in my name.
Ask and you will
receive, so that
your joy will be
completed.

B_2
judgment, because
the ruler of this
world is being
judged. (12.31 & 47)
12"I still have
many things to say
to you, but you
cannot bear it yet.
13When he comes,
i.e., the spirit of
truth, he will guide
you with the whole
truth; for he will
not be talking on
his own but will be
speaking whatever he
hears and announcing
to you what things
are coming. 14He
will glorify me
because he will
receive from me and
announce to you.
15All that the
Father has is mine;
that is why I said
receives from me and
announces to you.
16A little while
and you will see me
no more, and again a
little while and you
will see me. (14.19;
16.19) 17Then some of
his disciples said
to one another,
"What is he saying
to us, this 'A
little while (16.18)
and you will not see
me, and again a
little while and you

NOTES

16.18"little while" - referring to 13.33-14.3.

16.19"I said a little while ago" - the Greek phrasing is virtually identical to 16.16, but its sense is different. Most translations seem to contaminate 16.19 with the sense of 16.16, as did the final editor of the gospel.

16.20This breaks abruptly from 16.19.

16.23bSee 1 Jn. 1.4

A

to the Father."
29His disciples
said, "See now you
are talking openly,"
and "You are not
saying any figures.
30Now we know that
you know everything
and have no need for
anyone to question
you. We believe
this, that you came
from divinity."
31Jesus answered
them, "Now you
believe! 32Look, an
hour is coming and
has come so that you
will be scattered
each to his own, and
will leave me alone.
And I am not alone
because the Father
is with me. 33I
have spoken these
things to you so
that you will have
peace in me. You
have distress in the
world; but have
courage, I have
overcome the world."

17

B_1

1Jesus had spoken
these words, and
having raised his
eyes to heaven he
said, "Father, the
hour(16.32) has come.
Glorify your son, so
that the son may
glorify you, 2since
you have given him
power over all
flesh, so that he
may give to them all
you have given him -
eternal life. 3But
this is eternal
life, that they know
you, the only true
God, and him whom
you sent, Jesus
Christ. 4I
glorified you on
earth, having
finished the work
that you gave me to
do. 5And now Father
glorify me in your
own presence with
the glory that I had
before the world was
in your presence.
6I showed your
name to the people
of the world whom
you gave me. They
were yours, and you
gave them to me, and
they have kept your
word. 7Now they
know that everything
you have given me is
from you, 8that the

B_2

11 And I am no longer
in the world, and
they are in the
world, and I am
coming to you.(17.13)
Holy Father, keep
them in your name,
which you have given
me, so that they may
be one, as we.(17.22)
12 When I was with
them, I kept them in
your name, which you
had given me, and I
guarded them, and
none of them
perished but the son
of destruction, to
fulfill the
scripture.

16 They are not of
the world, just as I
am not of the
world.(17.14)
17 Consecrate them in
truth. Your word is
truth. 18 As you
sent me into the
world, I also sent
them into the world.
19 And I consecrate
myself for them,
that they too may be
consecrated in
truth.

20 Not only for
these do I pray, but
also for those who
believe in me
because of their

NOTES

17.3 See 1 Jn. 5.20

17.11-12 This is post resurrection.

17.13 See 1 Jn. 1.4

17.14 See 1 Jn. 3.13

17.15 See 1 Jn. 5.18

A

18 [1]Having said
these things Jesus
went out with his
disciples across the
Kidron Valley, where
there was a garden
that he and his
disciples entered.
[2]But Judas, his
betrayer, also knew
the place since
Jesus often met
there with his
disciples. [3]So
Judas, taking the
cohort as well as
the constables from
the high priests and
Pharisees, came
there with lanterns,
torches, and
weapons. [4]So Jesus,
seeing all that was
coming upon him,
went out and said to
them, "Whom do you
seek?" [5]They
answered him, "Jesus
the Nazorean." He
said to them, "I am
he." But Judas, his
betrayer, was also
standing with them.
[6]Now when he said to
them, "I am he,"
they drew back and
fell down. [7]So he
asked them again,
"Whom do you seek?"
They said, "Jesus
the Nazorean."

B_1

words that you have
given me I have
given to them; and
they accept and
truly understand
that I came from
you; and they
believed that you
had sent me.
[9]I pray for them.
I do not pray for
the world but for
them whom you gave
me, since they are
yours. [10]And all
mine are yours, and
yours mine; and I
have been glorified
in them. [13]But now
I am coming to
you(17.11) and I speak
these things in the
world so that they
may have my joy
fulfilled in
themselves. [14]I
have given them your
word, and the world
hates them because
they are not of the
world, just as I am
not of the
world.(17.16) [15]I do
not pray that you
take them from the
world but that you
keep them from evil.
[22]And I have
given them the glory
that you gave me,
that they may be one
as we are one:(17.21)

B_2

word, [21]so that all
may be one, as you,
Father, in me and I
in you; that they
also may be
one;(17.22) that the
world would believe
that you sent
me.(17.23)
[24]Father,(17.25)
what you gave me - I
wish that those may
be with me where I
am, so that they may
see my glory, which
you have given me,
because you loved me
before the beginning
of the world.

NOTES

17.24"where I am" - the time is post resurrection.

18.6The arresting party seems ready to fight the disciples.

A

Jesus answered, "I
said to you that I
am he. So if you
are looking for me,
let these go."[G]
[10]Then Simon Peter,
who had a sword,
drew it and struck
the servant of the
high priest and
severed his right
ear. The servant's
name was Malchos.
[11]Then Jesus said to
Peter, "Sheathe the
sword. Am I not to
drink the cup that
my Father has given
me?" [H13]They led him
to Annas first; he
was the father-in-
law of Caiaphas, who
was high priest that
year. [24]Then Annas
sent him to Caiaphas
the high priest.
[15]Simon Peter
followed Jesus, as
well as another
disciple. That
disciple was known
to the high priest
and accompanied
Jesus into the high
priest's courtyard.
[16]But Peter was
standing outside
near the gate. So
the other disciple,
the one known to the
high priest, went
out and spoke to the

NOTES

[G9]This was to fulfill what he had said, "I did not lose any of those whom you gave me."

[18.13]"him" - the word is located at the end of 18.12.

[18.13]"that year" - high priests held office for life. Caiapha was in office from 18 to 36.

[H14](It was Caiaphas who counseled the Jews that it was useful for one man to die for the people.)

[18.24]The proposal here, that 18.24 followed 18.13-14, pertains to the primitive text, not to the final Gospel, as with a similar proposal often made.

[18.15]The fact that the author was known to the high priest may account for his dwelling on Judas being the betrayer.

C_1

[19]Then the high
priest questioned
Jesus about his
disciples and about
his teaching.
[20]Jesus answered
him, "I have spoken
openly to the world.
I always taught at
synagogue and in the
Temple, where all
the Jews gathered,
and I spoke nothing
in secret. [21]Why
are you questioning
me? Question those
who heard what I
told them. See,
these know what I
said to them."
[22]When Jesus had
said these things,
one of the
constables, standing
by, slapped him,
saying, "Is that a
way to answer the
high priest?"
[23]Jesus answered
him, "If I spoke
evilly, testify
about the evil. But
if well, why do you
hit me?"

NOTES

[18.23]18.24 seems moved here from after 18.14 giving Peter another occasion to deny Jesus. The proposal here puts both denials (18.17 & 25) in the courtyard of Caiaphas.

A

door mistress and
led Peter in.
[17]Then the girl, the
door mistress, said
to Peter, "Aren't
you too one of this
man's disciples?"
He said, "I am not."
[18]But the servants
and constables stood
around, having made
a charcoal fire
because it was cold,
and they were
warming themselves.
Peter was also with
them standing and
warming himself.[I]
[25b]So they said to
him, "Aren't you
also one of his
disciples?" He
denied it, and said,
"I am not." [26]One
of the high priest's
servants, a relative
of him whose ear
Peter severed, said,
"Didn't I see you in
the garden with
him?" [27]Again Peter
denied it, and
immediately a cock
crowed.
[28]Then they led
Jesus from Caiaphas
to the praetorium.
It was dawn, and
they did not enter
the praetorium, lest
they become impure,
but might eat the

NOTES

[I25a]Simon Peter was standing and warming himself.

A

Passover. [29]So
Pilate came out to
them: "What charge
do you bring against
this man?" [30]They
answered him, "If
this one were not
doing evil, we would
not have handed him
over to you. [31b]We
are not permitted to
kill anyone."[J] [33]Then
Pilate reentered the
praetorium, called
for Jesus, and said
to him, "Are you the
king of the Jews?"
[34]Jesus answered,
"Are you saying this
on your own, or did
others talk to you
about me?" [35]Pilate
answered, "Am I a
Jew? Your nation
and high priests
handed you over to
me. What did you
do?" [36]Jesus
answered, "My
kingdom is not of
this world." [37]Then
Pilate said to him,
"So are you a king?"
Jesus answered, "You
are saying that I am
a king. I was born
and I came into the
world for this: to
testify to the
truth. Everyone who
is of the truth
hears my call."

C_1

[31a]Pilate said to
them, "Take him
yourselves and judge
him according to
your Law." The Jews
said to him,

NOTES

[18.31a]Pilate's reply is illogical as a response to 18.30; it would be obvious that the Jerusalem authorities had already judged Jesus by their Law.

[J32]This was to fulfill the statement of Jesus indicating what kind of death he was about to die.

[18.33]The charge that Jesus would be a king may be replaced by 18.31a.

[18.37]"I was born..." - the Greek text sets "you" and "I" in contrast; I have phrased the translation to do the same. See Lk. 22.70b.

A

38 Pilate said to
him, "What is
truth?"

C_1

36b "If my kingdom
were of this world,
my constables would
be fighting so that
I would not be
handed over to the
Jews. But now my
kingdom is not from
here."
38b Again he went
out to the Jews and
said to them, "I
find no guilt in
him. 39 But it is
your custom that I
release someone to
you on the Passover;
counsel me then.
Should I release the
king of the Jews to
you?" 40 Then they
called out again,
"Not this one but
Barabbas." But
Barabbas was a
guerilla.

NOTES

18.36b The first clause repeats 18.36a. There is also "the Jews" on the lips of Jesus, a Jew, and Pilate's question in 18.37 would be illogical with this in the basic text.

18.38b-40 This does not seem to belong to the primitive text because "Jews" is used for the authorities. That text also explains customs in a narrator's voice, unlike this.

A

19 And having
said this [1]Pilate
then took Jesus and
had him scourged.
[2]And the soldiers,
after weaving a
crown out of thorns,
placed it on his
head and threw a
purple cloak around
him. And approach-
ing him they were
saying, "Hail, King
of the Jews!" And
they slapped him.
[4]And Pilate went
out again and said
to them, "Look, I am
leading him out to
you, that you may
know that I find no
guilt in him."
[5]Then Jesus came out
wearing the thorn
crown and the purple
cloak. And he said
to them, "Look at
the man." [6a]When
the high priests and
constables saw him
they called out,
"Crucify! Crucify!"
[13]Then Pilate,
having heard these
words, had Jesus led
out, and he sat down
on the judgment seat
at the place called
Stone Pavement (in
Hebrew, Gabbatha).
[14a]It was the day of

C_1

[6b]Pilate said to
them, "Take him
yourselves and
crucify; for I find
no guilt in him.(19.4)
[7]The Jews answered
him, "We have a Law,
and according to the
Law he must die,
since he made
himself a son of
divinity." [8]When
Pilate heard this he
was more fearful,
[9]and he entered the
praetorium again and
said to Jesus,
"Where are you
from?" But Jesus
gave him no answer.
[10]So Pilate said to
him, "Are you not
talking to me?
Don't you know that
I have power to free
you and I have power
to crucify you?"
[11]Jesus answered
him, "You have no
power over me except
what was given you
from above.
Therefore, he who
handed me over to

NOTES

[19.9]According to this
version, Jesus is
still in the
praetorium, contrary
to 19.5.

A

preparation for the Passover, about noon. [15b]Pilate said to them, "Shall I crucify your king?" The high priests answered, "We have no king but Caesar." [16]Then he handed him over to them to be crucified.

So they took Jesus, [17]and carrying the cross himself he went out to the Skull Place, as it is called (which in Hebrew is Golgotha), [18]where they crucified him and two others with him on either side but Jesus in the middle. [19]Pilate also wrote a notice and had it put on the cross; it read, "Jesus the Nazorean King of the Jews."

[23]Then the soldiers, when they had crucified Jesus, took his clothing and divided them four ways, a portion for each soldier, and the tunic. The tunic was seamless, woven in one piece from the top. [24]So they said to one another, "Let's not

C_1

to you has the greater guilt." [12]From this point Pilate sought to release him, but the Jews called out, "If you free this one you are no friend of Caesar. Everyone who makes himself king opposes Caesar." [14b]And he said to the Jews, "Look, your king."[(19.5)] [15a]Then they called out, "Away, away, crucify[(19.6a)] him."

[20]Many of the Jews read this notice, since the place where Jesus was crucified was near the city, and it had been written in Hebrew, Latin, and Greek. [21]So the high priests of the Jews said to Pilate, "Do not write, 'King of the Jews,' but "He said, "I am King of the Jews."'" [22]Pilate answered, "What I wrote I wrote."

A

cut it but cast lots
for it." This was
to fulfill the
scripture, which
says, "They divided
my clothing for
themselves, and they
rolled dice for my
garments." So this
is what the soldiers
did.
25 Jesus’ mother
and his mother’s
sister, Mary wife of
Clopas, and Mary
Magdalene stood by
his cross. 26 Seeing
his mother and the
disciple whom he
loved standing by,
Jesus said to his
mother, "Mother,
there is your son."
27 Next he said to
the disciple, "There
is your mother."
And from that hour
the disciple took
her into his own.
28 After this
Jesus, knowing that
all was then
finished, said in
order to fulfill the
scripture, "I
thirst." 29 A jug
full of oxos was
at hand; so placing
a sponge full of the
oxos on hyssop they
offered it to his
mouth. 30 Then when

NOTES

19.20 "the Jews." Note "where..." - this reads as if the name of the place were never given.

19.26 "Mother" as a respectful English address; lit. "Woman."

19.29 "oxos" - a common drink, vinegar wine, that was good for quenching thirst.

A

Jesus took the oxos
he said, "It is
done." And bowing
the head he handed
over the spirit.
32Then the
soldiers came and
broke the legs first
of the one and then
of the other
crucified with him.
33But when they came
to Jesus, as they
saw he had already
died, they did not
break his legs,
34But one of the
soldiers opened his
side with a spear,
and immediately
blood and water came
out. 35And he who
has testified had
seen, and his
testimony is true,
and he is saying
that he knows it to
be true so that you
may believe. 36For
these things
occurred to fulfill
the scripture, "Its
bone should not be
broken," 37and again
another scripture,
"They will look at
him whom they
pierced."
41There was a
garden in the place
where he was
crucified, and in

C_1

31Since it was a
preparation day,
lest the bodies
remain on the cross
on the Sabbath (for
that Sabbath was an
important day), the
Jews asked Pilate to
have the legs broken
and the bodies
removed.
38After these
events Joseph, who
was from Arimathaia,
a disciple of Jesus,
but secretly out of
fear of the Jews
asked Pilate if he
could remove the
body of Jesus, and
Pilate permitted it.
So he went and
removed his body.
39Nicodemos who had
come at first at
night, also came,
bringing about a
hundred pounds of a
mixture of myrrh and
aloes. 40Then they
took Jesus' body and
bound it in cloth
with the aromatics,
as is the custom
among the Jews for
burial.

NOTES

[M]of the Jews

A

20 [2b]...and went
to Simon Peter and
the other disciple,
whom Jesus made his
friend, and said to
them, "They took the
Lord from the tomb,
and we don't know
where they have put
him." [3]So Peter and
the other disciple
went out and were
going to the tomb.
[4]Both were running;
the other disciple
outran Peter and
came to the tomb
first, [5]and bending
down he saw the
cloth lieing around.
However, he did not
go in. [6]Then Simon
Peter also came,
following him, and
he went into the
tomb and saw the
cloth lying around,
[7]and the towel that
had been over the
head was not lieing
with the cloth but
was by itself looped
around in one place.
[8]Then the other
disciple who had
come to the tomb
first went in, saw,
and believed. [9]For
they did not yet
know the scripture
that says that he

C_1

[1]On the first day
of the week Mary
Magdelene came to
the tomb early when
it was still dark,
and she saw the
stone removed from
the tomb. [2a]So she
ran...

NOTES

[20.1]A fragment from a another version; it speaks of a stone not mentioned before and does not have her look into the tomb though she later reports that the body was missing. See Lk. 24.1.

[20.2b]"we" - the speaker plus the two disciples. A different verb than usual is used to describe Jesus' favor for the disciple: *phileo* (before used to refer to Lazarus).

A

had to rise from the dead. [10]Then the disciples went home again.

C_1

[11]Mary stood outside near the tomb weeping. Then as she wept she bent down into the tomb [12]and saw two angels in white sitting, one at the head and one at the feet of where Jesus' body had lain. [13]And they said to her, "Madam, why are you crying?" She said to them, "They took my Lord away, and I do not know where they put him." [14]After saying these words she turned back and saw Jesus standing, and she did not know that it was Jesus. [15]Jesus said to her, "Madam, why are you crying? Who are you looking for?" She, presuming it to be the gardener, said to him, "Sir, if you carried him off, tell me where you put him, and I will take him." [16]Jesus said to her, "Mary." Turning she said to him in Hebrew, "Rabbouni!" (which means teacher). [17]Jesus said to her, "Don't cling to me,

C_1

for I have not yet
ascended to the
Father. But go to
my brothers and tell
them, 'I am
ascending to my
Father and your
Father, my divinity
and your divinity.'"
[18]Mary Magdelene
went announcing to
the disciples, "I
have seen the Lord,"
and the things he
said to her.
[19]When it was
evening on that
first day of the
week, when the
disciples were
behind closed doors
out of fear of the
Jews, Jesus came and
stood among them and
said, "Peace to
you." [20]Having said
this he showed the
hands and the side
to them. So the
disciples rejoiced
at seeing the Lord.
[21]Then Jesus said to
them again, "Peace
to you. As the
Father has sent me I
am also sending
you." [22]And having
said this he
breathed on them and
said, "Receive Holy
Spirit. [23]Whoever's
sins you forgive are

C_1

forgiven for them,
whoever's you retain
are retained."
[24]But one of the
twelve, Thomas,
called the Twin, was
not with them when
Jesus came. [25]So
the other disciples
were saying to him,
"We have seen the
Lord," but he said
to them, "Unless I
see the mark of the
nails in his hands
and place my finger
into the mark of the
nails and place my
hand into his side,
I will not believe."
[26]And after eight
days his disciples
were indoors again,
Thomas with them.
Jesus came though
the doors were
closed, and stood
among them and said,
"peace to you."
[27]Then he said to
Thomas, "Reach out
with your finger
here and see my
hands, and reach out
with your hand and
place it into my
side, and do not
become unbelieving
but believing.
[28]Thomas answered
him, "My Lord and my
God!" [29]Jesus said

C_1

to him, "Have you
believed because you
have seen me?
Blessed those who do
not see and are
believing."

30Jesus did many
other signs indeed
before his disciples
that are not written
in this book.

A_1

21

1After these
events Jesus
appeared[N] to the
disciples near the
Sea of Tiberias. He
appeared thusly:

2Simon Peter,
Thomas called the
Twin, Nathaniel from
Cana of Galilee,
Zebedee's sons, and
two others from his
disciples were
together.
3Simon
Peter said to them,
"I am going
fishing." They said
to him, "We are
coming with you
too." They went out
and climbed into the
boat, and that night
they caught nothing.
4But at dawn Jesus
already came to be
standing on the

B

31But these have
been written so that
you may believe that
Jesus is the Christ,
the son of God, and
that believing you
may have life in his
name.

NOTES

[20.19c]See Lk. 24.36.

[20.19-29]See Acts 13.31.

[20.31]See 1 Jn. 5.13

[N]again

A_1

shore; however, the
disciples didn't
know that it was
Jesus. 5Then Jesus
said to them, "Boys,
do you have any
fish?" They
answered him, "No."
6He said to them,
"Cast the net to the
right side of the
boat and you will
find." So they were
casting and they
were not strong
enough to haul in
any longer from the
abundance of fish.
7Then that disciple
whom Jesus loved
said to Peter, "It
is the Lord."
Hearing that it was
the Lord, Simon
Peter tied the outer
garment around
himself (for he was
stripped) and dove
into the sea. 8But
the other disciples
went by boat towing
the nets of fish,
for they were not
far from the land
but out about a
hundred yards.
9When they landed
they saw a charcoal
fire and fish lieing
on it, and bread.
10Jesus said to
them, "Take from the

A_1

fish that you just
caught." 11Then
Simon Peter went up
and hauled the net
ashore, full with a
hundred and fifty-
three big fish - and
with so many the net
was not torn.
12Jesus said to
them, "Come have
breakfast." But
none of the
disciples presumed
to question him,
"Who are you?"
seeing that it was
the Lord. 13Jesus
came and took the
bread and gave to
them, and likewise
the fish.[0]

15When they had
breakfast Jesus said
to Simon Peter,
"Simon Johnson, do
you love me more, or
these?" He said to
him, "Yes sir, you
know I make you a
friend." He said to
him, "Feed my
lambs," 16He said
to him a second

NOTES

[0]This was now the
third time Jesus
appeared to the
disciples, having
risen from the dead.

A_1

time, "Simon
Johnson, do you love
me?" He said to
him, "Yes sir, you
know that I make you
a friend." He said
to him, "Tend my
sheep." [17]He said
to him a third time,
"Simon Johnson, do
you make me a
friend?" Peter was
troubled that he
said to him a third
time, "Do you make
me a friend?" And
he said to him,
"Sir, you know
everything, you
understand that I
make you a friend."
Jesus said to him,
"Feed my sheep."
[19b]And having said
this he said to him,
"Follow me."
[20]Turning around
Peter saw the
disciple whom Jesus
loved following, who
also leaned at the
dinner on his chest
and said, "Sir, who
is it who is
betraying you?"
[21]So seeing him
Peter said to Jesus,
"Sir, what about
him?" [22]Jesus said
to him, "If I want
him to remain until
I come, what is that

B

[18]Amen amen I say to
you, when you were
young you girded
yourself and walked
where you wished;
but when you are old
you will stretch out
your hands and
another will gird
you and will bring
you where you do not
wish.[T]

to you? Follow
me." [23]Then this
saying spread among
the brothers that
this disciple will
not die. But Jesus
did not say that he
will not die but "If
I want him to remain
until I come, what
is that to you?"
[24a]This is the
disciple testifying
about these things
and who wrote them.[U]
But there are also
many other things
Jesus did, which if
written down one-by-
one I suppose the
world itself would
not have room for
the books that would
be written.

NOTES

[T19a]He said this to indicate by what death he would glorify God.

[U24b]And we know that his testimony is true.

Bibliography in the Sociology of Early Christianity

The works that are directly pertinent to this study are given in the end notes to the chapters. The scholarly commentaries on the Gospel of John provide extensive lists of works on that gospel; a characteristic feature of New Testament studies that social scientists and other readers will observe is that field's obsession with bibliographic adumbrationism. The purpose of this bibliography is to suggest useful background sources in the sociology of early Christianity - both the Jesus movement in Palestine in the 30s and the early Christian movement from the 40s onward.

Bartlett, David L.
"John G. Gager's 'Kingdom and Community': A summary and response." _Zygon. Journal of Religion and Science_ 13 (1978): 109-122.

Barton, Stephen C.
"Paul and the cross: A sociological approach." _Theology_ 85 (1982): 13-19.

Barton, Stephen C.
"Paul and the resurrection: A sociological approach." _Religion_ 14 (1984): 67-75.

Bendix, Reinhard
"Umbildungen des persönlichen Charismas. Eine Anwendung von Max Webers Charismabegriff auf das Frühchristentum." In Wolfgang Schluchter (ed.), _Max Webers Sicht des antiken Christentums. Interpretation und Kritik_. Frankfurt am Main: Suhrkamp, 1985, pp. 404-443.

Berger, Klaus
"Wissenssoziologie und Exegese des Neuen Tetaments." Kairos 19 (1977): 124-133.

Best, Thomas F.
"The sociological study of the New Testament: Promise and peril of a new discipline." Scottish Journal of Theology 36 (1983): 181-194.

Blasi, Anthony J.
"Role structures in the early Hellenistic church." Sociological Analysis 47:3: (1986) 226-248.

Blasi, Anthony J.
Early Christianity as a Social Movement. Bern and New York: Peter Lang, 1988.

Blasi, Anthony J.
Making Charisma. The Social Construction of Paul's Public Image. New Brunswick, New Jersey: Transaction, 1991.

Blasi, Anthony J.
"The more basic method in the sociology of early Christianity." Foundations & Facets Forum 9;1/2 (1993): 7-18.

Blasi, Anthony J.
"Office charisma in early Christian Ephesus." Sociology of Religion 56:3 (1995): 245-255.

Braun, Willi
Feasting and Social Rhetoric in Luke 14. New York: Cambridge University Press, 1995.

Bryant, Joseph M.
"The sect-church dynamic and Christian expansion in the Roman Empire: Persecution, penitential discipline, and schism in sociological perspective." British Journal of Sociology 44:2 (1993): 303-332.

Case, Shirley Jackson
The Evolution of Early Christianity. A Genetic Study of First-Century Christianity in Relation to Its Religious Environment. Chicago: University of Chicago Press, 1914.

Case, Shirley Jackson
The Social Origins of Christianity. Chicago: University of Chicago Press, 1923. [New York: Cooper Square, 1975]

Corley, Kathleen E.
Private Women, Public Meals. Social Conflict in the Synoptic Tradition. Peabody, Massachusetts: Hendrickson Publishers, 1993.

deSilva, David A.
"The Revelation to John: A case study in apocalyptic propaganda and the maintenance of sectarian identity." Sociological Analysis 53:4 (1992): 375-395.

DeSilva, David A.
"The construction and social function of a counter-cosmos in the Revelation of John." Foundations & Facets Forum 9:1/2 (1993): 47-61.

Duhaime, Jean
"L'univers social des premiers chrétiens d'après J.G. Gager." Social Compass 39:2 (1992): 207-219.

Duling, Dennis C.
"Insights from sociology for New Testament Christology: A test case." Society of Biblical Literature 1985 Seminar Papers 24 (1985): 351-368.

Ebertz, Michael N.
Das Charisma des Gekreuzigten. Zur Soziologie der Jesusbewegung. Tübingen: Mohr-Siebeck, 1987.

Ebertz, Michael N.
"Le stigmate du mouvement charismatique autour de Jésus de Nazareth." Social Compass 39:2 (1992): 255-273.

Edwards, Lyford P.
The Transformation of Early Christianity from an Eschatological to a Socialized Movement. Ph.D. thesis, University of Chicago. Menashe, Wisconsin: George Banta Publishing, 1919.

Edwards, O. C., Jr.
"Sociology as a tool for interpreting the New Testament." Anglican Theological Review 65 (1983): 431-446.

Elliott, John H.
A Home for the Homeless: A Sociological Exegesis of 1 Peter, Its Situation and Strategy. Philadelphia: Fortress, 1981.

Elliott, John H.
"Social-scientific criticism of the New Testament: More on methods and models." Semeia 35 (1986): 1-33.

Elliott, John A.
What Is Social-Scientific Criticism? Minneapolis: Fortress Press, 1993.

Esler, Philip Francis
Community and Gospel in Luke-Acts. The Social and Political Motivations of Lucan Theology. Cambridge: Cambridge University Press, 1987.

Esler, Philip Francis
"Political oppression in Jewish apocalyptic literature: A social-scientific approach." Listening. Journal of Religion and Culture 28:3 (1993): 181-199.

Esler, Philip Francis
The First Christians in their Social Worlds. Social-scientific approaches to New Testament interpretation. London: Routledge, Inc., 1994.

Fenn, Richard K.
The Death of Herod. An Essay in the Sociology of Religion. Cambridge: Cambridge University Press, 1992.

Fernandez Vargas, Valentina
"El púlpito como medio de communicación de masas. Los primeros tiempos: La génesis de la unificación Iglesia-Estado." Revista Intrnacional de Sociologia 37/29 (1979): 105-116.

Funk, Aloys
Status und Rollen in der Paulusbriefen. Eine inhaltsanalytische Untersuchung zur Religionssoziologie. Innsbruck: Tyrolia-Verlag, 1981.

Gager, John G.
Kingdom and Community. The Social World of Early Christianity. Englewood Cliffs, New Jersey: Prentice-Hall, 1975.

Gager, John G.
"Social description and sociological explanation in the study of early Christianity: A review essay." Religious Studies Review 5 (1979): 174-180. [Also in Norman Gottwald (ed.), Bible and Liberation. Political and Social Hermeneutics (Maryknoll, New York: Orbis, 1983), pp. 428-440.]

Gager, John G.
"Shall we marry our enemies? Sociology and the New Testament." Interpretation 36 (1982): 256-265.

Gewalt, Dietfried
"Neutestamentliche Exegese und Soziologie." Evangelische Theologie 31 (1971): 87-99.

Gooch, Peter D.
Dangerous Food. 1 Corinthians 8-10 in Its Context. Waterloo, Ontario: Wilfrid Laurier University Press, 1993.

Gottwald, Norman K.
"Social class as an analytic and hermeneutical category in biblical studies." Journal of Biblical Literature 112:1 (1993): 3-22.

Hadot, Jean
"Contestation socio-religieuse et apocalyptique dans le judéo-christianisme." Archives de Sociologie des Religions 24 (1967): 35-47.

Harrington, Daniel J.
"Sociological concepts and the early church: A decade of research." Theological Studies 41 (1980): 181-190.

Hock, Ronald F.
"Paul's tentmaking and the problem of his social class." Journal of Biblcial Literature 97 (1978): 555-564.

Hock, Ronald F.
"The workshop as a social setting for Paul's missionary preaching." Catholic Biblical Quarterly 41 (1979): 439-450.

Hock, Ronald F.
The Social Context of Paul's Ministry. Tentmaking and Apostleship. Philadelphia: Fortress, 1980.

Holmberg, Bengt
Paul and Power. The Structure of Authority in the Primitive Church as Reflected in the Pauline Epistles. Philadelphia: Fortress, 1980.

Holmberg, Bengt
"Sociological versus theological analysis of the question concerning a Pauline church order." In Sigfred Pedersen (ed.), Die paulinische Literatur und Theologie. Göttingen: Vandenhoeck & Ruprecht, 1980, pp. 187-200.

Holmberg, Bengt
Sociology and the New Testament. An Appraisal. Minneapolis: Fortress, 1990.

Horsley, Richard A.
"Popular prophetic movements at the time of Jesus, their principal features and social origins." Journal for the Study of the New Testament 26 (1986): 3-27.

Horsley, Richard A.
Sociology and the Jesus Movement. New York: Crossroad, 1989.

Houtart, François
Religion et modes de production précapitalistes. Bruxelles: Éditions de l'Université des Bruxelles, 1980.

Jaquette, James L.
Discerning What Counts. The Function of the Adiaphora Topos in Paul's Letters. Atlanta: Scholars Press, 1995.

Judge, Edwin A.
"The early Christians as a scholastic community." Journal of Religious History 1 (1960): 4-15, 125-137. ["Die frühen Christen als scholastische Gemeinschaft." In Wayne A.

Meeks (ed.), Zur Soziologie des urchristentums. Ausgewählte Beiträge zum frühchristlichen Gemeinschaftsleben in seiner gesellschaftlichen Umwelt (München, 1979), pp. 131-164.]

Judge, Edwin A.
The Social Pattern of Christian Groups in the First Century. Some Prolegomena to the Study of New Testament Ideas of Social Obligation. London: Tyndale, 1960.

Judge, Edwin A.
"The social identity of the first Christians: A question of method in religious history." Journal of Religious History 11 (1980): 201-217.

Keck, Leander E.
"On the ethos of early Christians." Journal of the Amrican Academy of Religion 42 (1974): 435-452. ["Das Ethos der frühen Christen." In Wayne A. Meeks (ed.), Zur Soziologie des Urchristentums. Ausgewählte Beiträge zum frühchristlichen Gemeinschaftsleben in seiner gesellschaftlichen Umwelt (München, 1979), pp. 13-36.

Kee, Howard Clark
Christian Origins in Sociological Perspective. Philadelphia: Westminster, 1980.

Kee, Howard Clark
Miracle in the Early Christian World. A Study in Sociohistorical Method. New Haven: Yale University Press, 1983.

Kee, Howard Clark
Knowing the Truth: A Sociological Approach to New Testament Interpretation. Minneapolis: Fortress, 1989.

Kee, Howard Clark
"Changing modes of leadership in the New Testament period." Social Compass 39:2 (1992): 241-254.

Kraemer, Ross Shepard
Her Share of the Blessings. Women's Religions Among Pagans, Jews, and Christians in the Greco-Roman World. New York: Oxford Univrsity Press, 1992.

Kreissig, Heinz
"Zur sozialen Zusammensetzung der frühchristlichen Gemeinden im ersten Jahrhundert u.z." Eirene. Studia Graeca et Latina 6 (1967): 91-100.

Kümmel, W. G.
"Das Urchristentum II. Arbeiten zur Spezialproblemen. b. Zur Sozialgeschichte und Soziologie der Urkirche." Theologische Rundschau 50 (1985): 327-363.

Kyrtatas, Dimitris J.
The Social Structure of the Early Christian Communities. London and New York: Verso, 1987.

Kyrtatas, Dimitris J.
"Prophets and priests in early Christianity: Production and transmission of religious knowledge from Jesus to John Chrysostom." International Sociology 3:4 (1988): 365-384.

Kyrtatas, Dimitris J.
"Slavery as progress: Pagan and Christian views of slavery as moral training." International Sociology 10:2 (1995): 219-234.

Lamb, Ruby Lee (Mrs. John M. Miner)
The First Three Years of Paul's Career as a Christian. Unpublished M.A. dissertation, University of Chicago, 1908.

Lampe, Peter
Die stadtrömischen Christen in den ersten beiden Jahrhunderten. Tübingen: Mohr, 1988.

Laub, Franz
"Sozialgeschichtlicher Hintergrund und ekklesiologische Relevanz der neutestamentlich-frühchristlichen Haus- und Gemeinde-Tafelparänese - ein Beitrag zur Soziologie des Frühchristentums." Münchener theologische Zeitschrift 37 (1986): 249-271.

Levine, Amy-Jill
The Social and Ethnic Dimensions of Matthean Social History: "Go nowhre among the Gentiles..." (Matt. 10:5b). Lewiston, New York: Edwin Mellen, 1988.

Lohmeyer, Ernst
Soziale Fragen im Urchristentums. Leipzig: Quelle & Meyer, 1921. [Darmstadt: Wissensschaftliche Buchgesellschaft, 1973.]

MacDonald, Margaret Y.
The Pauline Churches. A Socio-Historical Study of Institutionalization in the Pauline and Deutero-Pauline Writings. Cambridge: Cambridge University Press, 1988.

MacDonald, Margaret Y.
"Early Christian women married to unbelievers." Studies in Religion/Sciences religieuses 19:2 (1990): 221-234.

Maier, Harry O.
"The charismatic authority of Ignatius of Antioch: A sociological analysis." Studies in Religion/Sciences Religieuses 18:2 (1989): 185-199.

Maier, Harry O.
The Social Setting of the Ministry as Reflected in the Writings of Hermas, Clement,

and Ignatius. Waterloo, Ontario: Wilfrid Laurier University Press, 1991.

Malherbe, Abraham J.
Social Aspects of Early Christianity. Baton Rouge: Louisiana State University Press, 1977. [Second enlarged edition. Philadelphia: Fortress, 1983.]

Mantzaridis, Georges
"La naissance du dogme relatif à l'unité de l'Église." Social Compass 22:1 (1975): 19-32.

Meeks, Wayne A.
"The man from heaven in Johannine sectarianism." Journal of Biblical Literature 91 (1972): 44-72.

Meeks, Wayne A.
"The social context of Pauline theology." Interpretation 36 (1982): 266-277.

Meeks, Wayne A.
The First Urban Christians. The Social World of the Apostle Paul. New Haven, Connecticut: Yale University Press, 1983.

Messelken, Karl-Heinz
"Zur Durchsetzung des Christentums in der Spätantike. Strukturell-funktionale Analyse eines historischen Gegenstandes." Kölner Zeitschrift für Soziologie und Sozialpsychologie 29:2 (1977): 261-294.

Moxnes, Halvor
"Sociology and the New Testament." In Erik Karlsaune (ed.), Religion as a Social Phenomenon. Theologians and Sociologists Sharing Research Interests. Trondheim: Tapir, 1988, pp. 143-159.

Murvar, Vatro
"Towards a sociological theory of religious movements." Journal for the Scientific Study of Religion 14:3 (1975): 229-256.

Nielsen, Donald A.
"Max Weber and the sociology of early Christianity." In William H. Swatos, Jr. (ed.), Time, Place, and Circumstance. Neo-Weberian Studies in Comparative Religious History. New York: Greenwood, 1990, pp. 87-102.

Oakman, Douglas E.
Jesus and the Economic Questions of His Day. Lewiston, New York: Edwin Mellen Press, 1986.

Osiek, Carolyn
Rich and Poor in the Shepherd of Hermas: An Exegetical Social Investigation. Washington: Catholic Biblical Association, 1983.

Osiek Carolyn
What Are They Saying about the Social Setting of the New Testament? New York: Paulist, 1984.

Osiek, Carolyn
"The second century through the eyes of Hermas: Continuity and change." Biblical Theology Bulletin 20:3 (1990): 116-122.

Overman, J. Andrew
Matthew's Gospel and Formative Judaism: The Social World of the Matthean Community. Minneapolis: Fortress, 1990.

Petersen, Norman R.
Rediscovering Paul; Philemon and the Sociology of Paul's Narrative World. Philadelphia: Fortress, 1985.

Petersen, Norman R.
The Gospel of John and the Sociology of Light. Language and Characterization in the Fourth Gospel. Valley Forge, Pennsylvania: Trinity Press International, 1993.

Powell, Jefferson
"Social theory as exegetical tool." Foundations & Facets Forum 5:4 (1989): 27-40.

Richter, Philip J.
"Recent sociological approaches to the study of the New Testament." Religion 14 (1984): 77-90.

Riddle, Donald W.
"The martyr motif in the Gospel According to Mark." Journal of Religion 4 (1924): 397-410.

Riddle, Donald W.
"Environment as a factor in the achievement of self-consciousness in early Christianity." Journal of Religion 7 (1927): 146-163.

Riddle, Donald W.
"From apocalypse to martyrology." Anglican Theological Review 9:3 (1927): 260-280.

Riddle, Donald W.
"The messages of the Shepherd of Hermas: A study in social control." Journal of Religion 7 (1927): 561-577.

Riddle, Donald W.
The Martyrs: A Study in Social Control. Chicago: University of Chicago Press, 1931.

Riddle, Donald W.
"Die Verfolgungslogien in formgeschichtlicher und soziologischer Beleuchtung." Zeitschrift für die neutestamentliche Wissenschaft 33 (1934): 271-289.

Riddle, Donald W.
"Early Christian hospitality: A factor in the Gospel transmission." Journal of Biblical Literature 57 (1938): 151-154.

Rodd, Cyril S.
"On applying a sociological theory to bibical studies." Journal for the Study of the Old Testament 19 (1981): 95-106.

Rohrbaugh, Richard L.
"Methodological considerations in the debate over the social class status of early Christians." Journal of the American Academy of Religion 52 (1984): 519-546.

Rohrbaugh, Richard L.
"'Social location of thought' as a heuristic construct in New Testament study." Journal for the Study of the New Testament 30 (1987): 103-119.

Rowland, Christopher
"Reading the New Testament sociologically: An introduction." Theology 88 (1985): 358-364.

Rudolph, Kurt
"Randerscheinungen des Judentums und das Problem der Entstehung des Gnostizismus." Kairos 9:2 (1967): 105-122.

Russell, Ronald
"The idle in 2 Thess 3.6-12: An eschatological or a social problem?" New Testament Studies 34 (1988): 105-119.

Saldarini, Anthony J.
"The Gospel of Matthew and Jewish-Christian conflict." In David L. Balch (ed.), Social History of the Matthean Community. Cross-Disciplinary Approaches. Minneapolis: Fortress, 1991, pp. 38-61.

Saldarini, Anthony J.
Matthew's Christian-Jewish Community. Chicago: University of Chicago Press, 1993.

Sanders, Jack T.
Schismatics, Sectarians, Dissidents, Deviants: The First One Hundred Years of Jewish-Christian Relations. Valley Forge, Pennsylvania: Trinity Press International; London: SCM, 1993.

Schluchter, Wolfgang (ed.)
Max Webers Sicht des antiken Christentums. Frankfurt am Main: Suhrkamp, 1985.

Schoenfeld, Eugen
"Justice: An illusive concept in Christianity." Review of Religious Research 30:3 (1989): 236-245.

Schöllgen, Georg
Ecclesia sordida? Zur Frage der sozialen Schichtung frühchristlicher Gemeinden am Beispiel Karthagos zur Zeit Tertullians. Münster: Aschendorff, 1984.

Schöllgen, Georg
"Was wissen wir über die Sozialstruktur der paulinischen Gemeinden?" New Testament Studies 34 (1988): 71-82.

Schreiber, Alfred
Die Gemeinde in Korinth. Versuch einer gruppendynamischen Betrachtung der Entwicklung der Gemeinde von Korinth auf der Basis des ersten Korintherbriefs. Münster: Aschendorff, 1977.

Schütz, John Howard
"Charisma and social reality in primitive Christianity." Journal of Religion 54 (1974): 51-7.

Schütz, John Howard
Paul and the Anatomy of Apostolic Authority. Cambridge: Cambridge University Press, 1975.

Scroggs, Robin
"The earliest Christian communities as sectarian movement." in _Christianity, Judaism and Other Greco-Roman Cults. Studies for Morton Smith at Sixty_, Vol. II. Leiden, 1975, pp. 1-23.

Scroggs, Robin
"The sociological interpretation of the New Testament: The present state of research." _New Testament Studies_ 26 (1980): 164-179.

Smith, Robert H.
"Were the first Christians middle-class? A sociological analysis of the New Testament." _Currents in Theology and Mission_ 7:5 (1980): 260-276. [Also in Norman Gottwald (ed.), _The Bible and Liberation_ (Maryknoll, New York: Orbis Books, 1983), pp. 441-457.]

Stambaugh, John E., and David L. Balch
The New Testament in Its Social Environment. Philadelphia: Westminster, 1986.

Staples, Peter
"The cultural management of space and time in the narrative of the Gospel of Mark." _Foundations & Facets Forum_ 9:1/2 (1993): 19-45.

Stark, Rodney
"Jewish conversion and the rise of Christianity: Rethinking received wisdom." In Kent Harold Richards (ed.), _Society of Biblical Literature Seminar Papers_. Atlanta: Scholars Press, 1986, pp. 314-329.

Stark, Rodney
"The class basis of early Christianity: Inferences from a sociological model." Sociological Analysis 47:3 (1986): 216-225.

Stark, Rodney
"Antioch as the social situation for Matthew's gospel." In David L. Balch (ed.), Social History of the Matthean Community. Cross-Disciplinary Approaches. Minneapolis: Fortress, 1991, pp. 189-210.

Stark, Rodney
"Christianizing the urban empire: An analysis based on 22 Greco-Roman cities." Sociological Analysis 52:1 (1991): 77-88.

Stark, Rodney
"Reconstructing the rise of Christianity: The role of women." Sociology of Religion 56:3 (1995): 229-244.

Stowers, Stanley Kent
"Social status, public speaking and private teaching: The circumstances of Paul's preaching activity." Novum Testamentum 26 (1984): 59-82.

Stowers, Stanley Kent
"The social sciences and the study of early Christianity." In William S. Green (ed.), Approaches to Ancient Judaism. Atlanta: Scholars Press, 1985, pp. 149-181.

Taylor, Nicholas H.
Paul, Antioch and Jerusalem: A Study in Relationships and Authority in Earliest Christianity. (Journal for the Study of the New Testament, Supplement Series 66). Sheffield: JSOT Press, 1992.

Taylor, Nicholas H.
"The social nature of conversion in the early Christian world." In Philip F. Esler (ed.), Modelling Early Christianity. Social-scientific studies of the New Testament in its context. London and New York: Routledge, 1995, pp. 128-136.

Theissen, Gerd
"Wanderradikalismus: Literatursoziologische Aspekte der Überlieferung von Worten Jesu im Urchristentum." Zeitschrift für Theologie und Kirche 70 (1973): 245-271. [Also in Gerd Theissen, Studien zur Soziologie des Urchristentums. Wissenschaftliche Untersuchungen zum Neuen Testament 19 (Tübingen: Mohr, 1979); "Itinerant radicalism: The tradition of Jesus sayings from the perspective of the sociology of literature." In Norman K. Gottwald and Antoinette C. Wire (eds.), The Bible and Liberation: Political and Social Hermeneutics (Berkeley: Community for Religious Research and Education, 1976), pp. 106-141.]

Theissen, Gerd
"Soziale Integration und sakramentales Handeln: Eine Analyse von 1 Cor. 11: 17-34." Novum Testamentum 16 (1974): 179-206. [English translation in Gerd Theissen, The Social Setting of Pauline Christianity. Essays on Corinth (Philadelphia: Fortress, 1982), pp. 145-174.

Theissen, Gerd
"Soziale Schichtung in der korinthischen Gemeinde: Eine Beitrage zur Soziologie des hellenistischen Urchristentums." Zeitschrift für die neutestamentliche Wissenschaft und die Kunde der älteren Kirche 65 (1974): 232-272. [English translation in Gerd Theissen, The Social Setting of Pauline Christianity. Essays on Corinth (Philadelphia: Fortress,

1982), pp. 69-119.]

Theissen, Gerd
"Theoretische Probleme religionssoziologischer Forschung und die Analyse des Urchristentums." Neue Zeitschrift für Systematische Theologie und Religionsphilosophie 16:1 (1974): 35-56.

Theissen, Gerd
"Die soziologische Auswertung religiöser Überlieferungen: Ihre methodologischen Probleme am Beispiel des Urchristentums." Kairos 17 (1975): 284-299. [English translation in Gerd Theissen, The Social Setting of Pauline Christianity. Essays on Corinth (Philadelphia: Fortress, 1982), pp. 175-200.]

Theissen, Gerd
"Die Starken und Schwachen in Korinth: Soziologische Analyse eines theologischen Streites." Evangelische Theologie 35 (1975): 155-172. [English translation in Gerd Theissen, The Social Setting of Pauline Christianity. Essays on Corinth (Philadelphia: Fortress, 1982), pp. 121-143.]

Theissen, Gerd
"Legitimation und Lebensunterhalt: Ein Beitrage zur Soziologie urchristlicher Missionare." New Testament Studies 21 (1975): 192-221. [English translation in Gerd Theissen, The Social Setting of Pauline Christianity. Essays on Corinth (Philadelphia: Fortress, 1982), pp. 27-67.]

Theissen, Gerd
"Die Tempelwiessagung Jesu: Prophetie im Spannungsfeld von Stadt und Land." Theologische Zeitschrift 32 (1976): 144-158. [Also in Gerd Theissen, Studien zur Soziologie des Urchristentums.

Wissenschaftliche Untersuchungen zum Neuen Testament 19 (Tübingen: Mohr, 1979), pp. 142-159.]

Theissen, Gerd
Soziologie der Jesusbewegung: Ein Beitrag Zur Entstehungsgeschichte des Urchristentums. Theologische Existenz heut 194. München: Chr. Kaiser Verlag, 1977. [Sociology of Early Palestinian Christianity, translated by John Bowden (Philadelphia: Fortress, 1978); The First Followers of Jesus (London: SCM, 1978).]

Theissen, Gerd
"'Wir haben alles verlassen' (Mc X, 28): Nachfolge und soziale Entwurzelung in der jüdisch-palestinischen Gesellschaft des 1. Jahrhunderts N. Chr." Novum Testamentum 27 (1977): 161-196. [Also in Gerd Theissen, Studien zur Soziologie des Urchristentums. Wissenschaftliche Untersuchungen zum Neuen Testament 19 (Tübingen: Mohr, 1979), pp. 106-141.]

Theissen, Gerd
Studien zur Soziologie des Urchristentums. Wissenschaftliche Untersuchungen zum Neuen Testament 19. Tübingen: Mohr, 1979.

Theissen, Gerd
The Social Setting of Pauline Chrsitianity. Essays on Corinth. Philadelphia: Fortress, 1982.

Thompson, Leonard
"A sociological analysis of tribulation in the Apocalypse of John." Semeia 36 (1986): 147-174.

Tidball, Derek
An Introduction to the Sociology of the New Testament. Exeter: Paternoster, 1983. [The

Social Context of the New Testament (Grand Rapids, Michigan: Zondervan, 1984.)]

Vaage, Leif E.
Galilean Upstarts. Jesus' First Followers According to Q. Valley Forge, Pennsylvania: Trinity Press International, 1994.

Venetz, H.-J.
"Der Beitrag der Soziologie zur lektüre des Neuen Testaments. Ein Bericht." Methoden der Evangelienexeges. Theologische Berichte XIII (Zürich, 1985) pp. 87-121.

Verner, David C.
The Household of God: The Social World of the Pastoral Epistles. Chico, California: Scholars Press, 1983.

Wackenheim, Charles
"Trois initiateurs: Engels, Weber, Troeltsch." Social Compass 39:2 (1992): 183-205.

Wallis, Louis
"Sociological significance of the Bible." American Journal of Sociology 12 (1907): 532-552.

Wallis, Louis
"Sociology and theism." American Journal of Sociology 12 (1907): 838-844.

Wallis, Louis
A Sociological Study of the Bible. Chicago: University of Chicago Press, 1912.

Watson, Francis
Paul, Judaism and the Gentiles. A Sociological Approach. Cambridge: Cambridge University Press, 1986.

Wiefel, Wolfgang
"Erwägungen zur soziologischen Hermeneutic urchristlicher Gottesdienstformen." Kairos 14:1 (1972): 36-51.

Williams, D. H.
"The origins of the Montanist movement: A sociological analysis." Religion 19 (1989): 331-351.

Wire, Antoinette Clark
"Gender roles in a scribal community." In David L. Balch (ed.), Social History of the Matthean Community. Cross-Disciplinary Approaches. Minneapolis: Fortress, 1991, pp. 87-121.

Wuellner, W. H.
"The sociological implications of I Corinthians 1: 26-28 reconsidered." Studia Evangelica 6 (1973): 666-672.

Zeitlin, Irving M.
Jesus and the Judaism of His Time. Cambridge, England: Polity Press, 1988.

Zeitlin, Irving M.
1990
"Understanding the man Jesus. A historical-sociological approach." Ultimate Reality and Meaning 13:3 (1990): 164-176.

Index of Names

Index of Topics

Biblical Citations

TEXTS AND STUDIES IN RELIGION

1. Elizabeth A. Clark, **Clement's Use of Aristotle: The Aristotelian Contribution to Clement of Alexandria's Refutation of Gnosticism**
2. Richard DeMaria, **Communal Love at Oneida: A Perfectionist Vision of Authority, Property and Sexual Order**
3. David F. Kelly, **The Emergence of Roman Catholic Medical Ethics in North America: An Historical-Methodological-Bibliographical Study**
4. David A. Rausch, **Zionism Within Early American Fundamentalism, 1878-1918: A Convergence of Two Traditions**
5. Janine Marie Idziak, **Divine Command Morality: Historical and Contemporary Readings**
6. Marcus Braybrooke, **Inter-Faith Organizations, 1893-1979: An Historical Directory**
7. L. Wm. Countryman, **The Rich Christian in the Church of the Early Empire: Contradictions and Accommodations**
8. Irving Hexham (ed.), **The Irony of Apartheid: The Struggle for National Independence of Afrikaner Calvinism Against British Imperialism**
9. Michael D. Ryan (ed.), **Human Responses to the Holocaust: Perpetrators and Victims, Bystanders and Resisters**
10. G. Stanley Kane, **Anselm's Doctrine of Freedom and the Will**
11. Bruce Bubacz, **St. Augustine's Theory of Knowledge: A Contemporary Analysis**
12. Anne Llewellyn Barstow, **Married Priests and the Reforming Papacy: The Eleventh-Century Debates**
13. Denis Janz (ed.), **Three Reformation Catechisms: Catholic, Anabaptist, Lutheran**
14. David A. Rausch, **Messianic Judaism: Its History, Theology, and Polity**
15. Ernest E. Best, **Religion and Society in Transition: The Church and Social Change in England, 1560-1850**
16. Donald V. Stump *et al.*, ***Hamartia:*** **The Concept of Error in the Western Tradition, Essays in Honor of John M. Crossett**
17. Louis Meyer, **Eminent Hebrew Christians of the Nineteenth Century: Brief Biographical Sketches,** David A. Rausch (ed.)
18. James Jenkins, **The Records and Recollections of James Jenkins**, J. William Frost (ed.)
19. Joseph R. Washington, Jr., **Anti-Blackness in English Religion 1500-1800**

20. Joyce E. Salisbury, **Iberian Popular Religion 600 B.C. to 700 A.D.: Celts, Romans and Visigoths**

21. Longinus, ***On the Sublime***, James A. Arieti and John M. Crossett (trans.)

22. James Gollnick, ***Flesh* as Transformation Symbol in the Theology of Anselm of Canterbury: Historical and Transpersonal Perspectives**

23. William Lane Craig, **The Historical Argument for the Resurrection of Jesus During the Deist Controversy**

24. Steven H. Simpler, **Roland H. Bainton: An Examination of His Reformation Historiography**

25. Charles W. Brockwell, Jr., **Bishop Reginald Pecock and the Lancastrian Church: Securing the Foundations of Cultural Authority**

26. Sebastian Franck, **Sebastian Franck: 280 Paradoxes or Wondrous Sayings**, E. J. Furcha (trans.)

27. James Heft, S.M., **John XXII and Papal Teaching Authority**

28. Shelley Baranowski, **The Confessing Church, Conservative Elites, and The Nazi State**

29. Jan Lindhardt, **Martin Luther: Knowledge and Mediation in the Renaissance**

30. Kenneth L. Campbell, **The Intellectual Struggle of the English Papists in the Seventeenth Century: The Catholic Dilemma**

31. William R. Everdell, **Christian Apologetics in France, 1750-1800: The Roots of Romantic Religion**

32. Paul J. Morman, **Noël Aubert de Versé : A Study in the Concept of Toleration**

33. Nigel M. de S. Cameron, **Biblical Higher Criticism and the Defense of Infallibilism in 19th-Century Britain**

34. Samuel J. Rogal, **John Wesley's London: A Guidebook**

35. André Séguenny, **The Christology of Caspar Schwenckfeld: Spirit and Flesh in the Process of Life Transformation,** Peter C. Erb and Simone Nieuwolt (trans.)

36. Donald E. Demaray, **The Innovation of John Newton (1725-1807): Synergism of Word and Music in Eighteenth Century Evangelism**

37. Thomas Chase, **The English Religious Lexis**

38. R. G. Moyles, **A Bibliography of Salvation Army Literature in English (1865-1987)**

39. Vincent A. Lapomarda, **The Jesuits and the Third Reich**

40. Susan Drain, **The Anglican Church in Nineteenth Century Britain: Hymns Ancient and Modern (1860-1875)**

41. Aegidius of Rome, **On Ecclesiastical Power: De Ecclesiastica Potestate,** Arthur P. Monahan (trans.)

42. John R. Eastman, **Papal Abdication in Later Medieval Thought**

43. Paul Badham (ed.), **Religion, State, and Society in Modern Britain**

44. Hans Denck, **Selected Writings of Hans Denck, 1500-1527,** E. J. Furcha (trans.)

45. Dietmar Lage, **Martin Luther's Christology and Ethics**

46. Jean Calvin, **Sermons on Jeremiah by Jean Calvin**, Blair Reynolds (trans.)

47. Jean Calvin, **Sermons on Micah by Jean Calvin**, Blair Reynolds (trans.)

48. Alexander Sándor Unghváry, **The Hungarian Protestant Reformation in the Sixteenth Century Under the Ottoman Impact: Essays and Profiles**

49. Daniel B. Clendenin and W. David Buschart (eds.), **Scholarship, Sacraments and Service: Historical Studies in Protestant Tradition,** ***Essays in Honor of Bard Thompson***

50. Randle Manwaring, **A Study of Hymn-Writing and Hymn-Singing in the Christian Church**

51. John R. Schneider, **Philip Melanchthon's Rhetorical Construal of Biblical Authority: Oratio Sacra**

52. John R. Eastman (ed.), **Aegidius Romanus,** ***De Renunciatione Pape***

53. J. A. Loubser, **A Critical Review of Racial Theology in South Africa: The Apartheid Bible**

54. Henri Heyer, **Guillaume Farel: An Introduction to His Theology**, Blair Reynolds (trans.)

55. James E. Biechler and H. Lawrence Bond (ed.), **Nicholas of Cusa on Interreligious Harmony: Text, Concordance and Translation of** ***De Pace Fidei***

56. Michael Azkoul, **The Influence of Augustine of Hippo on the Orthodox Church**

57. James C. Dolan, **The** ***Tractatus Super Psalmum Vicesimum*** **of Richard Rolle of Hampole**

58. William P. Frost, **Following Joseph Campbell's Lead in the Search for Jesus' Father**

59. Frederick Hale, **Norwegian Religious Pluralism: A Trans-Atlantic Comparison**

60. Frank H. Wallis, **Popular Anti-Catholicism in Mid-Victorian Britain**

61. Blair Reynolds, **The Relationship of Calvin to Process Theology as Seen Through His Sermons**

62. Philip G. Kreyenbroek, **Yezidism - Its Background, Observances and Textual Tradition**

63. Michael Azkoul, **St. Gregory of Nyssa and the Tradition of the Fathers**

64. John Fulton and Peter Gee (editors), **Religion in Contemporary Europe**

65. Robert J. Forman, **Augustine and the Making of a Christian Literature: Classical Tradition and Augustinian Aesthetics**

66. Ann Matheson, **Theories of Rhetoric in the 18th-Century Scottish Sermon**

67. Raoul Mortley, **The Idea of Universal History from Hellenistic Philosophy to Early Christian Historiography**

68. Oliver Logan, **The Venetian Upper Clergy in the 16th and 17th Centuries**

69. Anthony Blasi, **A Sociology of Johannine Christianity**

70. Helmut Kohlenberger, **Twenty-five Years (1969-1994) of Anselm Studies**

GENERAL THEOLOGICAL SEMINARY
NEW YORK